Marjorie Merriweather Post—
When *She* Talked
E.F. Hutton Listened!

And so did her *other* three husbands—or anyone else blessed or cursed enough to cross her gilded path! Beautiful, shrewd, spirited and unstoppable, no woman in modern times lived a more glamorous life.

At age twenty-seven she took charge of the vast family fortune and rode it full-throttle until her astonishing end.

HEIRESS
The Rich Life of Marjorie Merriweather Post

"EXTRAORDINARY!"
—*Chicago Sun-Times*

"I LOVED IT! . . . full of wit and revelations of what it's like to be very, very rich"
—Cris Chase

WILLIAM WRIGHT

Heiress

THE RICH LIFE OF
MARJORIE MERRIWEATHER POST

PUBLISHED BY POCKET BOOKS NEW YORK

New Republic Books would like to thank the owners of the photographs used in the portfolio. The two photos taken in the Moscow Embassy are used courtesy of Elbridge Durbrow. The other photographs are used courtesy of Marjorie Durant Dye, Dina Merrill and David Close.

**POCKET BOOKS, a Simon & Schuster division of
GULF & WESTERN CORPORATION
1230 Avenue of the Americas, New York, N.Y. 10020**

Published by arrangement with New Republic Books
Library of Congress Catalog Card Number: 77-26168

ISBN: 0-671-82628-X

First Pocket Books printing August, 1979

10 9 8 7 6 5 4 3 2 1

For Harry Sions

ACKNOWLEDGMENTS

It is a delicate business eliciting information from a subject's family and friends without granting in return rights of review or assurances on the material's use. But there must be trust on both sides; people who loved or admired your subject are tempted to emend, while the author is tempted to cajole. These dangers double my gratitude to the many who made available their scrapbooks, letters, diaries, and memories. I would particularly like to mention Marjorie Durant Dye, Eleanor Barzin, Ellen Iverson, Cliff Robertson, Stanley Hutton Rumbough, Tim Durant, Margaret and David Close, James Griffin, Frank Moffat, Nettie Leitch Major, Hunter and Minnie Marston, Judge James Knott, John Logan, Major General Alden Sibley, Richard Pearson, Gerson Nordlinger, Clarence Francis, Loy Henderson, Elbridge Durbrow, Harry Winston, Count Vasily Adlerberg, Alice Leone-Moats, the Palm Beach Historical Society, and, for her great assistance in excavating Battle Creek, Amy South. I am especially grateful to Dina Merrill who had the courage to lead me to the fearless honesty of her niece Marwee ("Anything goes when the whistle blows.") and who unfailingly showed an artist's appreciation of the difference between a marble bust and a living woman with flesh, blood and freckles.

Ossabaw Island, Georgia   WILLIAM WRIGHT
November 1977

CONTENTS

PREFACE

If the three attributes that delineate most lives are brains, looks and financial resources, Marjorie Merriweather Post would qualify as a study in advantage. She possessed a sharp mind, a beauty that increased with age, and the kind of fortune that embarrasses the most enthusiastic capitalists.

Adding to her allure as a case history is a set of exemplary characteristics that render her a sturdy, serviceable laboratory creature. Foremost was the strength to command her fortune rather than fall hostage to it. Newspaper morgues are strewn with the remains of weaker individuals who were crushed by the harrassments and options of great wealth. Howard Hughes, Doris Duke, and Marjorie Post's niece and friend, Barbara Hutton, are a few of the more prominent casualties. Less extreme cases survive by cowering behind estate walls, clutching their Labradors and their scotches, hoping their existence will be overlooked so they will be permitted to lead out their lives of dull and anonymous opulence.

Marjorie Post fell into neither of these beleaguered camps. She knew who she was, and she knew what she wanted. Implementing a strong will was a rigid discipline and a genius for organization. Her life was governed by fixed principles of good sense, practicality, and propriety. Moderation and normalcy inform most aspects of her character. She was intelligent but not intellectual, she had humor but was not remarkable for either her wit or a grande-dame sharpness of tongue, she was sensual but not a sexual adventurer or pioneer.

Such pedestrian characteristics might be praiseworthy and qualify her for controlled studies in privilege; her beauty and wealth might have earned her tenure in magazines and gossip columns; her accomplishments in business, diplomacy, philanthropy, and collecting might merit a paragraph in *Who's Who*. None of this would justify a lengthy examination of her life if it were not for one additional facet: a gusto for her happy situation and a determination to extract from it the maximum for herself and those around her. She saw her wealth as a tool for converting the world through which she moved into enchanting flaw-free enclaves, and, in that other world just beyond her gates, for combating—to the extent her resources allowed—the manifold blights.

She waged this personal war against the world's blemishes by means of philanthropies and self-indulgences (both on a monumental scale) and with the planning, organization, and vigor of a giant corporation launching a new product. This impetus toward beautification linked such disparate actions as setting up a soup kitchen during the Depression, giving more than a million dollars to the National Symphony (she was almost tone deaf and, eventually, stone deaf), ordering ten thousand dollars' worth of new uniforms for her yacht's crew. Allegedly she sent Pat Nixon a fur coat, brushing aside the nonsense about the First Lady wearing a plain cloth coat. When daughter Dina Merrill was asked to confirm this, she responded, "I don't know, but anything's possible."

Marjorie Post took charge of her fortune when she was twenty-seven. Until she died in 1973 at the age of eighty-six, she rode it with a full-throttle, life-relishing zest. Wielding her checkbook with single-minded efficiency, she created the most lavish living pattern of modern times. She saw to it that her wealth was a happy event for herself and everyone around her. She was not afraid to be rich.

The money and her spirited spending of it were just the most distinguishing aspects of a life filled with outsized events and accomplishments. Her career serves as a spotlight into some of the more interesting pockets of contemporary history. With her second husband, E. F. Hutton, she was an energetic participant in the high-powered, unabashed social action of New York and Palm Beach in the twenties; she was instrumental in forming the General Foods Corporation, and she can take credit, or blame, for the development of frozen foods. As the wife of the United States ambassador to the USSR in the thirties, she was the first woman to represent the Americans to the Soviets.

For all this, it was her grandiose style of living that made Marjorie Post unique. Until her death, she maintained three enormous estates, each requiring a staff of between thirty-five and sixty. She had a four-motor turboprop plane for which she kept three full-time pilots. The art collection in her Washington house alone was sufficient to render this establishment, adding nothing, an important museum in the nation's capital. Until her last few months her party-giving was regal and constant.

She built two of the most remarkable houses in the United States and, in addition, maintained at various times a Fifth Avenue mansion, Long Island and Connecticut estates, the largest apartment in Manhattan, and a 16,000-acre South Carolina plantation. She built the most grandiose sailing yacht ever owned by a private individual. Along the way she acquired quantities of furniture and jewelry belonging to the French monarchs, vast amounts of rare Russian porcelains, and the most extensive collection of czarist treasure outside the Soviet Union.

When Queen Maud of Norway came aboard Marjorie Post's yacht and saw the three masts billowing with square-rigged sails, the crew of seventy-four lined up in crisp whites, the lunch table set with silver, crystal, and antique lace, she exclaimed, "Why, you live like a queen!"

The remark was self-promoting. While it is doubtful if any contemporary monarch lived in more luxury and pomp, Marjorie Post had certain advantages over most of them. She could go where she wanted when she wanted, and she had none of the royal chores and duties, tedious and endless, with which working monarches must justify their parliamentary stipends. If Marjorie Post chose, she could wander the world for six months of the year in her yacht. For years she did just that.

If she felt any inhibitions on her pleasure-seeking, they were not imposed by a badgering press or government; they stemmed rather from her own notions of sense and propriety. While these inner brakes may have been applied on occasion, they had scant effect on the overall spectacle of her life. Few monarchs had as many options; fewer still have had the will and capacity to pursue them so relentlessly.

Despite her advantage over royals, Marjorie Post had a lifelong fascination with them that bordered dangerously close to identification—particularly in the case of Marie Antoinette and Catherine the Great. In one regard, however, she was most similar to Ludwig II of Bavaria. Marjorie knew, as Ludwig did, that such a life-style was anachronistic and doomed; this very knowledge reinforced in both individuals a determination to postpone, as magnificently as possible, its ultimate extinction.

Marjorie Post's story, in addition to being a celebration of a charmed life, embodies many of the most beloved, if shopworn themes of American folklore: the humble, small-town beginnings segueing into polished palaces in world capitals; the shy, unprepossessing girl unfurling into a majestic beauty of drama and flamboyance; the nouveau riche who triumphs over entrenched society; and, the most cherished legend of all, the person possessed of everything but love. Marjorie Post's eighty-six years had enough story lines for a cry of Joan Crawford films.

An intriguing by-product to a life of great wealth is its disruptive effect on all who come near it. In addition to her prodigious generosity, Marjorie Post had a fairy-godmother tendency to meddle in the lives of those she liked. Often the effect she had on family, friends, and acquaintances resulted not from any action on her part, but merely from the shock waves thrown off by such a crucible of financial power.

The greatest hope of any biographer is that the life under scrutiny will yield up an insight into an aspect of human nature, one hitherto unclearly perceived. Marjorie Post holds out this hope, if only because she doesn't slip gracefully into any of the accepted categories of legends and heroes; yet she managed to hold the public's attention for fifty years. To dismiss this by saying that the rich have a certain fascination for many people is not explaining anything, only restating the question.

To be sure, the facts of a life like Marjorie Post's provide a lovely excursion into a pretty and unreal world. Then too we are willing to grant such fortunates a bit of limelight, on the premise that a superbly dressed woman or an exquisitely decorated drawing room raises the tone for the whole species.

There is a negative aspect to curiosity about the rich. Part of our nature is offended by one person's having so much in the face of real deprivation in the world. Another part, however, seems to take solace in the knowledge that someone, at least, is living like a god. Some groups codify this pooled-resources principle, making small sacrifices so that one of their number can lead a charmed existence; this might be called the Father-Divine or Reverend-Moon syndrome. Or the acquiescence to wealth might simply be characterized by the attitude of the Italian peasant who, on seeing a twenty-five-thousand-dollar Maserati flash by his scrap of land, doesn't shake his fist at the injustice of it all, but instead murmurs reverently, *"Magari"*— "Would that it were me."

Marjorie Post was not indifferent to the world's have-nots, but she was not haunted by them either. She gave large amounts to charity, and she was quick to assist, often anonymously, any friend or acquaintance in need. As for her personal extravagances, qualms were dispersed by the belief that her spending fed the economy and therefore helped the public at large.

However valid this theory, it relieved any guilt she might have felt about indulging her merest whim or most costly folly. And it is this lack of restraint to her life, as much as anything, that gives it interest for more earthbound mortals. Such a magical, wish-ful-filling existence says much, finally, about the economic realities that define the lives of the rest of us. And conversely, the absence of those realities in Marjorie Post's life, a life with as much pain and disappointment as most, says much about their unimportance in one's net balance of contentment and fulfillment.

Marjorie Post had none of the inhibitions of her fellow millionaires who felt that no good will come from letting the non-rich know too much about how the super-rich live. She used her advantages—physical, mental, financial—openly, fully, and free of guilt. With or without lessons in the roots of happiness, with or without indictments of a system that tolerates such outlandish privilege, with or without insights into whatever it is that draws our attention to the rich—Marjorie Post's life provides a series of savory dramas and a sixty-year tableau of what it means to have it all.

HEIRESS

Throughout most of her adult life, Marjorie Post had been one of the world's richest women, yet she kept abreast of the stock market and never lost her enthusiasm for turning a dollar. In her seventies, she was seated at a formal dinner in the baronial dining room of her Washington estate. The table was ablaze with gold candelabra and service, priceless porcelains and crystals; Marjorie herself was animated with enough jewelry to underwrite a Broadway musical. She shocked the sanitized State Department official to her left, a distinguished career diplomat, by leaning over and asking him, confidentially, very man-to-man, "Are you interested in making a little money?"

Estimates of Marjorie Post's fortune ran about $250 million, a figure that did not make her the world's richest woman, as she was quick to point out. "There are many people better off than I am," she said, "but I do more with my money. I move it around and put it to work."

When she went to Moscow in 1937 as the wife of the United States ambassador to the Soviet Union, newspapers around the world gasped at the two thousand pints of fresh cream Marjorie Post took with her. They didn't notice other imports she felt Russia might lack: fourteen deep freezers to be installed in her Moscow basement; two tons of frozen foods; a masseur; fresh flowers (shipped) in from Belgium); and her yacht the Sea Cloud, which she brought up the Neva River to Leningrad (and which caused logistical problems for her staff, who had to arrange entry documents for the seventy-four-man crew).

Barbara Hutton was very fond of Marjorie Post, her aunt-by-marriage, and would visit her frequently. Once, curled up at the foot of her aunt's bed at Mar-A-Lago, Barbara was bemoaning her seven failed marriages.

"You've had too many husbands, Barbara," Mrs. Post snapped. "You must be doing something wrong. You should try rotating the hips. It makes it much better for the man."

This was discussed for a while, then Barbara groaned, "You are older than I am, Aunt Marjorie, why is it you're so much stronger?"

Without a pause Mrs. Post replied, "Pioneer stock, dearie, pioneer stock."

For someone with a lifelong reputation for kindly equanimity, Marjorie Post could inspire fear in many. The apparition over a baby carriage of a befurred, behatted Mrs. Post was enough to detonate screaming grandchildren. With lawless youngsters, she never raised her voice; the glowers were enough. Adults, too, were wary of her black looks. Just about the only one who didn't seem intimidated was her son-in-law, Cliff Robertson, who says he was not afraid of her in the least.

"That's fine if he wants to believe that," says his wife Dina Merrill. "The fact is, he was terrified of her."

In the late 1950s, after Marjorie Post had married Pittsburgh industrialist Herbert A. May, she and her husband visited his good friend, Richard King Mellon, a principal heir to the Mellon fortune. The Mays' arrival at the Mellon home was preceded by several of Mrs. May's servants, who flew into action in the guest suite unpacking bags, laying out toiletries, pressing clothes. It was all a bit unnerving for the Mellon servants, who were undone completely when a Post maid ripped the sheets from the guest bed. As she handed a nonplussed Mellon maid the armful of clean sheets, she said with ill-concealed disdain, "Mrs. May won't be needing these."

Despite her massive philanthropy toward public institutions—the National Symphony, the Boy Scouts of America, C.W. Post College, Mount Vernon College, and many other organizations—Marjorie Post had her "private" charities, such as putting a number of young men through college. She was especially sympathetic to women accustomed to comfort whose old age had not been provided for. At one time she was said to have been supporting or substantially assisting thirty such women. Among them were several ambassadors' wives and Florenz Ziegfeld's widow, Billie Burke.

Marjorie had a grim competitive cord in her makeup, aspiring to the biggest and the best in everything she did. This trait energized her building and acquiring sprees. In her old age, it degenerated into childishness. Cliff Robertson's daughter Stefanie, when about eight years old, announced to her father that she would not be playing backgammon with Marjorie anymore. It seems that Granny repeatedly changed the rules so she could win.

In her last years, Marjorie Post grew increasingly deaf until she would often sit silently at the head of her dinner table while her guests conversed around her. Idly, she would pick up a butter plate or a teaspoon and start recounting its history, where she had bought it, to whom it had belonged. The guests, even those far down the table, would fall silent and listen.

Marjorie Post once told a friend that, throughout her life, her wealth had put a fence around her. She knew that people could get through the fence to befriend her, even marry her. What she didn't realize was that only a certain type of person would make the effort.

10

Marjorie Post was proud of her modest Battle Creek beginnings. She thought of herself as a simple midwestern girl who happened to have a lot of money. In spite of some epic extravagances, she would still buy shoes at Sears and pass up expensive skin creams in favor of castor oil.

But the pioneer practicality was clearly at odds with another self-view, one that led her to buy furniture and jewelry of the French monarchy, have portraits of Catherine the Great around her Washington estate, employ personal servants in numbers that at times topped a hundred, and rarely do anything—even go from one room to another—without attendants.

Perhaps the most telling glimpse of this other side is seen in the movie pavilion at her Washington estate, Hillwood. A bust of Marjorie Post is prominently displayed alongside a similar one of Marie Antoinette. The juxtaposition of the two marble *heads suggests that she felt a kinship with Marie Antoinette, but it was most likely a more subtle link than first supposed. Aside from a similar taste in jewels, furniture, and living arrangements, she knew they were both the last of their lines.*

CHAPTER ONE

Of all the commercial empires born during the last third of the nineteenth century, the breakfast-food bonanza that sprang up in Battle Creek, Michigan, is one of the oddest. The boom was typical of the Gilded Age. Even before it found its economic niche, Battle Creek, like most cities and towns, sniffed the air of fortune-making—an intoxicating mix of smoke, opportunity, and money lust that hung over the country. The moment belonged to the businessman. It was he—not the artist, the intellectual, or the statesman—who was the hero of the times.

Never again would the entrepreneur operate in such an aura of glamour or, more importantly, such an absence of restraints. Untroubled by labor laws, income taxes, public opinion, or scruples, the marauding businessman was threatened only by other marauding businessmen. This was a formidable exception. Interrelated industries offered tempting possibilities for extortion, bullying, and strangulation. Oil was at the mercy of the railroads; steel depended on heavy manufacturing.

Shrewd lawyers were set to fashioning the trusts, pools, and holding companies that accelerated moneymaking and eliminated the variables, particularly the peskiest variable: competition. Moral indignation was only aroused by the most flamboyant excesses; for the most part, the public was thrilled by the spectacle of men who, upon discovering opportunities, seized and exploited them. And to the ambitious, opportunity was everywhere, even in towns like Battle Creek; and it was available to everyone, even invalids like Charles William Post, Marjorie's father.

In building his cereal empire, C. W. Post embodied the more positive aspects of the businessman-hero. He was the dream capitalist in that he built his fortune on ingenuity, hard work, and pluck. He was not a privileged aristocrat, but an on-the-make salesman from a small midwestern town. Having made millions, he didn't tarnish his common-man luster by buying his way into society. Instead, he spent large amounts improving conditions for his workers, then turned his resources and his manifest shrewdness toward problems of the country at large.

Post's rise was relatively free of the dirty moves that propelled his fellow tycoons to the heights. His commerce was pretty much between him and the public. His independence from other businesses and, for years, his lack of competition, relieved him of resorting to the price wars and boardroom muggings of his brother moguls.

No irate laborer shot off his ear. He was never honored by legislation forcing him to change his methods. He was never summoned to J. P. Morgan's yacht, like the presidents of the New York Central and the Pennsylvania railroads, to be scolded and told to stop warring.

If the breakfast-food phenomenon lacked the rough stuff of the other robber barons, it got compensatory color from the bizarre list of characters who made up the cast. Then, as now, much ignorance surrounds the subject of food. The field attracts more than its share of charlatans, mystics, and nuts. They abounded in 1880, more numerous and more bogus even than those working the trade today—and a lot more eccentric.

In a day when Americans purchased their remedies from pitchmen talking fast from the backs of wagons, anyone with a little book-learning and a food theory could win adherents. If there was a religious angle— that is, if the theory came not from books but from a vision, a dream, or a voice in the night—so much the better. Battle Creek came to be known as the center for advanced notions on diet and health. When it did, many of these characters packed up their nostrums, their herb cures, their frayed leather volumes, and headed for Michigan. They produced some lovely drama.

Early in the 1900s, when C. W. Post was arriving at his tycoon status, he resented the press's characterization of him as a penniless traveling salesman who had cooked up an industrial empire on his wife's stove with a few dollars' worth of equipment and ingredients. It would have been hard for him to deny that his luck was down when he hit on Postum—too many people had seen him selling suspenders door-to-door from a wheelchair.

He later insisted that, at the time, he had one hundred thousand dollars in working capital at his disposal. This claim was undermined by his own accounts of launching a business on nothing but credit, salesmanship, and pluck. Still, he was not the insubstantial drifter the rags-to-riches enthusiasts would have us believe.

Post was born to a comfortable middle-class family in Springfield, Illinois. His father, Charles Rollin Post, had left his Vermont birthplace and, after a peripatetic youth that included the Gold Rush of 1849, settled in Springfield where he prospered in the farm-implement business. He married, then bought one of the town's handsomest houses; here he and his wife raised three sons: Charles William, who was born in 1854, followed by Aurrie and Carroll.

Rollin Post eventually outlived his oldest son by five years, and at the age of ninety-three would tell stories (sometimes to newspaper reporters or anyone who would listen) of his Springfield acquaintance with young Abraham Lincoln. A typical reminiscence was a description Post gave a newspaper interviewer:

Lincoln was very fond of a game of ball, and finding a vacant lot . . . between the blank walls of two four-story buildings, he passed a good deal of his leisure time there. When the balloting began, he naturally became very much interested and vibrated between the ball ground and the crowds surrounding the telegraph office. Soon a boy came bounding down the stairs and rushed to Mr. Lincoln shouting, "Mr. Lincoln, you are nominated."

Taking the message in his hands, he quietly looked it over and remarked, "Well boys, there is a little woman up at Eighth Street who will be interested in this. Please excuse me and I will go home."

Rollin Post was a member of the Springfield City Council; as such, he was part of the honor guard that met the Lincoln funeral train in Chicago and accompanied it to Springfield. Young Charlie Post grew up in this atmosphere of small-town prominence. In 1869, at the age of fifteen, he enrolled in college at Urbana but was so eager to set out on his own, he persuaded his parents to let him quit school a year later.

For the next twenty-one years, until he arrived as a moribund shell at the Battle Creek Sanitarium, his life alternated between bold business ventures and breakdowns, both nervous and physical. He was high-strung and driven. He had a probing, restless mind that analyzed—with the thought of improving—everything that came before it, from domestic details to commercial products. It seems to have been a natural reflex, but one that was excited by the hope of stumbling onto a fortune-making idea.

He had other assets valuable to a salesman. He was tall, handsome, and even in later years, fastidious about his slim, hard physique. His most remarkable feature was penetrating gray-blue eyes, which accentuated an overall intensity of manner. Few people ever remarked on Post's humor or charm, but few were unaware of his force and determination.

Looking for business prospects, Post traveled the Southwest where large sections were still wild. The Apache wars raged in New Mexico, and Geronimo was still at large. The Atchison, Topeka & Santa Fe line did not yet reach the West Coast. But parts—Texas, Kansas, Oklahoma—were rapidly becoming domesticated, and new cow towns like Dodge City and Abilene appeared to young men like Post to be good places for wealth, quick and legitimate.

The idea of pulling a fortune from the ground had by no means died out in the American consciousness

17

of the 1860s and '70s despite wholesale disappointments in California in 1849. New deposits of silver were discovered in Nevada, Utah, and Colorado, and men continued to flock to the mining fields. Eager as he was to be rich, Charles Post was never tempted by the tales of mineral strikes. His father had learned firsthand in California the impossible odds against such natural windfalls. He also learned that the odds in favor of riches from solid business were, in a burgeoning economy, excellent.

The industrial technology that had developed during the Civil War had unleashed a frenzy of commercial and industrial expansion with the war's end. Most significant was the spread of the railroads. In the thirty years following the war the amount of track in the country increased from 36,801 miles to 193,346 miles. The new network of cheap, efficient transport enabled the fusion of thousands of local businesses into corporate behemoths whose sales targets were the entire nation.

Many were ignited by the dream of nationwide businesses and the Vanderbilt-sized fortunes they could produce. It was during these years that John D. Rockefeller became disturbed by the spectacle of small oil companies competing so wastefully, and Frank Woolworth decided to repeat in other towns the success of his Lancaster, Pennsylvania, store. When J. P. Morgan bought out Andrew Carnegie to create the United States Steel Corporation in 1901, thereby consolidating all steel production in the United States, many were still alive who could remember when metalworking was the exclusive province of the town blacksmith.

The century's last thirty years was a time of staggering inventiveness. Bell developed the telephone, Marconi the radio, Edison the phonograph and incandescent bulb. By selling his reaper on a larger scale, Cyrus McCormick revolutionized the country's agriculture. This breakthrough would have particular relevance to the infant breakfast-food industry in that it sent grain productivity high and prices low.

These epic breakthroughs were the culmination of an American taste for innovation and novelty that, by the end of the century, had approached a national mania. The New World wanted new things, new methods, new habits. The better mousetrap had become the dream, not only of the businessman, but of the public as well.

Americans had not always been so restlessly forward-looking. In the mid-nineteenth century there had been a congressional move to close down the US Patent Office on the grounds that everything worth inventing had been invented. Prior to 1860, the total number of patents issued was 36,000; the thirty years after 1860 brought forth an additional 440,000. Each of these inventions carried the hopes and the possibility of a fortune.

Young Charles Post wanted to be part of all this. With a friend, he set up a hardware store in Independence, Kansas. The business flourished, but Post didn't like Kansas. He returned to regroup in Springfield where, in 1874, he married a lifelong friend, Ella Letitia Merriweather. She was twenty-one, a year older than Post. Ella's parents were dead; her father, a prosperous merchant, had left her an amount of money that did not make her rich but was sufficient to secure solid middle-class status.

Ella was small, almost tiny, and her taut, erect posture and sharp, prim features gave her a birdlike air. Large, deep-set gray eyes relieved her appearance of sternness. In striking contrast to her high-strung, frenetic husband, she was quiet and retiring. She was artistic, with a particular fondness for music; she played a respectable midwestern-parlor piano, sang well, and danced with professional grace. What little gaiety she may have had was burned from her by the ordeal of her marriage to Post, but throughout her sad life, she always loved to dance.

Not long after their marriage, Post took off again, this time traveling the Southwest, selling for a farm-implement company. The tools would be easier to sell, he decided, if they were designed better; thus evolved some innovations which he had patented. In this itinerant period, which lasted six years, Post met and struck up a casual friendship with Walt Whitman, who wrote Post a warm note and enclosed a photo of himself as a memento of their encounter.

Post decided that the big profits in business go to the manufacturer, not the salesman. This realization, sharpened by the first of his breakdowns, moved him to abandon selling. After recuperating in Springfield for a few months, he formed a company with his father, his brothers, and some friends to manufacture his farm-implement inventions. With his own business at last, Post drove himself feverishly.

The company prospered, but his restless creativity required additional outlets. He devised and built his own player piano, then a two-wheeled bicycle with equal-sized wheels. Both had been invented shortly before by others, but they were still unknown to the public. It is unlikely Post had any knowledge of the other bicycle; if he knew about the earlier piano, it could not have been more than third-hand knowledge of the principle involved. He and Ella would sit long hours at the kitchen table in their Springfield house cutting the holes in the paper piano rolls.

A fight over the stock of the Posts' new company depressed C. W. This, plus his manic productivity, brought on a more serious collapse. He retreated to the house, where Ella nursed him. With C. W. no longer running the company, it began to falter and finally went under. Debts were paid off, but the failure practically wiped out Post family assets.

This time Post's recovery was slower. His doctor, now ad-libbing remedies, recommended a milder climate. Partly for this reason, and partly because all the Posts wanted a fresh start, C. W. and his brother Carroll made a long tour through Texas in the fall of 1886 looking for a likely business.

They found it in Fort Worth, where a real-estate firm contracted the Post men to take over the management of a new community being developed east of town. The entire family, including an uncle and a cousin, decided to move immediately. His wife was pregnant, so C. W. elected to wait out her confinement in Springfield.

On March 15, 1887, after thirteen years of marriage, Ella gave birth to Marjorie Merriweather Post. She would be the couple's only child.

It was yet another year before C. W. and Ella joined the others in Texas. When he and Ella and their baby finally left Springfield for the last time, they did not go straight to Fort Worth but spent the winter in Southern California. There was no money for such a prolonged vacation. Clearly, Post's health demanded it.

Post, his wife, and daughter arrived in Fort Worth in February 1888. He immediately threw himself into land development—selling homesites, persuading businesses to lease or buy manufacturing sites. He also got involved in a blanket factory, which he'd lured to the site, and he was active in laying out the town. The whole project was, in a sense, a rehearsal for Post City, Texas—a model city Post was to create many years later.

His return to health and full-throttle activity lasted two years. Early in 1890, he collapsed again. This time a long year of convalescence in Fort Worth brought little progress. In desperation, his family got together the funds to send C. W. off to an institution that was gaining national attention in restoring health to the functionally incurable, the sanitarium of Dr. John Harvey Kellogg at Battle Creek, Michigan.

CHAPTER TWO

When C. W. Post was brought off the train at Battle Creek on a bleak winter's day in 1891, he was thirty-seven years old. Nothing in his life to that point suggested he had a future in food products; very little about his appearance suggested he had any future at all. The arrival in Battle Creek was his nadir, yet it marked the beginning of a drastic change in his fortunes. It is one of the many ironies that the Kelloggs had almost nothing to do with restoring Post's health but a great deal to do with his business success—to their lasting chagrin.

Battle Creek in 1891 was a pepped-up midwestern town with a handful of small industries and a lot of optimism. In that year the town's few trolleys switched from horse to electric power. It was not unusual for a farmer, tilling his field, to turn up an Indian arrowhead or a battle-ax. Indoor toilets were still a luxury. The local newspaper ran notices of church socials and cake sales and warned of the hazards caused by blocks of ice falling off the back of ice wagons and being left in the street. When the firemen's pet alligator was moved from his winter compartment to his outdoor pen for the summer, the event was written up.

About the only reason for the town's being known beyond a thirty-mile radius was the Battle Creek Sanitarium. This health establishment had been founded twenty-five years before Post's arrival by Seventh-Day Adventists after a guiding spirit of the group, Sister Ellen White, had a vision about God's idea of a balanced diet. Her message about good nutrition and its link with spiritual health became part of the Adventists' roster of eccentric tenets.

The sanitarium, originally called the Western Health Reform Institute, had been set up to implement these beliefs in an evangelical and, it was hoped, a money-making way. The enterprise limped along for years with its joyless dietary injunctions, halfhearted water cures, and much religious mumbo-jumbo. If they were to make a go of it, the elders decided, they would have to beef up the scientific standing of the place. They focused their sights on John Harvey Kellogg, the bright and ambitious son of an exemplary but poor Adventist family. The church financed Kellogg's way through medical school and shortly after his graduation, put him in charge of the health institute.

He made a quick and impressive success. As the sanitarium prospered, Dr. Kellogg revealed more and more signs of personal flamboyance—dramatic clothing, dictatorial manner, attention-getting pronouncements. His sanitarium and his surgical skill were making him a medical star, and he played the role like a fresh-minted Barrymore.

24

The Battle Creek Sanitarium became the favorite retreat of America's prominent and affluent ill, who told each other of miraculously renewed health, as well as good times at the convivial sanitarium; the press passed the news along to those who didn't have a sick rich friend. By the time C. W. Post and his wife and daughter arrived in Battle Creek, Kellogg was a celebrity and his sanitarium was a vast operation with hundreds of employees. More important for this story, the town itself was associated in the public mind with the most progressive ideas about health.

All of this alarmed and distressed Sister White, who saw in the prosperous health plant a resortlike godlessness that hadn't been the point at all. She also saw that her protégé's booming reputation was making him arrogant and even more defiant of God's messenger on earth, herself.

For years the battle raged between these two splendid old mountebanks—one an emissary from the shiny new god of science, the other holding credentials from a earlier deity—both with legions of disciples. Eventually Dr. Kellogg would ignore Sister White's injunctions about the sanitarium's operations; in 1891 he was still deferring to her. For example, the dining room at the sanitarium had a table where meat was served. When Sister White had a vision that the meat table must go, Dr. Kellogg acquiesced. He seems to have shared her faith in vegetarianism, but perhaps as a hotelkeeper, he also knew that grain was cheaper than beef.

To enliven his meatless menu, the doctor concocted a number of cereal dishes. One of his early health foods was a cake of baked wheat and cornmeal that was then shredded. It was all but identical to a product devised around 1863 by Dr. James Jackson at his health home in Dansville, New York. (Dr. Kellogg called his product Granula, an unfortunate choice,

25

since that was the name Dr. Jackson had used. Prodded by an immediate lawsuit, Dr. Kellogg changed the name of his product—to Granola.)

Later, Dr. Kellogg would claim to have stumbled on the prepared-breakfast-food idea when he was a medical student living in a room at Third Avenue and Twenty-Eighth Street in Manhattan. He had no cooking facilities and felt it would be a great convenience if grocers would sell cereals already cooked and ready to eat. If indeed he had so commercially refined an idea at the time, it does him little credit that he waited twenty years—and C. W. Post's example—to implement it.

Most of the Kellogg experiments dealt with cereal products for the sanitarium dining room. Dr. John Harvey and his younger brother, W.K., did develop a mail-order business for patients who wanted to continue their regimen at home, a project that the more enterprising W.K. was eager to expand. But Dr. John Harvey, who had already run afoul of the AMA for his aggressive commercialism, feared that pushing the food line, called Sanitas products, would jeopardize his highly successful sanitarium.

Coffee and other stimulants were forbidden at the sanitarium, so the Kelloggs devised alternative hot drinks from cereals. Here again, there was considerable precedent. Texas ranchers had been drinking a hot brew of wheat and molasses for years, as had Civil War soldiers. Coffee substitutes made from wheat had appeared in New England cookbooks as early as 1835. The Kelloggs' variation was named Caramel Coffee.

But the potion demonstrated another of Dr. Kellogg's nutritional credos. He seems to have believed that in order for a food to be healthy, it had to taste rotten. An example: Dr. Kellogg invented peanut butter; that is, he was the first to mash up cooked peanuts and call the goo peanut butter. Once, when Dr. John Harvey was away on a trip, W.K. did some experimenting on his own. He discovered that if the peanuts were roasted rather than steamed, as his brother had directed, the result tasted far better. The doctor was furious when he learned of the revision and ordered the more healthful steaming reinstated. His product died out. The peanut butter that is on every pantry shelf in America today is made from roasted peanuts.

Similarly, W.K. was always trying to sneak a little sugar into the cereal concoctions. The older Kellogg reacted as though the additive were hashish. The coffee substitute Dr. Kellogg approved was like his other improvisations: healthful perhaps, but in the eyes of many of his guests, undrinkable. No one was more disdainful of the brew than C.W. Post, who had been a coffee addict.

Still, Post was fascinated by the Kelloggs' food experiments. He visited the sanitarium's kitchens and watched the preparation of many of the health foods. The brothers were onto something and, characteristically, Post saw clearly what they were doing wrong. He approached Dr. John Harvey with a scheme for refining several of the Kellogg products and marketing them on a wider scale. Dr. Kellogg, torn as ever between greed and propriety (which in his case was a function of greed), turned Post down with a chilly definiteness.

The doctor's shortsightedness didn't discourage Post. He grew increasingly convinced that if he could come up with a product that could make Kellogg-type claims for health and yet be palatable, he could make a fortune. While still a patient at the sanitarium, he began his own experiments, using the basement of the Osgood Jewelry Store on Main Street for his concocting.

To economize, Post moved out of the sanitarium. With his wife and four-year-old daughter, he boarded for a time with a family named Haddock. Each day he could be seen being wheeled by his wife up Van Buren

Street to the sanitarium for treatments. Things were so tight for Post, at times he paid his bill to Dr. Kellogg with blankets from the now-defunct Texas factory.

After nine months of sanitarium care, Post was pronounced incurable. Dr. Kellogg told Ella Post he doubted that her husband had long to live. At this grim juncture, a letter from one of Ella's relations arrived, extolling the curative powers of Christian Science and offering the name of a practitioner in Battle Creek, a Mrs. Elizabeth Gregory.

Post was persuaded to see her. After an evening in her home he was so taken with Mary Baker Eddy's ideas about mental and spiritual health as expounded by Mrs. Gregory, he announced he was moving in with Mrs. Gregory until he was well. He brushed aside her pleas about the size of her house, her many children, and did just that. Post could play the vision game too. And his vision was that Mrs. Gregory had been called as his salvation.

The Post family has drawn a bit of a veil over C.W.'s symptoms. Marjorie would later refer to her father's stomach having given out. Others would talk vaguely of his exhaustion and depression. He himself, however, referred to his illness in letters to friends as "a nervous breakdown." We know that when he arrived at Battle Creek he came off the train on a stretcher. His long months in a wheelchair, Dr. Kellogg's prognosis, Post's grasp at religion—all suggest a very sick man.

One specific of his condition is known. He had an abhorrence of food that amounted to a phobia. There is a macabre irony in this. Three-quarters of a century later, after his daughter had realized the astounding life his food fortune made possible, she too developed an aversion to food.

Under Mrs. Gregory's care, C.W. Post's appetite returned quickly, followed shortly by his health and energy. One symptom lingered; his use of a wheelchair. Even after he left Mrs. Gregory's and, with his wife and daughter, set up a household of his own, he was seen being pushed by Ella from house to house, selling a new type of suspenders he had invented while still in Texas. His product, which improved the hang of trousers, had had some success before his breakdown, and Post was now seeking to revive it.

Today some Battle Creek residents recall that C.W. did not sell door-to-door to test market a new product. He simply needed the money. One old resident insists it wasn't suspenders, but girdles. Another resident, Mrs. Clara Bromberg, denies both stories. "No, no, no," she says, "not suspenders, not corsets, but shoestrings. He went door-to-door selling shoestrings!"

It was a long time ago.

Post was so enthusiastic about the Christian Science notions of mind over body, he reprocessed them in a book of his own called, *The Road to Wellville*. This was later distilled into a booklet called *The Second Man*. Both works are impossible to find today. Thirty years ago Alexander Woollcott implied this wasn't accidental. He reported darkly that even the Library of Congress copies had mysteriously vanished.

A co-opting of others' ideas was typical of Post. He didn't so much steal as re-invent. Under the force of his ego, anything passing through his brain was happening for the first time. While this brain was clearly a fine instrument for refining and rendering feasible half-worked ideas, it also seems to have filtered out any prior claims of authorship.

No sooner was Post on his feet than he decided to open his own sanitarium. Hadn't he cured himself after Dr. Kellogg had failed? With a small inheritance of his wife's he bought a property on the outskirts of Battle

Creek and opened his establishment in the existing farmhouse. He named it La Vita Inn.

To bring in income while waiting for the world's sick to arrive, he hired ten girls and began producing his scientific suspenders. A mail-order operation supplemented his door-to-door efforts, and the suspender business was soon doing nicely. He gave it outright to his wife.

As a healer, Post had some early success with Kellogg dropouts. Word spread that Post could succeed where Kellogg failed. Like the Kelloggs, Post put great emphasis on diet, but onto this nutritional foundation he built Christian-Science type philosophy. He also delved into the therapeutic possibilities of hypnotism. Battle Creek's reputation as a health center with spiritual overtones attracted all manner of fringe practitioners—spiritualists, clairvoyants, mesmerists. Post jumped right in and began hypnotizing his patients. He certainly had the physical equipment: gray-blue eyes that were incandescent and penetrating. Years later Marjorie remembered her father's hypnotizing her before trips to the dentist so she wouldn't feel pain.

With his sanitarium and suspender business running smoothly, Post returned to his search for a marketable coffee substitute. He read every book available on nutrition, health, and the chemistry of vegetable matter. He appears to have been sincere in looking for a formula that would be genuinely healthy. But he was first and foremost a businessman—which meant he was concerned with practicalities like uncomplicated manufacture, cost, and perishability.

The legends of Post starting the Postum Cereal Company with a total investment of sixty-seven dollars are a bit fanciful. That figure refers only to the cost of the ingredients and equipment for the final experiments. With an assistant, Shorty Bristol, Post worked over his formula for nearly a year, not counting his earlier experiments. After a time, Ella Post exiled her husband's roasting from her kitchen to the barn. He bought two used sheet-iron stoves, a coffee grinder, several sacks of wheat and bran, and ten jars of molasses. For slow-cooking the wheat, he constructed a special stove ten feet long. The wheat had to be constantly raked if it was to be evenly roasted. To help with this tedious and smelly job, the seven-year-old Marjorie would push the rake when she got home from public school. Later she would deliver paper bags full of Postum to Battle Creek stores.

For all Post's talk about releasing phosphates and the breakdown of glutens, his method was pretty much trial and error. He found that by cooking ingredients different lengths of time, he got markedly different results. He also learned that cooking the wheat, letting it cool, then cooking it again, changed the results still further. In one set of experiments, he heated the wheat in batches, each batch simmering five minutes longer than the previous one—from five minutes up to an hour. All of this took much time, patience, and more than sixty-seven dollars.

By the end of 1894 the proportions Post had arrived at were two-thirds bran, the remaining third a mixture of two parts wheat berries and one part molasses. He had found what he was seeking: a hot drink that was healthful, good-tasting, and economical.

On the little barn—which today sits in the General Foods complex of factories at Battle Creek—Post painted in bold letters: STARTED HERE JANUARY 1, 1895. As the McCormick reaper and other inventions were converting the American heartland into a vast and efficient cornucopia for dirt-cheap wheat and corn, C. W. Post pushed the technology one step further. He figured out how to convert them into gold.

CHAPTER THREE

With little cartons of Postum in his hand, Post called on E. H. Herrick, the most important wholesale grocer in Grand Rapids. Herrick was unimpressed. He pointed to unsold stacks of Kellogg's Caramel Coffee that had been taking up space for years. There was no market for such a product, Herrick said. Why not develop an item that people wanted? Post replied that he would create the demand.

The editor of the Grand Rapids *Evening News* was next. This time, along with his product, Post brought an alcohol lamp and fresh cream. There, in the editor's office, he brewed the Postum for twenty minutes, served a cup, and left with an advertising credit of one thousand dollars.

Post wrote his own copy, proclaiming the healthful

qualities of Postum and the toxic effects of coffee. His ads worked. Grocers were deluged with requests for Postum. Back in Battle Creek, he stepped up production. Post traveled to Chicago and repeated his Grand Rapids coup by persuading an advertising agency to extend him credit. Postum was catching on rapidly; still, cash problems were acute those first years.

Helping Post's nationwide ambition was the recent cross-hatching of the United States by railroad track, plus the networks of jobbers, wholesalers, and other set-ups for the broadest distribution of products. Post took quick advantage of this modernization of the merchandising process and traveled the Midwest, persuading wholesalers to handle Postum.

Clarence Francis, who worked for the Postum Company and was later chairman of the board of General Foods, remembers a story about this phase of Post's career: Post had gone to Kansas City to approach Mr. Seavey, of the large food-brokerage firm of Seavey and Flarsheim. Seavey was unenthusiastic about Postum but was persuaded by Post to accompany him to a prospective customer. The customer responded to the pitch and ordered fifty cases of Postum. He also asked to see a statement of Post's resources to assure himself that Post could make delivery. Post reached in his pocket and pulled out some change.

"Here are my resources," he said.

The buyer was unamused. He would have to rescind the order.

Seavey, who had watched the exchange, spoke up. "The firm of Seavey and Flarsheim will guarantee delivery."

By the fourth month of operation, sales for the Postum Company were over three thousand dollars. Within the next six months the figure jumped to six thousand dollars. In the second year sales totaled a quarter of a million dollars. By 1902 Post was a multimillionaire. His advertising outlay for 1909 was a million dollars, three-quarters of it in newspapers. He took in a profit for the year of $4 million, in a day when a stenographer made nine dollars a week and sugar cost a nickel a pound.

Post made more money more quickly than anyone ever had with a manufactured product. This is hard to understand, since few people drink Postum today. Its success is reflected in the vast sales of decaffeinated coffee. More than one-third of all coffee sold in the United States today is made by a variation on the decaffeinating process developed at the beginning of this century in France by Dr. Ludwig Roselius and named Sanka (*sans-caffeine*).

This statistic suggests there are multitudes who can't drink coffee but want a coffeelike product. Before Postum, there was no such thing. The scramble to keep the American mug full of hot beverage has now come full cycle with General Foods' announcement in April, 1977 that, in response to exorbitant world coffee prices, they would be putting out a coffee substitute called Mellow Roast. The product, introduced by a nationwide ad campaign, contains some coffee, but the main ingredients are wheat, bran, and molasses.

The key to Post's success, he was happy to concede, was advertising. Post used the medium in a totally new way, and the American economy has never again been the same. He was the first to create a widespread consumer demand where none had existed before—not simply for a new brand, but for an altogether new commodity.

Before Post set to work, advertising in America was, in large measure, placed by retail merchants trying to lure customers to their stores; it was the storekeeper's job to sell specific products. The few products that did advertise directly to the consumer, staples like Pears' Soap and Baker's Chocolate, did so in dignified "reminder" ads. The only ads that made an effort at selling were for patent medicines, and these went to the opposite extreme of haranguing, exhorting, threatening. It was from these ads Post borrowed much of his technique.

To push Postum, he backed the reader against a wall, planted a finger in his chest, and ranted: "You've got a lot of problems. You can't sleep, your nerves are on edge, you have no energy or zest for life. The cause of all this grief is a product for which you've been shelling out your money: coffee. My product offers all of the pleasure of coffee, none of the drawbacks. In fact, it improves your health. And it's cheaper, etc. etc. etc. . . ."

Post believed his drink to be of enormous benefit to mankind; no one should waste a minute before becoming a regular user. His exhortations sometimes reached fire-and-brimstone hysteria. In a singular burst of Darwinian eloquence he cried, "Does the coffee habit push you into the big crowd of mongrels, deaden what thoroughbred blood you may have? . . ."

His copy had a gusto and freshness that were then unknown. He deliberately used incorrect simple-folk grammar: "If the coffee don't agree . . ." He would capitalize words when he felt like it, and he crammed his headlines with shock words like KIDNAPPED! (your health) and upset typesetters with unorthodox lettering. "What do I care about typographical style?" Post once said. "What I want to do is get my message across to the man in the street." This kind of pronunciamento is common in advertising offices today; at the turn of the century it was unheard of. He summarized his ad technique: "Plain words for plain people." After a barrage of irrefutable arguments for buying Postum, Post's ads would finish with a tag line that floated across the bottom: "THERE'S A REASON." This incomplete thought suggests an array of conclusions—all favorable to Postum: There's a reason you feel wretched (coffee); there's a reason why you are starting to feel great (Postum); there's a reason why everyone's buying it (it does what it claims); there's a reason it does what it claims (fine ingredients, careful preparation). Another pioneer in the advertising business referred to Post as a hypnotic advertiser. Perhaps those evenings at La Vita Inn had been a warm-up for spellbinding an entire nation.

The great Chicago advertising man, Albert D. Lasker, is often credited with fathering modern marketing with his ad campaigns. But Lasker was a boy of fifteen when Post was writing the same kind of hard-sell copy that made Lasker famous. At his first job at the old Lord & Thomas Agency, Lasker was given the Michigan territory to solicit for business. He himself mentions visiting Battle Creek "scores of times," where he studied the success of Post's, and later Kellogg's ad campaigns. Innovations the textbooks attribute to Lasker—salesmanship in print, reason-why advertising, ending the days of passive, reminder ads—were all fundamental to Post's campaigns to sell Postum and later Grape-Nuts.

It is amazing that the Kelloggs stood by and watched Post's success for eleven years before bestirring themselves to imitate it. Others weren't so sluggish. In the first years of the new century some forty cereal companies sprang up around Battle Creek —some in tents, others never getting beyond the stock-issuing stage. One of these speculations, another coffee substitute named Javril, was the undertaking of Adlai Stevenson's father.

Other large food companies were already establishing national markets—H. J. Heinz (1869), Pillsbury (1869), Coca-Cola (1886); but many more came into being during the 1890s: Campbell's Soups, Carnation

Milk, Wrigley's Chewing Gum, Ralston Purina. The decade also saw the birth of a number of independently produced brand names that reached for national markets: Jell-O, Minute Tapioca, Maxwell House Coffee, Log Cabin Syrup. These last were eventually absorbed into the General Foods Corporation.

The activity wasn't lost on W. K. Kellogg. He persisted in urging his brother to take on Post in full competition, but Dr. John Harvey remained adamant, refusing to sully his white smock in the orgy of commercialism. The fraternal tug-of-war was aggravated by Kellogg's discovery of a process in 1895 (the same year Post arrived at Postum), that W. K. was convinced had enormous commerical potential. It was the flaking operation by which cooked corn or wheat pulp was roasted on large drums and then flaked off. It would eventually grind out Kellogg's Corn Flakes, Post Toasties, and scores of popular products. Still the doctor said no; he allowed an expansion of the Sanitas operation, but very gradually so as not to exercise the AMA.

In addition to Dr. Kellogg's professional inhibitions, the bizarre relationship between the Kellogg brothers also contributed to Post's eleven-year head start. W. K. was as drab and plodding as his brother was flamboyant and mercurial. Dr. John Harvey always dressed in a white suit, white shoes, and sometimes strolled the sanitarium grounds with a white cockatoo on his shoulder. W. K. remained in his shadow, working long hours, keeping the institution's books, putting out its publications, and running the food subdivision—all this for fifteen hundred dollars a year, while his older brother grew rich and lived like a duke.

An odd tableau summarizes their relationship. Dr. Kellogg enjoyed bicycling. As he pedaled he would have his fat younger brother huff and puff alongside him, reporting on business matters. This grotesque exercise in submission often occured in full view of patients relaxing on the sanitarium's long veranda.

Eventually, Dr. Kellogg grew bored with merely exploiting and humiliating W. K. and set out to destroy him. When a new factory for the Sanitas division was completed in 1902 and W. K. asked for fifty thousand dollars to pay the builder, Dr. Kellogg announced he had never authorized the expenditure. W. K. would have to pay the debt from his twenty-nine-dollar-a-week salary. That broke the bond. W. K. somehow raised the money, but he announced he would be leaving his brother's employ to start a cereal business of his own.

A strange accident delayed W. K. and gave Post a few more years to get control of the cereal market. The skirmishing that had continued unabated between Sister Ellen White and Dr. Kellogg since he'd come to the sanitarium now erupted into open war. Dr. Kellogg had remarked publicly that he considered the Sister's visions a form of hysteria that would cease when she reached menopause. (They did.) It was certainly no way to talk about God's messenger.

Nevertheless, the final break between the man of medicine and the woman of God was not over science or theology, but rather money. Sister White and the Adventist elders considered the sanitarium and its profits their property. They wanted its revenues to establish other Adventist sanitariums. Dr. Kellogg had little interest in this Howard Johnson approach to health or in watering down his reputation. He had even less interest in parting with his profits.

He engineered the rewriting of his charter to make his sanitarium nonsectarian and to forbid its revenues from being spent outside the state of Michigan. Both stipulations were necessary, he explained, to retain the tax-free status. When Sister Ellen realized that they were really ruses for thwarting her, she had a final vision about the imperious doctor and his ungodly health spa: She saw a sword of fire suspended over Battle Creek.

In 1898 and 1900 there were fires at two subsidiary sanitarium buildings. In 1902, just when W. K. Kellogg was setting out on his own, the sanitarium itself burned down.

In this picture of high-level feuding, it is hard to resist putting the torch in Sister White's hand. It should be pointed out, however, that in 1922, two years after the Sister's death, the Adventist Tabernacle of Battle Creek also burned to the ground. Whether these fires were caused by a divine sword, Sister White herself, or one of the devout who saw in the Sister's vision, not hysteria, but divine commands—the fact is that in a quarter of a century thirteen major fires broke out in Adventist buildings in Battle Creek, leaving only one building that predated Sister White's fire-alarm trance.

To help with the crisis of the burned-out sanitarium, W. K. Kellogg went back to work for his brother. He stayed another three years, continuing to produce the drab, goody-goody foods of the Sanitas Company. Then in 1905 he set out once again on his own. To get the rights to corn flakes, W. K. had to give Dr. John Harvey controlling stock in his new company, but here again, the doctor's infallible instinct for business blunders held true. In the financial panic of 1907, he ran short of cash and used his stock in the cereal company to pay staff. W. K. quietly trailed after him, buying up these random bits of stock, and took control. With this move, the Kellogg tortoise turned into the Kellogg hare.

Meanwhile, Post's eleven-year head start was filled with astonishing accomplishment. In 1898 he brought out Grape-Nuts which was an instant success. In 1906 Post introduced his first flaked cereal. Up to now, Post had shown a genius for names. It would be hard to imagine a better name for a new food than Grape-Nuts, suggesting as it does, two natural healthy foods everyone likes. Likewise the name Postum was not without hidden persuaders. The use of the family name suggested that the man stood behind his product; the *um* sounded like "yum-yum."

But with his new flaked cereal Post ran out of inspiration. He named it Elijah's Manna. Some say he was attempting to cash in on the Kellogg's religious connection. This seems unlikely, since the Kellogg example in business matters had proved to be a primer in bad judgment. In addition to its maladroitness, when the name appeared in Post's ad campaigns, it provoked an outcry of sacrilege. Grumbling about Bethlehem Steel, angel-food cake, and St. Joseph's Aspirin, Post changed the name to Post Toasties and raked in more millions. He started a paper-box company to produce his own packaging and expanded his sales to England and the Continent.

The stories persist that C. W. Post owes his success to the Kelloggs, from whom he stole his formulas. Naturally, the Kellogg faction sent up this cry from the beginning. Today, one of the most diligent proponents of the charge is C. W. Post's grandson-in-law, actor Cliff Robertson. Robertson is quick to tell how, while filming a documentary for General Foods, he encountered one of the original employees of the Postum Company who drew him aside and gave him the word on C. W.'s success. The word was *theft*. Straight poop. Eyewitness account.

Robertson is not the first son-in-law to try cutting his wife's fancy family down to size, but it is idle to assume a worker hired to make Post's products would necessarily be an authority on the origins of those products. The Kelloggs were clearly in the cereal-making game before Post. It would undoubtedly have appeared to the people of Battle Creek, ignorant of the earlier history of these food-processing ideas, that Post stole Kellogg inventions. The one innovation that might be considered original to the Kelloggs, the flaking process, was introduced in 1895. Post didn't bring out *his* first flaked cereal, Post Toasties, until 1906, well after other imitations had appeared on the market.

To cast further doubt on the larceny charge, the Kelloggs, for all their cries of theft, never launched litigation. They were no strangers to legal actions of this kind. In addition to losing Dr. Jackson's plagiarism suit over Granula, Dr. John Harvey eventually took his own brother to court to enjoin him from using the Kellogg name. (The doctor lost.)

The major elements of Post's accomplishments were all his own. Post saw the potential of convenient, ready-to-eat cereal products; he saw that they had to be made palatable as well as healthful, and that it was necessary (and possible) to short-circuit the middleman and sell directly to the consumer. In a sense, he left the Kelloggs back at the sanitarium, stirring their pots of corn mush.

Anyone intent on denigrating Post's success would do better to examine his ad campaigns. It was here he departed from respectability. So carried away was he with his products' curative powers, he began claiming that Postum would prevent appendicitis, blindness, and heart disease. The claims eventually landed him in court, but by the time Post was forced to tone down his scare technique, his products were well established.

Post's enemies, and later those of his daughter, did not have to evoke the patent-medicine hokum of the empire's beginnings to get in their jibes. They found sufficient cause for snickering in that a bowl of Post Toasties lacked the nobility of a railroad or real-estate swindle. But such petty distinctions are of interest only to dowagers with much time, much lineage, and little money of *any* origin. The many beneficiaries of Post largesse, including the legions who wined and dined for years on Post money, couldn't have been less concerned about how the money was made.

CHAPTER FOUR

Marjorie would have dreamlike recollections of living in a boardinghouse with an invalid parent who peddled suspenders door-to-door for a living. But the central spectacle of her young years was a dynamic father bursting into full-fledged tycoondom. C. W. Post adapted so quickly to the role, one suspects he had been rehearsing it mentally for years.

His response to riches, however, was outside the mold of other American moguls. By 1903, eight years after launching Postum, he had amassed a personal fortune of $10 million and it was still growing rapidly. He had no interest in using it to crack society, to build a great art collection, or to indulge himself with racehorses or yachts. He didn't even build himself a ducal mansion—the American millionaire's usual way of saying, "I've made it!"

Post saw his fortune as enabling him, not so much to own things, as to *do* things. His attitude contrasts with that of his daughter who, perhaps more than anyone of her time, surrounded herself with the trappings of great wealth. Instead of building estates, her father built an incongruously luxurious hotel in downtown Battle Creek, the Post Tavern, and, nearby, an office complex called the Marjorie Block. He built a community of model homes for his workers—the main street was called Marjorie Street—and sold them at cost.

He directed his energies and his fortune toward a number of causes. Having persuaded the world of the necessity of his products, he set out to change other things that weren't being done right. The Postum Company was only a year old when Post launched the first, and perhaps the most ambitious, of a series of crusades: to revamp the United States currency system. He had an ingenious and somewhat complicated idea for issuing currency that would circulate like traditional money until it was endorsed over to a specific firm or individual, at which point it would be worthless to anyone else.

The purpose of this scheme was to assist the country's vast mail-order business, which was losing revenue through mail theft or fear of mail theft. Few people had checking accounts and most post offices did not yet sell the little-used money orders. Post, who had suffered from the imperfection of the money system in his suspender business, set out to perfect it. That his idea would obviate checks and money orders and bankrupt most express companies and banks didn't deter him.

He waged his battle with the same weapon he had used to change public eating habits: advertising. In

newspapers all over the country he placed wordy dia-
tribes against the current system of mailing money,
including hard-sell explanations of his idea. Post was
the first individual to push a personal cause with extensive advertising. The campaign made him a personality to the public—which surely helped Postum sales
—and to other personalities. He received letters of
support from prominent figures, among them Mark
Twain. But notoriety was not his aim.

Post's researches into the currency matter introduced
him to rampant post office and congressional corrup-
tion. He was shortly caught in full-scale newspaper
melees with post office officials and powerful US
senators. Later struggles included a fight for truth-in-
packaging legislation, an effort to halt the impending
income tax, and, his last battle, combating organized
labor. (Post would say he was not against organized
labor, but *abuses* of organized labor, a list of actions
that seemed to include workers opening their mouths.)

As Post was becoming a colorful personality to the
nation's newspaper readers, he was also becoming a
glamorous presence on the streets of Battle Creek. He
had always been something of a dandy; now, immaculately suited and in a white Stetson hat, he sported the
panache befitting the town benefactor—the man who
was making Battle Creek known throughout the world,
not as a depressingly righteous health center, but as a
fast-buck boom town.

In the midst of her father's rise to wealth and national prominence, Marjorie had, in many ways, an
ordinary childhood in a small midwestern town. She
kept a rabbit hutch behind La Vita Inn and caught
moles to skin for her dolls' fur coats, her father instructing her in using the knife.

In later years, Marjorie would have few links with
these days in Battle Creek, but there were some. Walking home from school one day with a chum named

Myra, Marjorie caught her foot as the girls crossed the railroad tracks. A train approached, and Marjorie became too frozen with fear to do anything. Instead of running from the danger, Myra struggled calmly to free Marjorie's foot from the stuck shoe, succeeding just in time. Marjorie always kept in touch with Myra, bringing her an expensive present whenever she returned to Battle Creek. When as an elderly widow, Myra entered a nursing home, Marjorie sent word that her friend should have everything she wanted.

In the early years of Postum's success, C. W. began annual trips to Europe, often taking his daughter with him. The main purpose of these trips was to keep abreast of dietary developments, but he relished travel for its own sake. He also brought back some art, most of it second-rate, which he later used to decorate the lobby of the Post Tavern and the company offices.

With the Postum Company springing up around La Vita Inn, the Post family continued living there for a time. C. W. participated in community events as befitted the town's most prominent citizen. A newspaper account of 1898 describes a charity lawn party held at the house that featured a performance of Shakespeare's *As You Like It*. The write-up provides a rare glimpse of an eleven-year-old Marjorie: "a chubby-cheeked girl, with bangs across her forehead, who ran about the lawn on this special occasion."

Post very much wanted a son but seems to have been resigned to having only one child. Perhaps this was because of an estrangement from his wife that had been developing since his recovery. The marriage, never too solid, had been held together by its patient-nurse arrangement. Now that C. W. was not only well, but bursting with vigor and accomplishment, the retiring Ella was an encumbering presence in his life.

It was rare for the progenitor of such a large fortune to sire only one child and that one a female. This situation had much to do with Marjorie's future and the unique place she held among the twentieth-century scions of American fortunes.

Her only-child status also gave an odd cast to her up-bringing. C. W. confronted the no-son disappointment with his customary combination of logic and iconoclasm. He decided that the traditional view of female limitations was so much hogwash and determined to raise Marjorie as a boy.

Most remarkably—for the times—he started to take her with him to Postum Company board meetings when she was only eleven. Sometimes he would place her within earshot but out of sight; other times she would be a full participant in the meetings. Afterward he would quiz her on what had happened and on the significance of the decisions made.

He took her on business trips with him. When—to apprise himself of technological developments—he toured factories, Marjorie went along and was made to understand everything she saw. Post was determined to teach his daughter all aspects of the business she would one day inherit. The girl was flattered and fascinated.

Post showed his disdain for traditional notions about bringing up girls in other ways. Walking home from school each day, Marjorie and a companion were harassed by a local tough who reigned over a vacant lot on their path. C. W. resolved that Marjorie should handle this situation herself—daughter or not—and had her instructed in boxing. Marjorie soon put a stop to the taunting with a strong right.

Self-protection wasn't Post's only reason for boxing lessons. He was convinced the dependence and passivity of women was the result of the traditional style of rearing them. He showed the same contempt for these forms that he had shown for traditional forms of marketing. He took Marjorie hunting with him. He took her to prize fights, dressing her like a boy and pushing her hair up under a cap, since in those days women were not welcome at ringside.

Post continually reminded his daughter that she would one day be very rich. Although his own experience as a rich man was brief, he had many theories on dealing with wealth. Two maxims were emphasized: Money was to be spent; in spending it, she should trust no one. A corollary to the second was that one's only protection against being swindled was knowledge.

As an adult, Marjorie would adopt the money-spending precept with a convert's fervor. She adhered as well to the second, only so far as it related to trusting strangers—shopkeepers, art dealers, jewelers. She made a serious effort to educate herself about costly merchandise, even enrolling in courses on tapestries and, when building her yacht, marine engineering. On the other hand, when it came to trusting those close to her, she would have done better to retain a bit more of her father's cynicism.

Just when the century turned was a matter of some dispute. Purists said that 1900 belonged to the hundred years just ending, and that 1901 was the beginning of the twentieth century. Either way, 1901 was an eventful year with a markedly transitional air. Queen Victoria died, McKinley was shot, and Theodore Roosevelt took over the presidency. The English took time out from the Boer War to make boxing a legal sport, to negotiate an agreement giving the United States the right to build a canal across the Isthmus of Panama, and to participate in the Peace of Peking, thus ending The Boxer Rebellion. To lovers of the finer things these events were insignificant compared to the deaths of Toulouse-Lautrec and Giuseppe Verdi.

Europe was still agog over the Paris Exposition of

1900 where one of the star attractions had been the fifty-six-year-old Russian jeweler Peter Carl Fabergé and the collection of exotic Easter eggs that he had made for the Russian Imperial family. The rage in Paris for the women of fashion was a live fox as a pet; the demand was so great, foxes were sold on street corners. A thirty-year-old Marcel Proust gave a lavish dinner for Anatole France.

The robust action was on the other side of the Atlantic. The automobile was taking hold in the American consciousness. In Detroit, one Alexander Winston set a new track record for cars of fifty miles per hour, and Henry Ford would soon quit his recently launched Detroit Automobile Company and form the Ford Motor Company. J. P. Morgan decided it was time to impose his brand of sense onto the burgeoning American steel industry and formed US Steel. The Wright brothers were building their heavier-than-air device; an oil strike in Beaumont, Texas, launched that state's oil boom. On the popular front, ping-pong became the newest rage, women risked arrest by smoking cigarettes in public, and Carrie Nation continued her hatchet raids on Kansas saloons. A blare of ragtime and the release of five thousand homing pigeons marked the opening of the Pan-American Exposition at Buffalo, New York, where the principal attraction would be the assassination of President McKinley.

Battle Creek, Michigan, was not to be left out of the changing-times hubbub. It celebrated the new age by getting its first two automobiles, then showed it wasn't quite finished with the past by hosting Buffalo Bill Cody's stampede of 250 cowboys, Indians, and Cossacks. Businesses were thriving; each month a new food company was established. Proof that the prosperity was not all gossamer was the opening of Charlie Post's luxurious new Post Tavern.

Each room had a connecting bath and its own

telephone; no hotel in New York City could claim that. The lobby had leather furniture as well as genuine antiques and oil paintings brought back from Europe by none other than C. W. himself. With Post's rapid rise, Battle Creekers saw no reason why they should not follow Chicago along the path to big-city glory. Indeed, with his hotel, they were halfway there.

Today traffic is still halted in downtown Battle Creek while a freight train lumbers across a main street, telephone numbers have five rather than seven digits, and the only air transportation available is a two-engine turboprop. But in 1901 it all looked infinitely possible.

Townspeople had barely recovered from Post's hotel bedazzlement when he completed a large office building, and later, a theater, which opened with a gala comedy performance starring the leading actress of the day, Maxine Elliott. She was a friend of Post's—seventy-five-year-old gossip has them more than just friends. Gossip also says she later asked him to build her a theater, and when he refused, replaced him with J. P. Morgan, who did.

The opening night of the Post Theater was fourteen-year-old Marjorie's first taste of the Great World. Before the curtain opened, her father had her take a rose to each lady holding a box seat; and at the curtain calls Marjorie presented Miss Elliott with a large bouquet of roses. If C. W. Post was the king of Battle Creek, he was seeing to it that his daughter was a hard-working princess. The local paper launched a seventy-year tradition by reporting what Marjorie was wearing: a blue crêpe de chine dress with embroidered roses.

As her husband's pace accelerated, Ella Post spent more and more time away from Battle Creek, traveling for her health, it was reported. C. W. was now in a position to give Ella everything she wanted, except for himself; as she had a great fondness for sightseeing, music, and the arts, travel seemed to be the answer.

Marjorie, still in school, remained with her father, and her Aunt Mollie, Carroll Post's wife, became her surrogate mother. Marjorie would adore the jovial, hefty woman as long as she lived. But the girl's world was her father.

These years must have been a daddy's-girl fantasy for Marjorie. C. W.'s preoccupation and pride in his daughter could be seen, not only on the buildings and streets named after her, but in more customary forms of fatherly doting: He alone ordered her dresses from fancy New York and Chicago stores, chose her hair style, and offered her constant from-the-shoulder advice.

Marjorie's hero ruled a vast industrial complex, hired hundreds of workers, fed an entire town's prosperity, was at the center of national controversies; his name appeared on breakfast tables across America—this dashing man had focused his Olympian attention on a teenage girl with plump cheeks and bangs. He would explain the world to her, decide if she were to have lace trim on a new dress, pluck her from boring schoolrooms, and spirit her off to Europe or California—and to cap off his godlike condescension, he would make her privy to his divine mysteries: the operation of the company that produced all that money.

Marjorie loved her mother, and the rift between her parents caused her much pain. But surely one part of the teenage girl exulted in the mother's banishment that left her alone with this glorious father.

The dream was short-lived, god-men being what they are. The father-daughter idyll was broken by the entrance of Leila Young, a beautiful young Battle Creek girl who worked as a secretary at the Postum Company, and whose widowed mother ran a boardinghouse. C. W. had an alert eye for pretty faces and, since regaining his health, was not shy about pursuing them. With this particularly pretty face already on the payroll and Ella touring Europe, it was easy to the point of inevitability.

C. W. fell resoundingly in love with Leila and hired her as a companion for his daughter—adding baby-sitter affront to Marjorie's more personal wound—and later as his private secretary. The dress boxes from Chicago were opened with less gusto.

In 1902 C. W. moved from Battle Creek to Washington and entered Marjorie in a girl's finishing school there, the school that would later become Mount Vernon College. To be near her daughter, Ella Post also moved to Washington, setting up a separate residence. Although C. W. wanted a Washington base to continue his lobbying, at the same time he was searching the Northeast for a pleasant place to build a home that was, he said, to be for his daughter. In Greenwich, Connecticut, he found an ideal combination of rural charm and convenience to New York City. In 1903 work was begun on a house.

In 1904 C. W. divorced Ella and married Leila. This was merely legalizing the existing situation. Still, Marjorie was all but crushed, according to her oldest friends. It was natural that she would be thrown together with her step-mother, but time and proximity did little to ease the pain. Marjorie always blamed Leila for her parents' divorce; the indictment was shared by most of Battle Creek.

C. W.'s reaction to such gossip was typical; he lobbied against it. In a testimonial dinner given him by his employees, he seized the occasion to discuss his personal affairs:

In concluding this family talk, I am going to take up a personal subject. It is not considered good taste to discuss private and domestic affairs in public. I am going to break that rule this evening

52

because my family affairs have been made public in perhaps every newspaper in America. The papers have all been kind except the labor sheets and a little lonely society paper that has been lambasting me for about three years because I would not advertise in it. Many of the statements have been erroneous, some laughable, and, in the so-called society paper, willfully and maliciously false. The paper devoted a column or more to derogatory remarks about Postum and Grape-Nuts and a tirade against me for taking as my wife a poor girl that had earned her living as my private secretary. It was gracious enough to say she was a tall, graceful person and one of the most beautiful women ever seen in Washington.

Mark you, I was condemned because I had separated from a former wife and married a poor girl. Such statements, without explanation, give the public a false and harmful impression of the individual and the facts of the case. I propose to stand before my people as just what I am, no more and no less, and to this end the following facts are given:

When scarcely out of our teens, the first Mrs. Post and I were married, and in less than a year found a childish mistake had been made, and that we both lacked mature judgment in the selection of a life partner. Therefore many years ago we found it better to live apart most of the time, while in public we appeared together. We each had high esteem and regard for the qualities of the other, but the home-making element was not there and we never occupied a house as our private home. The nearest approach was at The Inn, and that was a public institution. My daughter has from babyhood been chum and companion of her father and about five years ago while trying to care for her, it became necessary to have someone with her at the noon hour and at four when she came from school. Not a housekeeper, but a companion that would see that she was warm, comfortable and contented. After a consultation with Leila's parents, we secured her to come each day at noon and stay over the evening dinner with Marjorie. Then she added to her other duties that of private secretary, looking after and assisting me in the preparation of papers, public addresses, etc., and became a regularly installed member of our little family.

During those days, my friends, I caught glimpses of what a peaceful, contented home might be, if nature happened to supply the members of the home circle with temperaments that harmonized. . . .

For five years I have had almost daily opportunity to observe the traits of a gentle, womanly character whose presence with Marjorie and I meant peace. Let it be remembered that many years before this a practical separation had occurred, caused by no individual or person but by old Mother Nature herself. A large volume of bonds was placed in trust for the use of the former Mrs. Post, the income for life being enough yearly to keep a dozen families, and sufficient to indulge her desire for travel to any limit. She is happy and contented and we have had no occasions for the usual acrimonious contentions customary in separation. On the contrary, I frequently hear of the kind expressions from her, and I have a steady and profound regard for the many sterling qualities of her character.

The public generally seems to think a man of means should marry a wealthy society woman, and the so-called society paper that criticized me rather sneered at the fact that I married a new wife

that was a poor girl and earned a living as my
secretary and the fact that she ever worked seems
to trouble it. I can't possibly imagine what use I
would have for a society pet that would drag an old
work horse around nights to social functions and
make him listen to the drool about the latest kind
of necktie, cut of riding pants "ye know," and all
the tiresome stuff the dudes feed on.

Marjorie was seventeen when her father remarried.
Her own life at school in Washington continued rou-
tinely. She attended parties, sometimes impressive ones
like dances at the US Naval Academy nearby at An-
napolis. As was the custom, she would not go with any
particular boy, but rather with a group of friends, her
mother often chaperoning. (Ella Post was such a good
dancer, she was as popular at these parties as her
daughter.)

As the house in Greenwich, named the Boulders,
neared completion, C. W. would meet his daughter
there to check on its progress and make plans for its
furnishings. They stayed in a hotel and became acquainted with a few of the local people. One in particular, a pleasantly bland young man named Edward
Bennett Close, took a keen interest in the midwestern
girl. Close was from a socially prominent Greenwich
family and had just graduated from Columbia Law
School. He journeyed to Washington to see her again.
When they attended a party together on the evening
of his arrival, it was the first time Marjorie had ever
worn her hair up. She had never had a beau before:
Ed Close now filled that role.

Close was liked by most people, but at that age was
not overly burdened with charm or good looks. He also
tended toward plumpness—all in all, a stopgap Prince
Charming for a disenfranchised princess. His only distinction was his family background. A Close had been

the first settler of Greenwich, and the boy's mother had been a Brevoort, a proud old Knickerbocker family.

Close seems to have fallen completely in love with Marjorie, and his puppydog devotion was not wasted on the emotionally buffeted schoolgirl. One evening in the Greenwich hotel, Close asked C. W. Post if he could speak to him alone. To steady her nerves during this crucial conference, Marjorie went to visit an older woman who lived in the hotel and who had befriended her. Marjorie would always be sentimental about people who shared dramatic moments in her life, and although their lives grew quite separate, she kept in touch with the woman for many years. Ed Close emerged from the talk with C. W.'s consent to his marrying Marjorie.

The following year, 1905, they were married in a fashionable wedding at Grace Episcopal Church in Manhattan. Marjorie was eighteen, Ed twenty-three. The Manhattan land on which Grace Church stood had been given to the parish by his great-great-grandfather. The Closes were longer on lineage than money, making them feel superior to itinerant midwesterners, however rich.

This attitude was apparently shared by many of the Close relatives and friends who attended the wedding. A Close uncle, too old or too proud to whisper, was heard to say as Marjorie came down the aisle, "She's a rather pretty little thing, considering who she is and where she's from." The remark made its way to Marjorie, who was deeply stung by it.

Even though she spent a lifetime showing such eastern snobs she was a person to be reckoned with, such social distinctions do not die out easily. Even today her two daughters by Close are quick to establish that one half of their pedigree is East Coast aristocracy. Although well aware that their wealth and whatever renown they possess comes from their link with Marjorie Merriweather Post, they prefer not being lumped in with the Battle Creek emigrés or with their half sister Dina Merrill, who is midwestern on both sides.

If C. W.'s second marriage drove Marjorie to an early wedding, it also cast a cloud over the celebration itself. Ella Post refused to attend the ceremony if Leila did. C. W. would not come without his new wife. In the impasse, Marjorie sided with her mother. The man who still began letters to his daughter, "Dear Little Sweetheart . . ." and referred to her as "My small pal of long ago"—who named streets after her and who would make her one of the world's richest women— stayed away from her wedding.

CHAPTER FIVE

Greenwich in 1905 was on its way to being the top suburb for rich New Yorkers, suggesting C. W. Post may have had more in mind than pretty scenery and convenience to Manhattan when he started building Marjorie's house in 1903. As early as the 1850s a number of summer resort hotels sprang up along the Greenwich shore of Long Island Sound, attracting wealthy city dwellers. Some of the summer visitors became so enchanted with the clean country air, the waterfront with its quaint inlets and harbors, and the gentle green hills, they bought property and built houses. As travel by car and train improved, Greenwich became less and less a seasonal place, except for the very rich who saw a few late Manhattan parties a year as reason enough for an in-town residence.

By 1905 Greenwich had such distinguished settlers as William Rockefeller, his two sons, and a pride of company presidents. The hills, quaintly referred to then as "back country," blossomed with large estates that were closer in spirit to English manors than gentleman farms or city dwellers' summer refuges.

The house that C. W. Post built for his daughter cost three hundred thousand dollars. It was huge but, strangely, not overpoweringly pretentious. Such a charge is avoided by the simple, unmonumental architecture—gabled roof, sprawling shape, chunky stone construction. A rather long drive passes a gate house, then some huge rocks that give the place its name. The drive follows a stream through woods, and finally a clearing reveals the house. The rooms are vast but low-ceilinged and informal. The style can best be characterized by the lack of a terrace, veranda, patio, or lanai—but the presence of the longest front porch in the history of domestic architecture. It is the dream house of the richest man from a small midwestern town, set down in the wooded rolling hills of the affluent East.

The stables sat directly behind the house and were every bit as unstinting. Elsewhere on the property was a small lake. C. W. had built onto the house a large apartment for himself and Leila. The interior decor throughout had many of the day's fashionable touches: satin walls in the master bedroom and, in the dining room, wall panels of blue velvet divided by gold braid. Cooks, maids, butlers, coachmen, and grooms totaled thirteen, which was a modest staff in those days when a maid's salary was less than three hundred dollars a year. Marjorie would never again live so simply.

Marjorie's marriage interfered little with her closeness to her father, who was a frequent visitor at the Boulders. For his part, C. W. kept her involved in his business trips. The year following the wedding, he took his daughter and son-in-law to Texas. Ever since his days in Fort Worth, C. W. had dreamed of creating his own city. Now that he had his fortune, he set about implementing this vision. In Garza County of the Texas Panhandle region Post bought a number of ranches totaling some 230,000 acres. Here he broke ground for Post City. C. W. spent millions developing this dream, a book could be written about it, but it never became the Utopia he envisioned.

On this early inspection tour of the land, C. W. Post and the young couple traveled to within seventy-five miles of their destination by train, completing the journey by mule-drawn wagons. A storm arose suddenly and the convoy—tycoon, heiress, and mules—took refuge in an abandoned shack for the night. When they arrived at the site selected for the town, they spent days planning the arrangement of buildings and roads, occasionally taking a break to go bear hunting.

For the most part, Marjorie's young married days were more conventional. She and her husband settled down to the comfortably dull existence of a wealthy suburban couple. The highlight of her Greenwich week was Monday night at the Metropolitan Opera or an occasional party. Close had his own circle of friends— the thinned-out blood of the Field Club set—and had little interest in expanding it. It is doubtful if Marjorie would have known how to branch out even if she had wanted to.

Up to now her life had been school in Battle Creek, followed by a few years at an undistinguished finishing school in Washington. Her lack of polish was a marital sore point. Ed Close worked on Marjorie's diction to try and rid her of her midwestern accent, and he never lost the opportunity to instruct her on "the way things are done."

He also kept a lid on her spending. C. W. had never discouraged his daughter from spending money, provided she didn't waste it, but every time Marjorie stirred to break loose and enjoy her wealth, Ed would talk her out of it. Their daughter Eleanor can remember her father's continuing struggle against what he called her mother's tendency toward ostentation. Close was so consistent about this, he seems to have been masking a personal quirk, a tendency toward withdrawal, behind injunctions about propriety.

Into this slough of respectability C. W. would arrive in a swirl of empire-shaking celebrity. He would regale his daughter with tales of fighting senatorial dragons, labor-leader Goliaths—then pull her aside for a rich person's confab on improvements to the Boulders, new conveniences she should buy, or trips she should take. He would stay for a few days, running the world from his Connecticut headquarters, then disappear to Battle Creek, California, or Europe. While Marjorie had a strong feeling for Close, he represented a haven. The thrills and glamour in her life still came from her father.

In July 1908 the Closes' first child arrived, a girl they named Adelaide. Seventeen months later, a second daughter, Eleanor, was born. Marjorie and Ed Close were thrilled; so was C. W., who quickly set up trust funds for the two girls. A photograph taken when they are roughly three and four shows them on the lawns of the Boulders, both atop a pony held by their mother. They are chubby, pretty children with great billows of curly hair unrestrained by floppy ribbons that hung to the side. Marjorie appears handsome in an ordinary way. She still had the fullness of face that prevented her from being a real beauty.

Eleanor recalls C. W. Post as a severe, forbidding man. She once tried to liven up one of her grandfather's visits by throwing a pet cat on his shoulders as he sat reading. Sixty years later she remembers with a shudder the fierce look he gave her with his blue, laser eyes.

61

Recollections of her grandmother Post were more pleasant: Ella singing lullabies to her and Adelaide in a pure, lovely soprano.

In contrast with his daughter's domestic idyll, C. W.'s life with Leila was fast-paced and glamorous. From 1902 on he took less and less part in the affairs of the Postum Company, leaving operations to his "cabinet," a hand-picked group of executives headed by his brother Carroll. He devoted his time to travel, crusades, and the development of Post City. The newspapers gave his activities extensive coverage.

He and Leila kept apartments in Battle Creek, Washington, Chicago's Blackstone Hotel, and a new location they favored increasingly, Santa Barbara. Rumors circulated that C. W. was once again playing around; various actresses were mentioned. Whether or not the rumors were true, Leila Post believed them, and they made her angry. In Chicago the Posts met a man named Lawrence J. Montgomery whom they befriended; in 1913 Post hired him to manage the Post Tavern. Before long, rumors had it that Leila had found in Montgomery a shoulder to cry on.

Early in 1914, as Post was to deliver an anti-income-tax speech in Philadelphia, the newspapers announced that he had collapsed. It was a recurrence of his old breakdown pattern: severe depression and acute stomach trouble. With Leila, he went to Santa Barbara to recuperate. After a time, the stomach trouble flared up again, and Post was rushed to the Mayo Clinic in Minnesota by special train. The president of the Santa Fe Railroad arranged for a pilot train to clear the tracks so Post's train could make record time. Headlines around the country proclaimed the "MILLIONAIRE'S RACE WITH DEATH."

Post was operated on for appendicitis, and he returned to Santa Barbara to convalesce. His mental state was as bad as it had ever been. Doctors left orders that Post should not be alone, nor should he have access to weapons.

Somehow a rifle from his gun collection eluded the ban. Left alone one day while Leila went shopping, Post dressed himself immaculately and lay rigidly and formally on the bed. He put the rifle in his mouth and pulled the trigger with his outstretched hand. He was sixty years old.

The suicide of this embodiment of the American dream caused a sensation throughout America and Europe. Post had a beautiful wife, an adoring daughter, the attention of the public in matters that concerned him. He had built and owned outright a giant corporation that was making him richer every day. Now he was building his own city. His name was mentioned in the press as a presidential possibility. That such a colossus should suffer the ultimate despair stunned the nation.

As soon as the news reached Marjorie and Ed Close, vacationing in Palm Beach, they rushed to Santa Barbara. Marjorie's stoicism and ability to function in the face of such a disastrous end to the man who had been her entire world suggests she had been braced for such a calamity.

Even with C. W.'s history of instability, there is considerable mystery surrounding his death. To this day the people of Battle Creek do not feel the story makes sense. Why was he left alone? they ask. What was a severely depressed man doing with a rifle? Some accounts said that Post believed he had cancer (he did not) and could not face a lingering death. Others weave a more gothic plot: Post discovered that Leila was having an affair with Montgomery (whom she married two years later), and in despair took his life. Some versions insist that she had not gone shopping but had gone off to meet Montgomery.

It is neither possible to unearth the unknown facts

nor build the known ones into an unchallengeable story. Most relevant here is Post's thirty-year history of breakdowns and depression. Whatever it was that got him to pull the trigger—cancer, infidelity, *Weltschmerz* —there is no doubt that the potential for self-destruction had always been with him.

Years later Marjorie would openly discuss her father's suicide with friends. She would speculate that, had he stayed closer to Christian Science, as she herself tried to do, he would never have killed himself. She was not always so forthright about this grim episode in her family history. In her later years she commissioned a friend, Nettie Leitch Major, to write a biography of C. W. Post. Mrs. Major included a detailed description of the suicide with all its horrific details. When Marjorie read the part in the manuscript about the suicide, her head stayed lowered on the page, although she had obviously finished reading. Finally she spoke.

"Oh, Nettie, do we have to include this?"

"But Marjorie," Mrs. Major protested, "it was a headline in every paper in the world. How can it be left out?"

Mrs. Major saw that there were tears starting down the cheeks of the elderly Mrs. Post. "But it was so long ago," she said. Then, more forcibly, "You'll think of some way, Nettie."

Mrs. Major's biography refers to C. W. Post's "passing away" and avoids the merest hint of suicide. "When I saw what it was doing to her," Mrs. Major said, "I couldn't have done it."

MINNIE MARSTON:

I got married in Port Chester in 1909, and someone brought Marjorie Close to my wedding. I'd never met her before. No one knew her. She didn't go out or give parties. She had had an odd childhood, and she was still under the domination of her father, who was something of a Turk. He'd brought her up but always kept her near him, taking her with him on business trips, to board meetings, but she had no upbringing really, no social graces. She was a terrible dresser.

I was from the East and she was very midwestern, but we were about the same age and we took to each other right away. She was down-to-earth and she loved people although she was shy. She didn't know how to let her hair down or to have a good time. But she loved to do simple things. My husband and I had a very modest house in Port Chester with only one servant—nothing like her place in Greenwich—but she loved coming over for visits.

Nobody much liked C. W. Post. He was an awfully austere man, not social at all. And he had very little humor. A man with a purpose, with a lot of purposes. He was always very nice to younger people, particularly to young men on the way up. He went out of his way to help them. He liked Ed Close and got him involved in the Postum Company.

When C. W. divorced Ella Post, it almost killed Marjorie. She adored her mother. Her Aunt Mollie helped bring her up. Marjorie was still suffering from this when she met Ed Close. He was the only beau she'd ever known. He was nice enough but very quiet and retiring, a great mouse of a man. He was conservative—a real Greenwich type—he just wanted to stay home or maybe see his friends at the Field Club.

I would encourage Marjorie to liven up her life. I would say to her, "Come on, Marjorie, you never have any fun." She'd laugh. She wanted to, but she didn't know how. And Ed Close was always restraining her.

One time I got her to take a house with us in Palm Beach. It was just a small place with a few bedrooms on Sunset Avenue. It was simplicity itself—nothing pretentious about it. I remember we had two colored women working for us—that was all. It was in the days when the only way to get around Palm Beach was those bicycle chairs that black men pedaled you around in. Marjorie had no trouble adjusting to the simple life. She adored that house. And she enjoyed meeting people . . . all kinds of people. She didn't have a snobbish bone in her body. She didn't know anything about society in those days, and she didn't care about it either. Yet she wanted to be different than she was. She wanted a more exciting life, but she didn't know how *to go about it. And Ed Close was throwing cold water on her ideas, telling her things weren't done that way in the East. . . .*

When they would have fights, Marjorie would turn up on our doorstep in Port Chester. She would spend a few days with us until tempers quieted down. We were a haven for her. She didn't know that many people.

Because of the big estates and the grandeur—she loved grandeur—everyone always forgets about her simple down-to-earth side. Some years later when I was traveling down to Palm Beach in her private railroad car I heard a mouse in my room, and I was terrified. I went next door to her room and woke her up.

"Move over, Marjorie," I said, "you've got company for the night." She loved it.

CHAPTER SIX

At the time of C. W. Post's death in 1914, Marjorie was twenty-seven years old. She had a devoted husband, two healthy, comely daughters, an estate with nursemaids, servants, grooms, horses, and dogs. She now became owner of a cereal company worth $20 million.

C. W.'s end, compared with the prolix tangles produced by his daughter's death almost sixty years later, was fiscally tidy. He had already put the cereal company in Marjorie's name, so his death merely changed her ownership from titular to actual. He had set up trust funds for his first wife, his granddaughters, and his parents.

A good portion of his non-Postum holdings—including the Post Tavern, the office building, and other properties adding up to the amount of some $5 million—he left to his wife Leila, who lived out her days as one of Battle Creek's richest citizens and benefactors. She provided the town with money for an arboretum and a hospital; both were given her full name—Leila Post Montgomery—but are known in Battle Creek with sexist condescension as the Leila Arboretum and the Leila Hospital.

Perhaps with the notion of reconciling his wife and daughter, C. W. left his Texas lands to them jointly, but the arrangement struck Marjorie as messy. Some years later she suggested to her lawyers that they sue Leila for her stake in the Texas acreage; Marjorie's lawyers talked her out of it.

C. W.'s will had one other oddity: a sizeable bequest to one John Post in Texas, whom Post referred to as a "foster son." If her "foster" brother was ever known to Marjorie, she remained quiet about it. At the funeral in September 1973 her daughter Eleanor was approached by a young man who introduced himself as a cousin from Texas.

"He was absolutely charming," she recalls. "I suppose he was a son of John Post. I had him sit with me at supper. Later he disappeared. I don't remember his name."

As the shock of C. W.'s suicide subsided, Marjorie and Ed Close decided to establish a residence in Battle Creek, where Ed would represent his wife on the Postum board. In spite of C. W.'s coaching his daughter on the business—in spite of her outright ownership of it—her presence on the board was not wanted.

In those days, no one thought this strange. The slight was largely a matter of form; her husband and her Uncle Carroll Post kept her briefed on all plans, and no major decisions were made without her approval. But little stewardship was needed from either

Close. The company was prospering under C. W.'s "cabinet," so the couple's Battle Creek sojourns grew briefer and less frequent. They settled back at the Boulders, where they stepped up their socializing, including more frequent forays into Manhattan. Marjorie soon took a Park Avenue apartment to avoid late drives back to Greenwich.

Now with her own unfettered fortune, Marjorie felt increased stirrings to expand her operation. Close countered with firmer lectures on ostentation. His restraining hand met with less patience, and there were many fights. Increasing the friction was Marjorie's growing belief that her husband had a drinking problem; though friends of the period say there was no truth in this. The contradiction may be explained by Marjorie's distorted view of sophisticated vices of this kind. She abhorred liquor and drunkenness and continued to do so throughout her life. Ed Close liked to have a few drinks. From Marjorie's teetotaling Christian Science vantage point, the slightest sign of inebriation appeared rampant alcoholism.

Dina Merrill provides a glimpse of this aspect of the Close marriage with a story her mother told years later. The couple was staying in a New York hotel after a party at which Ed Close had drunk too much. In the middle of the night, he got up from bed to go to the bathroom but mistakenly took the door to the corridor instead, and found himself outside. So disgusted was Marjorie with her husband's condition, she locked him out for the rest of the night.

Disregarding the husband tugging at her sleeve, urging her to stay home, Marjorie began building a circle of friends, attending parties, and giving a few. She had made her first visit to Palm Beach in 1909, an occasion in American social history equivalent to Lenin's arrival in Moscow eight years later.

At first she and Close stayed at the Royal Poinciana.

The luxurious establishment had been the world's largest hotel when Henry Flagler built it fifteen years earlier, and by so doing, created the resort of Palm Beach out of sand and jungle. To launch his beach town, Flagler had imported a trainload of Vanderbilts and Whitneys in March 1896. The social tone of the place has been in slow but constant decline ever since. Nevertheless, Flagler quickly established the island as *the* place for the very rich; in that regard it has never stopped booming.

It is hard to think of Palm Beach as ever having been quaint. Today it has all the charm of a new Cadillac. In the early days, however, there was no road to the island, only a train spur that crossed Lake Worth on a causeway. Flagler would permit no horses; the only transportation was the afromobile, the unhappily racist name for three-wheeled chairs pedaled by black men who sat behind the passenger.

A few years after the opening of the Royal Poinciana, Flager built another hotel, the Breakers, which, in a reconstruction, still sits on the ocean. A small trolleylike train ran through the dense tropical growth between the two hotels. A few cottages clustered around the newer hotel. That was Palm Beach.

By the time Marjorie began coming to Palm Beach, the town had grown somewhat, but it was still a wilderness compared to the manicured toy village it is today. Marjorie loved to bicycle, and she took long rides through jungle trails that teemed with red bugs, land crabs, spiders, and coral snakes. On later visits, like those with the Marstons, Marjorie and Ed Close would lease a small house. In an interview years later, Marjorie waxed coy about how this was managed financially. "We young marrieds would save our money all year long so we could rent a cottage for a few weeks and all be together."

The Close marriage plodded along, helped by the

71

brightening presence of the two little girls and by the fundamental good nature of both Marjorie and Ed. Most of the time the tensions caused by the mismatch of will, ambitions, and temperaments remained in check. The bucolic stalemate was disrupted by Ed's departure to France in 1917. Then an accident capped the Greenwich era.

One night Marjorie was summoned home from a Greenwich dinner party to find the house on fire. Her daughters and servants were safe, but the Boulders was in flames. Faulty wiring had ignited a wall, and as the children were being rushed from the house, one wing burst into flames. By the time the fire was brought under control, the main house was severely damaged.

This calamity was the wrench Marjorie needed to break away from her suburban sentence. She decided to buy a house in Manhattan and make that her principal seat. We can be sure the decision was hers. Ed Close wanted nothing more than to be left alone to tend his garden and dabble in business schemes; the girls loved Greenwich with its brook, lake, and ponies. Marjorie's eye fell on the Burden mansion at the corner of Fifth Avenue and Ninety-second Street, the kind of gigantic pile that today we find hard to believe once housed a single nonroyal family. Marjorie was starting to think as big as her fortune.

To test out the house, Marjorie rented it for a winter with the Burden furniture still in it. With the disdain big new money feels for less big, older money, the Close family snickered at the way the Burdens had tried stabilizing the legs of antique chairs by tying them with string.

The house passed the test and was purchased. Marjorie filled its enormous rooms with French furniture and covered the walls with tapestries, first taking courses at the Metropolitan Museum of Art down the street. She seems to have found her way into the felt-lined back rooms of the fanciest shops quite quickly as rare and esoteric merchandise caught her eye. About this time she bought a quantity of lace that had belonged to the Hapsburgs for many generations and had traditionally been worn at Hapsburg weddings. Adelaide would wear it at her wedding before her mother presented it to the Metropolitan. There was a taste for historically significant jewelry too, a particular fondness for Bourbon diamonds.

Marjorie was taking charge. She countered any back-to-Greenwich movement on the part of her husband and daughters by giving the Boulders—still a valuable property even with a partially burned house—to the Lanier family to use as a school. She was also beginning to see in her fortune possibilities beyond buying houses, jewels, and antique lace. When the United States had entered World War I Marjorie put up funds to finance and equip the base hospital at Savenay, which, by the end of the war, had become the largest American hospital in France. Her patriotic largesse was kept a secret.

In the decade she had been married to Close, Marjorie had developed considerably from the shy midwestern girl overawed by her aristocratic husband and his eastern friends. Her growing self-assurance put an even greater strain on the marriage. By the time Close had left to serve in France, the marriage was too weak to survive the separation. After Close's return, the relationship limped along for a time, but even his French Medal of Honor couldn't compensate for other lacks.

One night in 1919 Minnie and Hunter Marston returned from a trip to find Marjorie established in their Port Chester home. Tearfully she told them that her marriage to Ed Close was finished. She wanted to stay with them "until the furor dies down." The furor was mostly from friends and relatives; the press had not yet deemed Marjorie's domestic arrangements of national import.

Marjorie and Ed remained friendly after their divorce and even after his remarriage. When later twin sons were born to his second wife, Ed came down with a serious kidney ailment. Marjorie telephoned her successor.

"Well, my dear," she said, "you'll have to take care of Ed. You just send the twins over to me, and I will take care of them for you." (The offer was neither accepted nor appreciated by Betsy Close who, for the next fifty years, would resent Marjorie's attentions to her family.)

Rumors say that Marjorie settled a large sum of money on Ed Close, making it unnecessary for him to work for a living. He went on to a distinguished career in public service, spending many years in France, where he managed the American Hospital and became a connoisseur of wines. Later, when he again settled in Greenwich, he look a number of charitable and church-related posts and proved himself to be a man of administrative ability and character.

Marjorie appreciated his good qualities and, throughout her life, maintained a strong affection for her first husband. She also knew he was not the man to replace the void in her life left by the death of her dynamic, charismatic father; neither was he the man with whom to cut loose and enjoy her fortune.

Now over eighty, Close's widow lives in Greenwich, resentful still of her predecessor's many acts of generosity to Close and his second family. "She was a terrible woman," Betsy Close snaps. "She was married to Ed Close for fourteen years, and I was married to him for thirty-five, but in those thirty-five years she never left him alone for a minute!"

Her dislike is understandable. People who knew Ed Close well say that he had a strong feeling for his first wife until the day he died. Even then Marjorie infuriated Betsy Close by the simple but upstaging act of attending Ed's funeral.

By divorcing Close in 1919, Marjorie had, in a sense, ended her childhood. An exciting but overbearing father was dead, an admirable but mismatched husband was disposed of. The life of Marjorie Merriweather Post was about to begin.

CHAPTER SEVEN

A convenient way to categorize Marjorie Post's life is by her four marriages—the Close years, the Hutton years, the Davies years, the May years—and then her final years as Mrs. Post. Such male-oriented classifications make sense in the case of her second marriage to Edward F. Hutton. Many of the main events of her life occurred during this marriage—the creation of the General Foods Corporation, the purchase of her sprawling Adirondacks camp and her Long Island estate, and a building binge of three separate entities. Each of these would become in its category a record-holder for magnificence: a Palm Beach estate, a Manhattan apartment, and an ocean-going yacht.

The marriage also produced a child who would become Marjorie's favorite, Nedenia Hutton, now known as actress Dina Merrill. Ed Hutton and Marjorie were married for fifteen years, but his influence was present in her style and in her emotions until the day she died.

There was something Gatsbyish about Hutton. He was not born to society but, having scored an early business success, moved easily among the denizens of Oyster Bay and Park Avenue. In the Roaring Twenties social barriers were lowered for people who were fun, or successful; Ed Hutton was both.

Hutton had grown up in Cincinnati, moving with his family to New York when he was fourteen. He went to work on Wall Street as a teenager, and by the time he was twenty-one, he had already started his own brokerage company. The Hutton firm was a quick success, and when he met Marjorie twenty years later, he had amassed considerable wealth, with his own yacht and shooting plantation in South Carolina. His former wife had died, leaving him with a son, Harcourt, then eighteen and a student at Hill School. The boy was later killed in a riding accident.

Hutton was a man's man; like many of that breed, he was adored by women, a tribute he was assiduous in returning. He was not tall, but to some he was unusually handsome; an athletic body and an aggressive charm combined with a somewhat formidable sex appeal.

Dashing, exuberant, vital—Hutton replenished in Marjorie's life the male excitement that had been lacking since the death of her father. Yet Hutton was quite different from C. W. Post, and different in ways that define the altered personality requirements for big-business success in their respective eras. As a turn of the century capitalist, C. W. Post had the right combination of creative ingenuity, toughminded aggression, and determination to forge a major industry out of nothing. An easy popularity was no more a part of his bag of assets than it had been with John D. Rockefeller, Andrew Mellon, or any of the other empire founders.

Hutton, on the other hand, had a comparable business acumen, but he wielded it against a different set of attributes. He had the affability and charisma to unite groups of highly successful and talented men in a common effort. The difference may only have been a matter of style, but Hutton's was the style needed to forge a giant corporation like General Foods from a pride of smaller companies. It is doubtful if Hutton would have been sufficiently single-minded to start the Postum business, and it is doubtful whether C. W. Post would have been politician enough to create General Foods.

While Ed Hutton was unquestionably a self-made man, his younger brother Franklyn seems to have been another kind. The Hutton family had scraped together the money to put one son through Yale. For some reason, the favored son was Franklyn. Ed got only some courses at a commercial college. After an undistinguished turn as a Wall Street broker, Franklyn married Edna Woolworth, one of the richest heiresses in America. The only child of that marriage, Barbara Hutton, would hold the attention of heiress-watchers for fifty years.

That these two brothers from Cincinnati would marry two of the richest girls in the country raises certain uncharitable suspicions. The odds would seem to be against two such fiscally significant marriages just happening in the course of true love.

We don't have to make Hutton a scoundrel to imply that Marjorie's fortune may have had something to do with his infatuation. The Wall Street cronies he moved among all knew that there were plenty of young women walking around with looks, brains, *and* fortunes. If you were going to fall in love, it might just as well be with one of them. If this remarkable young man watched his unremarkable brother leapfrog over his own success by the simple ploy of marrying a fortune, why not counter that deft move? And just because he owned a 100-foot yacht didn't mean he wouldn't like a 300-foot one.

Neither Adelaide nor Eleanor Close have any recollection of seeing Ed Hutton in attendance on their mother while their father was in France. It was natural that Hutton and Marjorie should meet; both were active in the youthful, new-rich circles in Manhattan. Whether he made his intentions known while she was still married is not known, but Dina Merrill later said her mother never ended one relationship unless she "had a place to perch."

Once Marjorie had made her decision to end her marriage to Ed Close, Hutton shifted into the gear that made him one of the most successful businessmen of his day. Minnie Marston recalls a trip to California with Marjorie at this time. At each train stop, there would be flowers and cables from Hutton. C. W. Post would surely have approved of this go-getter approach. In this instance, Hutton was not selling to an indifferent prospect. Years later, and after four marriages, Marjorie would confide to intimates that she had never felt such a strong physical attraction to any other man.

Mrs. Alfred Kay, one of Marjorie's contemporaries, remembers meeting her and Ed Hutton in 1920 at an informal dinner at the estate at Palm Beach's then grande dame, Mrs. Edward T. Stotesbury. The Huttons had just returned from their honeymoon trip around the world.

"We had never met either of them before," Mrs. Kay recalls, "but they were so obviously in love, so happy and so full of enthusiasm for their trip, they captivated us all." Then she adds, "It's too bad they split up. I really thought they would make it."

It is interesting to note that Marjorie had been visiting Palm Beach for eleven years and had not yet met Mrs. Kay, originally a Warden from Philadelphia with Standard Oil money, and securely entrenched in Palm Beach society. Ed Hutton would bring such inconspicuousness to an end.

"With Ed Hutton," says Minnie Marston, "Marjorie encountered something completely new to her. He was socially ambitious." C. W. Post had no use for society. Ed Close had been born to it and bored by it. Hutton, on the other hand, loved it; and, of course, knowing the right people was basic to the brokerage business.

For all his keenness for the high life, Hutton maintained a simple side. Even when he was ensconced as the lord of the most elaborate estate in Palm Beach, he used to enjoy walking down the beach to a pier called Gus's Baths, where he would spend hours fishing and passing the time of day with the old codgers who loitered there.

Ed Hutton had other enthusiasms that were not shared by his socialite neighbors. Sometime later, he backed a young black fighter, and Dina Merrill recalls her father taking her over to West Palm Beach to see him fight. This is an ironic throwback to the fights her mother was taken to years earlier. Dina finds it logical: "Both men wanted sons."

Mercenary motivations, and vainglorious ones aside, the Huttons threw themselves into the grand social life because they were both bent on having fun, all that their youth, money, and the Roaring Twenties could dish up. The decade—in addition to its good-times rampage—had an unusual tolerance for the big rich and their excesses. In those postwar years the country seemed to take a pride in the bumper crop of millionaires the lusty economy was throwing up. There was less feeling of censure about the indulgences of the wealthy than at almost any other time. "If you have it, flaunt it; just remember that I might have it next month."

The Huttons were well set up to make a social splash. They were young, attractive, and rich. They both had friends among the socially prominent. Although her money was new and his newer, and although they were both originally from the Midwest, their property would seem to be an adequate support system for a society *Anschluss*. It turned out to be the merest nucleus from which the Huttons would expand their living arrangements in the next decade—to one of the most opulent lifestyles the world had ever seen.

CHAPTER EIGHT

"I think everyone took right away to Marjorie and Ed Hutton," recalls Mrs. Kay. "There was no feeling about them being newcomers. Of course, they *were* newcomers, but Palm Beach never asked about your background—unless you became close friends and a curiosity about it would be natural . . . but on the party circuit here, nobody much cared. It wasn't Philadelphia or Boston or any place like that."

When Mrs. Kay talks about "newcomers" she doesn't mean new to Palm Beach, she means to society. With the Huttons' few connections and many assets, Marjorie began entertaining—the circle-expanding, position-enchancing sort of party-giving that meant attracting as many of society's bright lights as possible.

As Mrs. Kay implies, this was easier in Palm Beach

than it would have been in Manhattan or Long Island. An enormous help to Marjorie in Palm Beach was the patronage of the resort's reigning queen, Mrs. Edward T. Stotesbury, a woman who was to have an effect on Marjorie's life comparable to that of Ed Hutton's.

Edward T. Stotesbury was a senior partner in Drexel and Company, J. P. Morgan's Philadelphia connection. Neither Stotesbury nor his wife was old Philadelphia. To compensate for this dereliction, they built a Versailles-like spread outside Philadelphia in Chestnut Hill, an estate so grandiose it moved Henry Ford to say after a visit, "It is always a great experience to see how the rich live."

In Palm Beach the Stotesburys commissioned the whimsical architect Addison Mizner to build his first private villa, something many people urged him to do after the success of his design for the Everglades Club, Paris Singer's Moorish-fantasy. The Stotesburys' Palm Beach estate took up twenty-five acres and ran from the ocean to Lake Worth (as would Marjorie's Mar-A-Lago). It had about forty rooms, numerous courts and patios, an under-lit swimming pool, a forty-car garage, seventy servants, and a private zoo containing twenty-five monkeys and squadrons of parrots and parakeets. The house cost over a million dollars, which, in 1920 was, well, over a million dollars. Thinking the expense was getting out of hand, Edward Stotesbury limited his wife to a Palm Beach operating budget of twelve thousand dollars a week.

Even with two palaces open for business, the Stotesburys' were never accepted by Philadelphia society. But in Palm Beach, which Cleveland Amory calls society's back door, their, or rather her, victory was absolute. The triumph was not because of the palatial mansion—although wholesale displays of wealth have never been a drawback in Palm Beach—but because of Mrs. Stotesbury's great personal charm.

Mrs. Stotesbury's unequivocal success in Palm Beach and her failure in Philadelphia presages Marjorie's own social successes and failures in years to come. As Mrs. Kay points out, resorts are easier to invade than cities. For one thing, they don't reach as deeply into history or have as many venerable clubs and other institutions —the Philadelphia Assembly, for instance, or Boston's Chilton Club: difficult places for goats to pass as sheep. The general mood of a resort is more relaxed; associations have fewer long-term ramifications, and the power-base of the mighty is located elsewhere. A Philadelphian who finds Palm Beach growing too vulgar can always retreat northward to Hobe Sound. He can't however, think of quitting the city of Philadelphia just because a lot of the wrong people have gotten in. Where could he go?

In any case, Mrs. E. T. Stotesbury was *numero uno* in Palm Beach in the twenties, and she took a great liking to the pretty young cereal heiress from Battle Creek. Mrs. Stotesbury's friendship was important to Marjorie, not just because of the entrée it gave her— she probably would have had that sooner or later. Marjorie loved and admired Mrs. Stotesbury and used her as a model to emulate as hostess, grande dame, and big spender.

Years later when Mrs. Stotesbury's health and money were running out, she said to Marjorie, "You'll have to carry on now, dear." It was clear that she meant for her friend to succeed her as Queen of Palm Beach. Marjorie took this anointing seriously.

There was considerable difference in hostess style between the two women. Mrs. Stotesbury would buzz merrily through her parties—a kiss here, a squeeze there—making everyone feel relaxed and welcome. Marjorie lacked this ice-breaking knack, and it's doubtful whether or not she ever wanted it. Her warmth toward her friends was manifest more in the open-

handedness of the hospitality she offered them. In years
to come her style would be to serve the finest foods
and wines in exquisite settings, to anticipate her guests'
smallest wants, and to smile benignly down from above
on those she had made happy.

There were personality differences as well, most
noticeably Mrs. Stotesbury's lack of self-importance.
One story illustrates her rare, for Palm Beach, unpre-
tentiousness. She had a new cook whose imperious
nature and temper so frightened her, she dreaded having to talk with him. The only way she could bolster
her courage for a conference, she told a friend, was to
get all dressed to go out. Then, sitting in her finery
high in her Victoria she would say to a footman, "Oh,
before we go, I'd like a word with the cook." The cook
would be summoned, and they would have their talk,
Mrs. Stotesbury looming above him, abristle with
feathers and jewels, maybe even with a riding crop in
one hand in case negotiations broke down over a
béchamel. Mrs. Stotesbury could laugh at her own ruse.

On another occasion she found herself in the middle
of a group of men bragging about the smart business
deals they had made. "My only astute business move,"
she volunteered, "was to marry Mr. Stotesbury."

In later years when Mrs. Post assumed the grande
dame role, she too could poke fun at herself and admit
to friends costly blunders or other faux pas, but she
never quite developed the good-humored ease with her
own foibles that so characterized Mrs. Stotesbury.

With Mrs. Stotesbury's sponsorship,
Marjorie and Ed Hutton quickly developed into one of
the brightest teams of the Palm Beach action. Their
name was becoming more widely known for business
reasons as well. E. F. Hutton & Co. opened an office in
the Royal Poinciana Hotel, and the firm advertised in
Palm Beach and New York.

The couple's presence was felt in New York social circles. In 1921, only a year after the Huttons' marriage, society columnist Maury Paul listed the fifty names he considered Old Guard society and another fifty for whom he created a new term, Café Society. The Old Guard were predictably the Vanderbilts, Goelets, Van Rensselaers; Paul's Café Society includes some names which today sound Old Guard: Mrs. William P. Burden, Mrs. John R. Drexel, Jr., Mrs. Jay Gould, Mrs. Joseph Widener, Mrs. Edward T. Stotesbury—and Mrs. Edward F. Hutton. That Marjorie was listed as one of the top members of *any* society in New York shows she had traveled far, not only from Battle Creek, but from her Greenwich retreat as well.

It is wrong to create the impression that Marjorie's motive in building her Florida palace and expanding her style of living was social advancement, or even merely the pursuit of fun. While these aims were omnipresent and intertwined, they were mixed with other aspects of her personality. She took the genuine delight of the natural-born hostess in creating beautiful settings—spaces made enchanting with crystal candlelight, and silver urns filled with fresh flowers. With her wealth she could further indulge this impulse to have her richest fantasies of beauty and elegance transformed into permanent structures of gold leaf, marble and stone. So few of us are in the palace-building position, it is hard to appreciate the temptation of such a financial capability.

Of course, there was in this considerable vulgarity. As Dina Merrill would point out years later, her mother had so strong a sense of the dramatic, such a theatrical view of herself, that she saw these ornate, drop-dead environments as backdrops for her act, stage sets for her own long-running vehicle.

Another less self-aggrandizing motive lies behind the urge to create fairy-tale castles, and to entertain lavishly in them. Majorie aimed at taking over the lives of her guests for the duration of their visits and converting them into existences buoyantly luxurious and stubbornly unreal. That she would do this even more often and more enthusiastically when the recipient was not one of her fellow plutocrats—someone from the every-day world—is a telling insight into her instincts as a hostess and as a person.

There was a strong proviso to her generosity: Guests should behave. In later years, when her entertaining become both more frequent and more lavish, it was not unusual for Marjorie to go up to a couple who were dancing suggestively and say, "Either stop that or leave." This was not merely the crotchetiness of age. At the large debut ball she gave for her niece Barbara Hutton, she rebuked the entire guest list of young New York bluebloods. To entertain the group, she had hired the well-known dancer, Argentina, to perform. The noise and disinterest the party showed the dancer so infuriated Marjorie she went to the bandstand and had the conductor stop the performance. Taking the microphone, she told her guests that if they didn't quiet down and show respect for this distinguished artist, she would end the party.

As fairy princesses go, however, her kindness overcame her disciplinarian instincts. If smothering your guests in luxury and consideration is a form of aggression, Marjorie was the most aggressive hostess who ever lived. In the incredible vacations from reality she provided her friends at Mar-A-Lago, Topridge, and on her yacht, the *Sea Cloud* we see her getting her highest pleasure from waving her General Foods wand and transporting guests to magical palaces where they would awaken like beggars in the Arabian Nights who suddenly find themselves the Caliph's best pal.

An early example of her work as a genii involved a relative of Pearsie's, the children's nurse, a young man named Alden Sibley, who was a cadet at West Point. When Marjorie Hutton learned that the boy could not get home for Christmas, she invited him to be her guest at her Fifth Avenue house, although the Huttons would be in Palm Beach for the holidays.

Today, retired after a distinguished army career, Major General Sibley remembers with clarity the visit Marjorie had arranged for him: "I had never seen anything like it, that incredible mansion right on Fifth Avenue, the rich furnishings. She had put me in Mr. Hutton's bedroom, which I remember had hunting prints around the walnut-paneled walls; each print had a little light over it. On the dresser were a pile of invitations for me to all the most important debutante balls. She had left a car and chauffeur at my disposal. Everything had been arranged down to the smallest detail. She hadn't stopped by wrangling me the invitations; she had arranged for me to be one of the escorts of the girl making her debut. Not only was it an honor, but it put me at the center of things. That way I got to meet some people before going to the party."

Marjorie had lived in a Battle Creek boardinghouse and slept on a canvas cot in Texas. She knew what it must have meant for a young southerner of ordinary circumstances to come from the ice-water austerity of West Point to a Fifth Avenue palace; to be waited on by twenty servants; to be driven about Manhattan in a chauffeur-driven limousine; to wine, dine, and dance each night with the most attractive debutantes in New York. She was under no illusions that this was the way things always were for him or anyone else. That she could provide such luxury for a few days, perhaps the only such days in an entire life, was and would always be one of her greatest satisfactions.

It is tempting to assume Ed Hutton was behind Marjorie's explosion of extravagance if only because it dates from his tour of husbandly duty. He had a flamboyant side, and he had already shown a taste for the rich and their enthusiasms. Arguing against his role as big-spending advocate was the dismay he sometimes expressed at his wife's checkbook rampages. Dina Merrill quotes him as saying when he, like everyone else, was agape at the newly finished Mar-A-Lago, "I wanted a cottage by the sea and look what I got."

Hutton may have been talking out of two sides of his mouth. It is possible he encouraged his wife; then hearing the derision for follies were provoking, portrayed himself as a somewhat appalled bystander. He may also have influenced his wife's buying spree in a more indirect way. Marjorie was very much in love with her broker husband; maybe she felt magnificence was the way to please him. No one builds a new house when a marriage is deteriorating.

A burgeoning fortune may have been the main cause of her burst of spending. She may have been spending more because she was making more. When Hutton became chairman of the Postum Company board in 1923, he began a program of acquisitions. Marjorie said this had been her father's intention. In 1925 they bought the Jell-O Company and shortly thereafter, Swans Down Cake Flour and Minute Tapioca. With these moves, under Hutton's direction, the company was prospering as never before. Helping it all, of course, was the bullish economy of the twenties.

Behind all of these reasons for her epic extravagance —and all surely played a part—was the overriding if unenlightening reason that she did it because she wanted to.

Few channels of activity were open for a woman in the twenties. There was no feeling that a woman, especially a rich one, should "do" anything. Still Marjorie might have turned her wealth and energy toward cultural patronage, art collecting, social causes, or philanthropy. Before she was finished, she would become involved in most of these. But in 1920, because of the mood of the country, her marriage to Hutton, and her own impulses at the age of thirty-three, she guided herself into a course of pleasure and fun and monumental self-indulgence.

CHAPTER NINE

The year after Marjorie and Ed Hutton were married they bought Camp Topridge in the Adirondacks and Hillwood, a princely estate on Long Island's socially robust North Shore. Topridge—with its three lakes and forty buildings—alternated with Hutton's yacht to ease the couple through the hot summer months. Hogarcito, a large house in Palm Beach, got them through the winter; the Long Island estate, the Fifth Avenue mansion, and the 16,000-acre South Carolina plantation filled the chinks of spring and autumn.

Five residences and a yacht would seem adequate to deal with the social and meteorological fluctuations of a mere twelve months. If not, there were trips abroad or a stay at one of the American or European spas that had recently won Marjorie's favor. Occasionally, the Huttons would run out to Battle Creek to check on the smooth operation of C. W. Post's giant money-making machine. All this moving about required transport. To make land travel as deprivation-free as possible, Marjorie bought and outfitted a private railroad car, which had its own staff.

Camp Topridge was built on Upper St. Regis Lake (which it shared with several other families); but two other lakes were located completely within the Hutton property. Marjorie had visited this part of the world during summers when she was married to Close. She expanded the existing camp to some forty buildings, including thirty guest cabins. Each was outfitted luxuriously in different styles; the most distinguishing feature was a panel of buzzers, each labeled with a different service, or activity. A guest had only to push a button to arrange for swimming, fishing, boating, hunting, hiking—or to summon forth a barber, hairdresser, masseur, stenographer, or dance instructor. In later years, the panels of buttons were replaced by a more modern telephone system (forty-eight extensions) with the same services available.

The Long Island estate, Hillwood (a name Marjorie later gave to her Washington showplace), was basic Wall Street baronial. The main house was a rambling affair in Tudor half-timbered style. There were stables, another large house on the property, and extensive formal gardens.

To entrenched New York society, the Huttons were regarded as rich newcomers. While their looks and charm brought them a certain amount of acceptance, they could never be at the social summit. Since they were supremely successful at Palm Beach, it was natural then that Marjorie would build her most elaborate seat at Palm Beach. Then, too, New York offered existing buildings that fit her majestic needs; Palm Beach did not.

Years later, explaining why she had built Mar-A-Lago, Marjorie said that her daughters were entering their teens and their many beaux and houseguests made Hogarcito inadequate. This is a bit like Shah Jahan's saying he built the Taj Mahal because he had no place to put the remains of his wife. In fact, the daughters were dismayed to be moving so far from the Breakers and the social action.

If you look at Hogarcito today, you get a sense of Marjorie's restless need. The house is large, with a courtyard, fountains, and gardens. It sits on the edge of the rolling green lawns of the Everglades Club golf course. It is an establishment that few millionaires would sniff at. Impressive as it was, it did not provoke gasps; Marjorie wanted a place that did.

In the first winters of her marriage to Hutton, Marjorie began planning her beach house. The Huttons were friendly with Florenz Ziegfeld and his wife, Billie Burke, and through them with Joseph Urban, the set designer for the Ziegfeld Follies. Urban was a Viennese who claimed to have designed buildings for Emperor Franz Joseph, a credit sure to arrest Marjorie's attention.

The Huttons commissioned Urban to design them a large estate. A previous houseguest, a highly imaginative artist named Ju-Ju de Blas, had run up a series of sketches of possible styles and moods for the house. These were incorporated into Urban's ideas. Marjorie also took an active part in this design stage. Today, when you walk through the tangle of odd corridors, angled rooms, and inexplicable staircases you get the impression that her contribution was not insignificant.

A design agreed upon, she next set out to find a piece of land. As always when embarking on a spending extravaganza, Marjorie tempered her extravagance with a Battle Creek practicality. She studied the problems of local construction and learned that, for most of the island, it was a matter of building castles in sand. But there were spots, she discovered, that had an undershelving of rock. She set real-estate man Lytle Hull to finding such a lot.

He took her to see some acreage at the south end of the island, far from the resort's developed areas. Marjorie would later tell how she and Hull were forced to crawl on their hands and knees over the land, the jungle growth was so thick. This picture has greater impact when envisioned against the opulent tableaux the lady and the land made together years later.

The land passed her inspection. In addition to the necessary coral underpinning, it was large enough: 17.7 acres that ran from the ocean—where it had 450 feet of beachfront—through to Lake Worth.

Marjorie engaged a young local architect, Marion Sims Wyeth, to assist Urban with the more technical aspects of the mansion's design. Palm Beach had had a taste of talented but erratic architects, Addison Mizner's habit of omitting an essential feature from each of his houses had become his trademark. In one two-story mansion, he had neglected to include an interior staircase. Marjorie wanted no such omissions. Later, when Mar-A-Lago was considered by many to be a monstrosity, Wyeth claimed responsibility for the kitchen wing only.

Construction began in 1923. Over the next four years, as the building and grounds took shape, Palm Beach was agog at the part Spanish, part Moorish, part Arabian Nights fantasy that was being fashioned from three shiploads of Italian stone and that rose from the beach up to a sandcastle tower seventy-five feet tall. Marjorie was on her way to having her own permanent Ziegfeld Follies set.

With such a grandiose construction project under way, Marjorie's building compulsion would seem to be appeased for a time. Not at all. The year after starting Mar-A-Lago, she had her Fifth Avenue mansion torn down and an apartment building put up. For her own use, she divided the top three floors into seventy rooms that would constitute the most elaborate apartment in Manhattan.

The late real-estate giant Douglas Elliman once commented an Marjorie's astute business sense. When it was pointed out to her how much the house cost her for a few months' use a year, he said, she moved the house to the top of a profitable apartment building.

Such concern over cost seemed out of character. Economy had little to do with this decision, according to her daughter Eleanor. When Marjorie had first moved into this location, traffic and buses reached only as far as Seventy-second Street. But by 1924, the bus line passed Ninety-second Street, as did rushes of fuming and noisy cars. Eleanor remembers her mother once chiding her and her sister for making so much noise in their third-floor room when she was trying to nap in her bedroom below them. Eleanor protested that the little noise the girls were making was nothing compared to the noise from Fifth Avenue.

Marjorie said, "Things you *can't* do anything about, you put up with. You don't put up with things you *can* do something about—and I can do something about you."

For most people this would seem to be admirable wisdom; in Marjorie's case the reasoning had a fallacy —she was coming to have as much control over bricks and mortar as she had over her daughters. She tore down the mansion and put eight floors between her and the Fifth Avenue tumult. It wasn't economy she was seeking, only a nap.

With two daughters growing into attractive women, a husband she adored, an expanding circle of friends, and a number of properties to maintain and build, Marjorie's attention was turned inward toward her family and her own interests. She traveled less. Her politics were a filial echo of her father's hard-rock capitalism. Her grasp of the political and social issues of the day was just sufficient to get her through dinnerparty chitchats. It is surprising then that it was during these selfish twenties when she was at the height of her self-absorption, that she should do the one thing that had the greatest effect on the rest of mankind.

In the summer of 1925 the Huttons were cruising in their yacht off the New England coast. One evening, their chef served them a goose that Marjorie thought particularly succulent and tasty. Perhaps it was the wrong season of the year or perhaps the length of time they had been at sea; in any case she thought it was odd that a goose in such condition was available and asked her chef about it. He told her he had purchased the bird in Gloucester, Massachusetts, from a man who had developed a new way of preserving foods. The Huttons had eaten a frozen goose.

Marjorie had never heard of such a thing. She was fascinated. Could vegetables be preserved this way? Fish? Her immediate thought—as it would have been with anyone accustomed to planning elaborate meals— was her own table. But like her father, she reasoned that any improvement over the old way of doing things, any idea that could improve and simplify her life, must have a similar possibility for many lives and should therefore have strong commercial potential.

In the 1974 edition of the *Encyclopaedia Britannica,* the entry on food preservation describes at length the discovery and development of the canning process and notes the various individuals responsible. About frozen foods the author states only that the "process was developed in the early part of the twentieth century."

The freezing concept, like that behind C. W. Post's cereal concoctions, had been around for a long time before its mass-market possibilities were realized. Freezing foods to preserve them had been done for centuries by Eskimos and other northern peoples. But the notion seems to have eluded more technologically advanced areas.

Marjorie's encounter with that frozen goose would come to have an effect on the world's eating habits even greater than C. W. Post's development of cereals. She told her chef she wanted to meet the man from Gloucester. They returned to the mainland and looked him up. His name was Clarence Birdseye.

Thirteen years earlier, Birdseye had done a stint as a fur trader in Labrador. One day he caught a fish and was astonished to watch it freeze instantly in the −40 degree temperature. He left it on his front porch for several days. Later, to thaw it out, he tossed it into a bucket of water. He was even more astonished to see the fish swim around.

Birdseye felt he had stumbled on a major secret of nature, perhaps the secret of immortality. He soon came to realize that he had only discovered frozen spinach. Still, that could be more lucrative than trapping animals, so he returned to Gloucester to launch the frozen-food industry.

No one was interested. The public had never heard of frozen foods and had no place to store them. At the time Marjorie encountered Birdseye, his company, the General Foods Company, was foundering. Marjorie saw the opportunity immediately and suggested to her husband that they buy the company. Ed Hutton was negative. For frozen food to become widespread, not only would households have to purchase a freezer, an expensive piece of equipment, but so would the thousands and thousands of small independent grocers who sold food in those presupermarket days. Besides, Hutton argued, no matter what you tell housewives about the bacteria-arresting effects of freezing, they would be afraid to serve their families six-month-old meat.

Marjorie proved to be her father's daughter. She didn't care what the public had or had not done before. She didn't care about the practical considerations. She thought it was fantastic that you could have fresh green peas in January. She urged her husband to buy Birdseye's company.

Clarence Birdseye, not doing well, was only too happy to get out, and he named a figure in the neighborhood of $2 million. To humor his wife, Hutton presented the idea to his Postum board of directors, a group of men as knowledgeable about food marketing as any in the country. Their decision: Frozen foods would never catch on.

Marjorie did not let up. Rarely did she intrude herself into the affairs of her company, but this time she was convinced she was right and her businessmen were wrong. It took four more years, but in 1929 the board decided to take a chance. Their hesitation was costly. Birdseye's fortunes had improved, and to acquire the company, they now had to pay $22 million.

The purchase was a major step for the Postum Company, and Hutton used the resulting corporate upheaval to do something he had been considering for some time—to bring all the Postum companies together under the name General Foods Corporation. The new conglomerate, producing all the basic foodstuffs for America's kitchens, was to become the largest food company in the world.

It is easy to toss about words like "inevitable" and "self-evident," when discussing new ideas that have triumphed. To create General Foods, Hutton had to overcome the chauvinism and proud independence of old-line food companies. And there were other pitfalls, known and unknown, to the conglomerate idea.

But Marjorie's vision of the future was even bolder, demanding as it did a capital outlay for both retailer and consumer and the conquest of a fear of being poisoned. Even C. W. Post had only asked the public to invest twenty-five cents in a new food product. Considering the business realities his daughter was bucking, her obstinate determination is a thrilling endorsement of the spoiled rich woman as industrial visionary. If the United States ever gets around to adopting five-year plans, there should be at least one Marjorie Merriweather Post on the planning board.

CHAPTER TEN

From 1925 to 1929 the Huttons drummed out a crescendo of activities that paralleled the nation's boisterous rush toward the Crash. Mar-A-Lago was under way, General Foods was growing and the birth of their daughter Nedenia only seemed to intensify their exuberant high living. To cap it all off nicely, Marjorie decided on scrapping her husband's yacht and building one far more splendid.

C. W. Post had been interested in yachting but never got around to buying one. Now his daughter, with a husband who was an enthusiast, decided she would have a yacht that would be the ocean-going equivalent of Mar-A-Lago, a boat that would make other yachtsmen gape. She began reading up on marine architecture and doodling with deck plans. In 1926 in the German port of Kiel, work was begun on the most magnificent sailing yacht ever built for private individual. The entire interior arrangement of staterooms, salons, galleys and companionways was designed by Marjorie.

By the end of that year, her other project, Mar-A-Lago, was taking on its finishing touches. Since it would be such an integral part of Marjorie's life, as well as an $8 million insight into her fantasy system, it is worth a quick tour.

Guests pass through an imposing and fanciful gate on South Ocean Boulevard and proceed up a drive lined with coconut palms. In later years the main gate would be opened only when Marjorie was in residence, a signal akin to the flying of national flags over royal residences.

Entering the house you come into a spacious hall with centuries-old Spanish tiles that line the walls to a height of eight feet. (There are some 36,000 such tiles embedded into those walls.) A hooded fireplace with a bust of Homer on one side, Hadrian on the other, dominates the room. High on the walls are ten plaques of coats of arms related to the Post and Merriweather families that Marjorie had unearthed with the help of complaisant genealogists.

Huge cypress doors lead into a monumental drawing room that soars more than two stories to an overwhelming ceiling of intricately carved gold leaf, a copy of the famous "Thousand-Wing Ceiling" in Venice's Accademia. The room was proportioned to accommodate seven tapestries from a Venetian palace, which give a hushed and lugubrious feeling; yet clumps of heavy padded furniture scattered around make the vast space seem comfortable, almost cozy. The whole effect is very much like one of the movie palaces of the twenties that Urban and other romantics designed and that were, in turn, probably trying to resemble a fantastic private palace like Mar-A-Lago.

101

The drawing room is the most stupendous feature of a stupendous house and is surely one of the most remarkable rooms in any American residence. Marjorie delighted in the impact the room made. She would often conceal herself in the second-floor gallery on one of the small balconies high against the gold ceiling to observe guests' reactions when they first entered the room.

Marble steps lead up to a wide window alcove where an enormous expanse of plate glass frames the lawn and the ocean. When the glass (which had been specially made in Pittsburgh and with great difficulty was transported to Florida by a chartered truck) was being coaxed into position, it shattered. The months-long process had to be repeated.

The dining room, a copy of the room in Rome's Chigi Palace that Mussolini used as an office, was almost as lavish. Marble columns rose up the walls, separating Venetian sea murals; two colossal gold chandeliers hung over a spectacular table, a tour de force in *pietra dura* that had been custom-made in Florence to Urban's design and came to be known as the "million dollar table." There were large gold candelabra on the table and side tables, plus gold tea and coffee services. Carved beams separate oil paintings of sea and sky set into the ceiling.

A modest library is lined with antique pine paneling and holds a portrait by Sir Joshua Reynolds. The drawing room open onto an enclosed space called the Monkey Loggia because of some carved stone monkeys that perch near the ceiling (one next to the library wears glasses and is reading a book). Throughout the house appear intricate carvings in wood and stone, mostly the work of Viennese sculptors, Franz Barwig and his son, who spent three years at Mar-A-Lago fashioning the rich ornamentation.

There were four master-bedroom suites; the one

designated for Marjorie was of a Versailles lavishness. On the ground level, it was reached by the covered loggia that circles around the mansion's Lake Worth side. Inside, a sitting room was followed by two enormous bedrooms, side by side, one for Ed and one for Marjorie. Each had its own bath, but Marjorie's was more than just that.

One passed from her bedroom through a corridor (from which open various closets and a commode), ending up in a large semicircular room with windows overlooking the lawns and gardens that stretched to the lake. This room was a combination bath and office. It had a bathtub and dressing table, but it also had a desk and a phone. Here Marjorie would spend her morning with her secretary and masseur, exercising, putting together her toilette, writing letters, composing memos to the staff, making phone calls.

On the second floor of Mar-A-Lago a number of other bedroom suites open off the partially covered semicircular walk that tops the loggia below. Each of the major bedrooms is decorated in a completely different style, contributing strongly to the cries of "bastard" that met Mar-A-Lago's unveiling. One is in an old Dutch style with much heavy carved oak and Delft tiles—Marjorie's mother had loved Delft—set into the walls and into the head and footboards of the twin beds. Another suite is Spanish; another, perhaps the most incongruous in the predominantly Spanish-Moorish ambience, is a large room (in the formal English architectural style of the brothers Adam) that looks as though it could have graced the Governor's Mansion at Williamsburg.

A bedroom suite on the ground floor is perhaps the most fanciful of this free-wheeling architectural fantasy. It is "Deenie's House," also known as the Sleeping Beauty Suite, a series of rooms that open off the loggia next to the entrance to the Huttons' bedroom

103

complex. Leading into these rooms is an iron gate. After the Lindbergh kidnapping an armed guard was stationed here at all times. Inside is a large sitting room and two bedrooms—one for Nedenia, one for her nurse.

Dina's bedroom was an oval-shaped space that focused on a fireplace in the form of an outsized beehive. Rich ornamentation in plaster relief trailed around the walls: pink roses on twisting vines. Two bright yellow plaster canaries peeked out from the green plaster foliage.

The carpet was specially woven after illustrations Urban had once done for a book of fairy stories: elves, knights, and ladies in tall hats with veils trailing from the peaks.

Climaxing the storybook apparition was Dina's bed. Four posts of intricately carved and silvered wood passed through a canopy, then converged in a point where several carved squirrels played. Door handles in the room were also squirrels of silvered wrought iron. The suite is the apotheosis of the impulse that sends parents out to buy a toy-soldier lamp for baby's dresser.

It only adds to the fantasy to realize that living in this walk-in music box was a remarkably pretty child with golden hair and a happy disposition. And while bathing in the high-cholesterol perfection of it all, it is not irrelevant to point out that one of Dina's mother's best friends—a frequent visitor to Mar-A-Lago during this period—was the actress Billie Burke. With the filming of *The Wizard of Oz,* Billie Burke embodied every child's idea of a perfect fairy godmother. On the nurse's day off, the actress used to help Marjorie take care of Dina. Perhaps she warmed up for her sweet chats with Dorothy and Toto by practicing on Dina in the Sleeping Beauty Suite.

Behind Mar-A-Lago is a nine-hole golf course (reusing the same fairway) that stretches to Lake Worth and a boat dock. To either side, paths wend through lush tropical gardens. The patio has a large fountain and stone steps, with a blue flood-light installed in the tower to ensure all-phase, all-weather moonlight.

To the front a lawn stretches down to South Ocean Boulevard, a gentle upsweep in the lawn concealing the road but not high enough to block the view of the Atlantic Ocean. On the other side of the road is a length of beach which has a large swimming pool, built in later years by her fourth husband, Herb May. Actually Marjorie preferred the congeniality of the pool at the Bath and Tennis Club a few yards to the right. A tunnel passed under South Ocean Boulevard so that both the ocean and the club could be reached from the main house without negotiating public roads.

With the twenty-seven servants' rooms, guest rooms and caretakers' cottages, the entire estate could house seventy people. It was set up to operate with a staff of sixty, including day help, but in peak entertaining periods, the staff rose to eighty.

During the Korean War, twenty-five years after Mar-A-Lago was built, Marjorie installed four bomb shelters underneath the house. The largest was for the servants, and all were outfitted with bunks, toilets, and provisions.

In the mid-1920s Mar-A-Lago cost over $8 million. In the late 1960s, a tax assessment of $1.5 million was considered so low that a public outcry moved the assessors to amend it to $4 million. For 17 acres of prime oceanfront real estate to be worth half of what it had been worth forty years before suggests that separate economic laws govern white elephants.

When Mar-A-Lago was finished in January 1927, all of Palm Beach was stunned. Some recovered enough from their shock to snipe and snicker at the lavishness of it all. The greatest put-down was attributed to Harry Thaw, who is said to have taken one look at the mansion and remarked, "My God, I shot the wrong architect." Unfortunately for historical accuracy, Thaw died in Miami three years before Mar-A-Lago was completed. But conservers of wit, remembering the line and seeing Mar-A-Lago, assumed Thaw must have said it about Marjorie Post's creation. The Huttons celebrated the opening by a round of large parties all of which were given fawning attention by the local press in the following manner:

With the guests garbed in a bewildering variety of exquisite costumes and the magnificent setting of their estate, Mar-A-Lago, as a background, Mr. and Mrs. Edward F. Hutton's dinner preceding the fancy-dress ball at the Everglades Club last evening was one of the most colorfully beautiful events of this exceedingly colorful season. The fairy-like setting of their patio was chosen for the occasion, and everything conspired to make the scene perfect in every lovely detail. The waxy petals of a wealth of orange blossoms . . . and of pink oleander, which also was used in profusion, blended in an exquisite perfume that brought thoughts of a Persian garden, and the vivid hue of bougainvillea added its exotic charm to the scene. Mrs. Hutton was a charming figure in her Louis Fifteenth gown of blue taffeta, trimmed with rare old lace and silver.

The writer then catches her breath long enough to tell us the names of all two hundred guests present, a list that includes the Stotesburys, Jimmy Donahue, the Franklyn Huttons, the John Phippes, the Hunter Marstons, the Paris Singers, the John Pillsburys, Mrs.

William Randolph Hearst, Billie Burke, Addison Mizner, Jimmy Cromwell, and Evalyn Walsh McLean.

You can almost hear the orchestra pumping away at songs from Rodgers and Hart's *A Connecticut Yankee* or Jerome Kern's *Show Boat,* the season's two hit shows. Marjorie's photo albums for this period display a series of pictures of dancers Ruth St. Denis and Ted Shawn, the modern dance sensations of the day, striking exotic postures around the courtyards, fountains and gardens of Mar-A-Lago.

Palm Beach was now the Huttons'. It was natural that they should encounter in their ever-broadening circles the many titled Europeans who were working the gilded salons of Newport, New York, and Palm Beach. Since America had first produced an affluent class, the rich had automatically turned toward Europe for instruction on culture, taste, refinement, and the art of opulent living. This reflex was still much in force in the twenties.

Marjorie Merriweather Post from Battle Creek, Michigan, was not immune to the glory imparted by the lips of a count or a duke on the back of her midwestern hand. As many aspiring hostesses had learned before her, what better way to short-circuit the Vanderbilts and Van Rensselaers and other parochial snobs? Give up on them and go straight to the mother lode of European aristocracy, a hungry group who laughed at America's petty social distinctions but did not laugh at fortunes like Marjorie's.

She was a pushover for blue-blooded flattery, and like many mothers of the period, she didn't see why her daughters shouldn't marry one of the titles. After all, she was bringing into her homes Marie Antoinette's earrings and Franz Joseph's teacups, why should she not have a little of the living commodity?

Adelaide was a prime target for the titled marauders. Her mother presented her to society at a 1927 ball which was one of the most lavish of its day. The walls of New York's Ritz were covered with orchids, beverages gushed upward, sideward, downward, and two orchestras kept elbows pumping. Adelaide neatly side-stepped co-option by her mother and an out-of-work prince; the day after her debut she announced her engagement to Tim Durant, a young man who had gone through Yale on an athletic scholarship.

Eleanor, with her remarkable beauty and her trust funds from C. W. Post, was another prime candidate. But she had inherited something else from C. W.—a mind of her own. She was not cooperative with the blue-blooded sharks her mother found for her.

One in particular, a Bulgarian prince both odious and cross-eyed, offended Eleanor's sense of suitability. At a dinner at the Ritz in New York, Eleanor bribed a waiter to spill hot soup over the prince's white tie and tails. When reminded of this incident fifty years later in Paris, she was quick to justify her move: "I never had to go out with him again." And then she added, "I thought it was a hot sauce."

If the cross-eyed prince was discouraged, Eleanor's mother was not. She corralled as many titles as she could lay a glove on and entertained them frequently. One such occasion was a lunch Marjorie gave at the Bath and Tennis Club for the Grand Duke Alexander, brother-in-law of the late Czar Nicholas II. Among the guests were His Royal Highness Cyril of Bulgaria, Baron and Baroness Von Einem and Lady Wavetree—all of whom were no doubt as conversant with Dun and Bradstreet as they were with the *Almanach de Gotha*.

The high spirits of the twenties did not elude Marjorie and Ed Hutton; they were at the center of the era's mood, if perhaps not to the goldfish-swallowing degree. Marjorie would often have ballet dancers—her particular favorites—to her Manhattan home for lunch and then spend the afternoon creating impromptu ballets, the entire group, hostess included, pirouetting through the vast rooms and up and down the sweeping stairs.

In 1927 Charles Lindbergh made his solo flight over the Atlantic, transatlantic phone service was begun, and the Holland Tunnel completed, thereby subjecting Manhattan to fifty years of illegally parked New Jersey cars.

In 1928 the American Telephone and Telegraph Company transmitted the first television picture, a development Herbert Hoover pronounced of no commercial value. The publication of *Lady Chatterly's Lover* marked the demise of Victorian morality, and Evelyn Waugh's novel about the high-jinks of the idle rich (*Decline and Fall*) delighted readers on both sides of the Atlantic.

The year's hit Broadway play was Philip Barry's *Holiday* in which the hero is reluctant to work while young, preferring instead to play, perhaps going to work at fifty when it didn't much matter what he did. To 1928 audiences it seemed a reasonable point of view.

That same year Marjorie presented her daughter to the Court of St. James's and brought the entire cast of a Broadway musical to Palm Beach to entertain her guests at a party, a hospitable gesture that is still evoked at that resort as a benchmark of entertaining munificence. (The cast remembered it too; they were all given a week's vacation at Mar-A-Lago after their performance.) Ed Hutton and the Postum board effected the acquisition of Calumet Baking Powder, La France laundry bluing, and Maxwell House Coffee. Meanwhile in Kiel, hundreds of Germans hammered, riveted, and arc-welded away on the *Sea Cloud*'s 316-foot hull.

In 1929 came the purchase of Clarence Birdseye's

company and the formation of the General Foods Corporation. Then, in October, the Crash.

Almost overnight the nation's securities and stocks lost $26 billion in value. Both General Foods and E. F. Hutton & Company were rocked by the debacle, particularly the latter; but both were able to survive the impact. The Huttons' income, which had been sky-rocketing to obscene proportions, was reduced to a mere princely level. For a while the couple would have to journey to New York to see a Broadway show rather than having it brought to them.

It is some gauge of the economy of the United States during the twenties—and Marjorie's share of it —to recall that in 1914 she had inherited a company worth $20 million. During the ten years from 1920 to 1930 her personal expenses had almost equaled that amount; yet she was leaving the decade, the Great Depression notwithstanding, richer than she had entered it.

CHAPTER ELEVEN

The collapse of the stock market in 1929 presented a dilemma to the Huttons as it did to all of the rich who still had any choice: continue their scale of living and court censure, or curtail it and throw more people out of work. The revenues from General Foods and E. F. Hutton & Company dropped, but the situation was far from grave. Still, to keep Mar-A-Lago open meant spending capital, and 1930 was not a propitious time to liquidate stock. Marjorie resolved to keep Mar-A-Lago going.

She was not oblivious to the grim straits of a good many Americans, nor was she unaware of the press criticism her palace-running would bring here. She showed a life-long taste for lavish living, but according to Minnie Marston, had no trouble adapting to simpler living arrangements. There is little reason to doubt that her decision to maintain the grand style was based, at least in part, on altruism.

Back in the first days of the Depression Marjorie saw that she could do more to help the situation than merely maintaining her life style. Through the Salvation Army, she set up and financed a food station in New York's Hell's Kitchen where, from 1929 until 1935, the destitute could get a hot meal. Stories circulated at the time that she had financed the kitchen with money saved on canceled insurance premiums. She had stored her jewelry in a vault for the duration of the Depression; the insurance savings were not sufficient to underwrite the food station, but the move typified her effort to find ways to economize without putting anyone out of work.

These actions may have been gestures. The publicity from her soup kitchen was so great—newspapers referred to her as "the Angel of Hell's Kitchen"—one might suspect that she was creating a public-relations smokescreen for her undiminished lifestyle. This is unlikely. For one thing, the rich of the time felt little responsibility for the nation's predicament. The government had gotten the country into the mess, with their attitude, and the government could get the counry out of it. The rich saw no connection between their good fortune and the majority's hardships.

Another consideration undermines a cynical explanation of Marjorie's charity. Before the Crash, when scant attention was given either the excesses of the rich or the privations of the poor, she had shown herself compassionate and generous to needy people or causes. With the Depression, she felt obliged to make public explanations of her costly lifestyle, giving frequent comments to reporters about her reason for keeping up Mar-A-Lago and other pricey pursuits. She initiated her ambitious program for directly assisting the destitute. In these two actions alone she showed herself to be far more concerned and responsible than many of her fellow millionaires. All her available cash went toward maintaining her large payroll.

In addition to the gloom cast by the nation's economic plight, Marjorie had a more personal problem. Eleanor eloped with a man the Huttons had vetoed, an unknown writer and perfume salesman named Preston Sturges. Sturges's background was colorful; his mother had been best friend and companion to Isadora Duncan. He perpetuated that bohemian tradition to a degree the Huttons strongly disapproved. A story suggests the Huttons' dislike may have gone beyond mere questions of suitability. When it was clear that Sturges's intentions with Eleanor were serious, Ed Hutton called him in and asked if Sturges would be able to support Eleanor in the manner to which she was accustomed.

Sturges replied, "I would hope in better taste." It wasn't just Sturges's sassy tongue that turned the Huttons against him. He was penniless, unemployed, and endowed with a reckless impulsiveness that would have worried any parents. Eleanor married him in spite of her parents' refusal, an act of defiance that so angered her mother, she disowned her daughter completely.

Sturges and his former heiress settled in a Third Avenue walk-up where they had plenty of visitors—strays both human and animal that Sturges would drag home—but not enough to eat. All of this soon changed when Sturges's play, *Strictly Dishonorable,* became a Broadway hit. With his first royalty check Sturges bought Eleanor a diamond bracelet; the present brought little delight, since the money was desperately needed for back rent and food. Eleanor immediately hocked the bracelet to pay bills and wondered if her mother had been right about Sturges.

When the money started coming in faster than Sturges could think of ways to throw it away, the couple moved to Paris. There Eleanor, hospitalized for appendicitis, received a visit from her emotional husband. Shortly after her surgery, Sturges swept his wife from her bed to show her the magnificent view of Paris from her window. In the process he opened up her sutures.

Eleanor had never had to worry about money, and Sturges had no disposition to; in a year they went through the quarter of a million dollars he had made on his play. Fortunately, Marjorie relented and made up with her daughter before the groceries ran out. The Sturges marriage ended a short time later.

From Sturges's point of view the match had been a childish mistake. In a letter to actress/writer Chris Chase shortly before his death thirty years later, Sturges wrote: "In 1930, I was in Palm Beach—at the Everglades Club and various places—helling around and romancing a very rich young girl I would have been better off never to have married—her name was Hutton, I believe."

It is fortunate that Marjorie Post did not antagonize the public in the first months of the Depression the way her niece Barbara Hutton did. If she had, an event in December 1931 might have brought lynching parties after her. Her incredible yacht—christened the *Huzzar V,* later renamed the *Sea Cloud* —sailed into New York Harbor for the first time. Perhaps Depression-stunned New Yorkers (like the people of Leningrad five years later) couldn't believe that this magnificent ship belonged to one person.

Marjorie had booked passage on the *Monarch of Bermuda* to meet her new toy part way across the Atlantic before it arrived in New York. She writes of her encounter in her album for 1931: "Saw ship for first time from the deck of the *Monarch of Bermuda* morning of November 30, 1931. She was lying in the harbor and before we could see her, we saw her great masts and yards—great kick!! She came up to all our expectations (which rarely happens). Furnishings were in progress. We had ten days on board setting, arranging, etc., and loved every minute of it."

The bill for the barque was $1 million, plus an import duty of ninety-five thousand dollars. The overall length was 350 feet. There were four masts. In full sail the yacht looked like a square-rigger from pirate films, only no square-rigger was ever this large. Imposing as the sails were, they were insufficient to power the ship; four diesel engines assisted the wind.

The ship's main salon had an open fireplace, antique furniture, and works of art, including some Sèvres china that had to be glued in place to protect it against high seas. The guest staterooms were not like ship's quarters, but rather spacious bedrooms in a private home. Each had regular beds, not bunks, and each had an electric fireplace. Also on board was a movie-projection room, a barber shop, and a schoolroom for Dina.

For all the gold and marble fixtures, the thick carpeting, and the oak paneling, the ship's real opulence was reflected in unseen technological features: the gyroscope stabilizer, the ship-to-shore telephone, and the watertight bulkheads that could be closed automatically from the bridge (an almost unheard of feature at that time).

To be run the way Marjorie desired, the ship required a crew of seventy-two; the number would sometimes be higher. The men would have to be outfitted in uniforms about which Mrs. Hutton was most particular, renewing them frequently. The large crew necessitated considerable paperwork each time the ship went to a foreign port because of the need for special visas and other entry documents.

While owning a yacht has long been a clichéd image for great wealth, it is difficult to appreciate what it means to own a ship like the *Sea Cloud*. With a ship of this size you can live in great comfort and splendor as you are conveyed about the world—destinations, arrival, and departure times based on little more than your whim. You do not have to move in and out of accommodations, you bring them with you. You can take along as many of your friends and family as you care to have around. You can also take whatever you want in the way of personal services—doctors, hairdressers, rhumba instructors, astrologers—only paying them if you feel, as Marjorie did when she brought such people along, duty-bound.

With an oceangoing yacht you travel about the world with your wardrobe, not in suitcases, but in closets and dressers. You are waited on not by strangers but by your own staff, trained to respond to your foibles. You can also bring along your wine cellar, your library, your record collection, your pets, your favorite chair, your chessboard, your exercise machine. As an argument for self-indulgence on the most breathtaking and monumental scale, a sea-going yacht is hard to beat.

When they travel, most of the rich are sadly shorn of their ego-bolstering props. Estates, servants, paintings, racing stables, must be left at home. But with a yacht, the greatest ornament of your wealth is right there with you, whether you are in Oyster Bay, Cannes, Tierra del Fuego, or Leningrad. Some millionaires have enormous rushes of pride as they cut the ribbon on a new hospital or museum bearing their name. It is hard to imagine what Marjorie felt as she stood on the deck of the *Monarch of Bermuda* and for the first time saw the *Sea Cloud* come into view.

The enthusiasm of both Huttons for the yacht led them to view their other five establishments as places for social and family responsibilities. The *Sea Cloud* was for fun. The Huttons' Christmas card of 1931 was sent from on board the yacht. A year later, while Franklin Delano Roosevelt was taking office for the first time, Marjorie ordered the *Sea Cloud* to meet her in Havana for a leisurely cruise of the Caribbean with some friends. The winter months would be spent in New York and Palm Beach where Hutton could stay on top of business, but summers were aboard the *Sea Cloud* and the summers grew longer and longer.

The next few years the Hutton family spent so much time sailing around the world, it appeared they were staying at sea until the Depression went away. Some ten scrapbooks of the voyages show photos of North Africa, Southern Europe, South America. There are pictures of remote monasteries with long descriptions in Marjorie's own hand of the buildings and their artistic significance.

The mood on the *Sea Cloud* these first years was casual and relaxed, the Hutton family minimizing their social distance from the crew. At the frequent at-sea parties and sporting events and in the daily routine, Marjorie and Ed affected an air of easy informality.

A former third mate can recall, after forty-five years, sitting on the yacht's rear deck with Fred the chauffeur who was waiting to take his mistress ashore at Tahiti for some shopping.

As Marjorie approached the chauffeur called out, "Here comes my girlfriend."

"Come along, Fred," she said, tugging at a white glove, "We have a lot to do."

Fred jumped to his feet and, with arch courtliness, offered his arm. Picking up the style, Marjorie ceremoniously took his arm, and the two swept off merrily.

One photo suggests the degree of personal luxury for the *Sea Cloud*'s passengers. The picture is of an athletic young man, blond and handsome, in the uniform of a *Sea Cloud* officer. Underneath Marjorie has written, "Lindstrom—who keeps us well pulled and stretched and rubbed." If this suggests a bit of big-rich decadence, another entry in the album probably places with greater accuracy the yacht's sin level. A red page has been inserted in the album; on it Marjorie has written: "Red-letter day! Deenie smoked her first cigarette. For such a good reason. Tunis, the Souks!! So while waiting for Daddy to buy postals, we indulged—all three of us: Deenie, Mother and Mrs. Titler. Cheers! No one was seasick."

If Dina Hutton had been born plain and dull, she would still have been fussed over and pampered as few children have been. It was her mother's nature to spoil anyone she loved. But Dina was bright, pretty, and the child of her lovematch with Ed Hutton. Her mother went a bit crazy.

Friends of Marjorie's say they never saw a child so swathed in laces and frills, like something out of the 1890s. As she grew a bit older, Dina developed an exhibitionistic streak that was fanned by her doting, theatrical mother. The result might have been a show-offy scene-stealer who would have boggled a stage mama. Instead, it produced a hardworking, dedicated actress.

Her own suite at Mar-A-Lago, a personal nurse-maid, and round-the-clock bodyguards would seem sufficient to isolate Dina permanently from all of her contemporaries. The years she spent as the only child aboard the *Sea Cloud* further removed her growing-up period from any other. We get a glimpse of this rare childhood in a note she received years later from a former crew member:

Malmö, Sweden
Jan. 3, 1967

Dear Deenie,

Once upon a time a little girl arrived aboard a big sailing ship at Honolulu and all the town was full of flags and shouting and guns and noise. The little girl asked the third officer what all the fuss was about. "It is my birthday," said the young officer. "It is the sixth of April."

The little girl laughed but her governess said, "No, it is the birthday of President so-and-so."

Both answers were right and the little girl made a birthday cake and we all had a lovely evening around the main mast. It was in the days of kidnapping and proudly I rode behind the little girl in Honolulu and Miami with a gun in my pocket. At the Royal Waikiki I had a room beside hers and we rode the surf board together and Mrs. Campbell taught us the hulu-hula.

Yes, the little girl stayed in my memory through life. A couple of years she was part of my life, a lovely thing with high forehead and laughing eyes. It was 1933 and 1934. And so in Newsweek I saw the face again and all the memories came back, the same laughing eyes. . . . I took a look at the old pictures—you fishing, you riding on the turtle in a dress designed by me, you together with your mother and Princess Kwananakoa. . . . I must write Deenie, I must congratulate her to her happiness and I must ask her for a picture, a designated picture. If you ever go yachting in European waters, I will be more than happy to become your captain. Remember, I am your true friend and will so remain forever. I wish you all the best, dear Deenie.

Faithfully yours,
Steig Flöden

Contributing to Dina's popularity with the crew were the events and parties she organized to relieve the boredom of long stretches at sea—fancy-dress competitions, boxing matches, and other sports contests—all with advance preparations and build-up. Everyone took part, but the festivities were as much for the crew as for the *Sea Cloud*'s passengers.

Many of the miles tallied by the yacht in the early thirties were of a touristing, see-the-world nature. Occasionally trips would grow social. Returning from a voyage to the Pacific, the *Sea Cloud* put in at Los Angeles, where the Huttons entertained such Hollywood nobility as Will Hays and Hal Roach, who with his wife came along for a cruise to Alaska.

Marjorie was fascinated with Hollywood. Some years later she took Dina and a young friend, as well as the Hunter Marstons, to Hollywood. They toured several studios, both Dina and her mother hoping for a call to replace an ailing Norma Shearer or Carole Lombard. Things did not work out that way. Errol Flynn took a worryingly unprofessional interest in the teenage Dina, and the only member of the party who aroused producer interest was Minnie Marston's banker husband. Later, when Dina's keeness on acting grew serious, her mother became less playful about the profession.

When the *Sea Cloud* was in one of the Hutton's home ports, the couple used it to throw large parties. In New York it might be a bash for the General Foods executives or on Long Island a reception to show off their boat to old friends. (In order to get to the North Shore, it had to sail out into the ocean and circle Montauk; the masts were too high to clear the East River bridges.)

In recollecting one of the business parties on board, a General Foods executive speaks of the *Sea Cloud*'s informal, cozy atmosphere, which was largely due, he said, to the personalities of Marjorie and Ed Hutton.

120

Yet even in these carefree Hutton days the ship could rise to more stately occasions. Once in the Baltic the Huttons gave an on board lunch for the Queen of Norway.

For all the ship's luxury, it still provided enough rough moments to permit the family to feel like sportsmen rather than coddled sybarites. Minnie Marston recalls arriving at Havana in seas so high the yacht could not enter the harbor but had to spend the night tossing offshore. Marjorie came to her stateroom and said, "Come on! I'll show you how we can get some sleep." She instructed crew members to move their beds onto the deck.

"Marjorie and I slept up there right under the main mast," Mrs. Marston recalls. "The roughness wasn't nearly so noticeable."

The mishaps could be more serious. Crew members invariably suffered injuries. On one cruise to Bermuda, a grim pall was cast over the party by an eighteen-year-old crew member's falling from the rigging and landing on the deck. He was killed instantly.

Ed Hutton's exploratory impulse did not, regretfully, stop with yacht trips to uninhabited islands. He had a sharp eye for a pretty woman, and after a decade of marriage, he began pursuing his interest to a degree Marjorie could not ignore. Her family, looking back at the disintegration of this marriage, thinks she was dangerously unmindful of the perils of leaving an attractive, lusty husband untended.

"She would announce to him that she was going to Vichy for a few weeks," her granddaughter Marwee recalls. "Hutton would tell her he couldn't get away that long and suggest they run down to Mar-A-Lago for a few days instead. She'd say, 'No. I'm going to Vichy.' No sooner was she out the door than he was on the phone to a lady friend."

"Or some lady friend was on the phone to him," Dina adds. "There were a lot of women around just waiting for Mother to leave town."

Marjorie was first alerted to her husband's infidelities by the usual gossip. Her reaction was to try playing detective herself to see if the rumors were true. When Hutton's sport hit too close to home—that is to say, when he grew interested in houseguests and housemaids—her sleuthing involved some farcical ploys like threads tied across doors and wired beds. Her investigations came to a sudden halt one sunny afternoon at Mar-A-Lago when she caught him hard at it with a chambermaid in the bedroom adjoining her own.

The cause of the final breakup was a young woman named Dorothy Metzger who, with her husband, had been a frequent houseguest at Mar-A-Lago, Topridge, and on the *Sea Cloud*. She was twenty-eight and quite beautiful. When divorce action was finally launched, the corespondent cited by Marjorie was, according to the newspapers, "described but not named." The description was not of Dorothy Metzger but of a young woman of twenty who weighed 104 pounds. This ploy might have been to save Metzger (whom Hutton later married) from the scandal; the corespondent could have been any of the female population of Manhattan or Palm Beach.

The divorce distressed the Huttons' friends, even those who knew the extent of his meanderings. Most felt that the couple was ideally matched and had a deep feeling for each other that would have grown over the years if Marjorie could have been more philosophical about Ed's weakness. Sadly, she had not yet reached such a dispassionate point in her feelings for him. Both of them were people of strong sexual appetites; while hers was obsessively monogamous, his was quite the opposite.

She remained intensely bitter for a long time after

the divorce and even tried to turn Dina, who was shattered over the breakup, against her father. Hutton did not retaliate, but always spoke affectionately of her mother to Dina. He did, however, have a mean and devious last word. Hutton owed Marjorie $4 million, and she had waived repayment on the understanding that he would leave Dina a comparable amount in his will. When he died, he left Dina nothing.

Dina felt that her father had intended to honor this obligation, but as he grew old and slightly senile was persuaded by his last wife to alter financial arrangements in her favor. Dina felt strongly enough about this to launch legal action against Dorothy Hutton, settling out-of-court.

There is no doubt Hutton adored his only surviving child. He also knew that she would be comfortable no matter how he wrote his will. He probably assumed Dina would understand his tactic, that it had nothing to do with sentiment or paternal affection; it was strictly a business matter between him and her mother.

Meanwhile another cloud intruded itself into Marjorie's azure skies. Adelaide's husband, Tim Durant, had been set up with a seat on the New York Stock Exchange by his mother-in-law. At the time of the Crash, when many unseemly deals were exposed to the light, he was discovered to have been playing fast and loose with Adelaide's fortune, with no one's approval. He had lost most of it.

Durant's standing was already low with his wife's family in that he had produced one daughter, the formidable Marwee, but no sons. Durant and Adelaide were divorced, he decamping to Hollywood to become paid chum and factotum for Charlie Chaplin, a job that put him at the center of film-colony action. Today he is an old man living not far from his daughter's Santa Monica beach house. He and Marwee have not spoken in years, and he is not mellow about his tour of duty with the very rich. He doesn't mention his Wall Street difficulties but pins his dismissal on his failure to produce a son.

"The Post family were like all families into making big money," he said. "They become ruthless. It spills over into their personal life. A son-in-law must produce a grandson. If this one can't do it, get rid of him and get one that can. But Marjorie Post was a wonderful gal. She had a strong character, and she influenced me in many ways she never realized. She had courage, spirit—and many bitter disappointments. . . ."

In a vein that suggests he may have found his proper milieu in Hollywood of the thirties, he added, "She was terrific-looking. I remember her once calling me into her lavish dressing room to talk about something. She was sitting there in a lacy peignoir, her light-brown hair falling down her back, surrounded by all that luxury—I could have jumped her right there. . . ."

After her divorce, Adelaide brought Marwee to live at her mother's estate on Long Island. They occupied the other house on the large Hillwood property, taking meals at the main house. Marwee fired off the opening salvo of a long career of hell-raising by snipping off her dog's tail.

The final years of Marjorie's marriage to Hutton were humiliating, anxious, and painful. His bird-dog reflexes were so finely honed, he gave reason to suspect that even his beautiful stepdaughter Eleanor might not be considered off limits. The failure of both Adelaide's and Eleanor's marriages was a cause of nagging worry to Marjorie, and the headstrong, asocial personality of her only granddaughter was beginning to alarm her.

On the brighter side, Dina was a source of pride, the enjoyment of the *Sea Cloud* never waned, General

Foods was doing well, and the country's chances of pulling out of the Depression were looking up.

All of her life, Marjorie was an avid collector of photos, clippings, and other memorabilia of her life, an impulse that grew stronger with the launching of the *Sea Cloud*. In one of the albums is a photo of Marjorie sitting alone at a large table that had been set up on her ship's deck. She is working on her albums—cutting, pasting, writing. The picture is taken from slightly above, so we can see the corners of billowing sails, then on beyond her work table to the whitecaps rushing by the ship's rail.

The picture clings to the imagination: one woman, alone on her yacht, diligently recording this odd life that was at once magnificent and vulgar, enchanted and hurt-filled, godlike and banal—and finally with about as much point as any other life—while her ship plowed its way across the globe.

DINA (I):

When I was very small I
was allowed to sit with my mother in the mornings
when she was doing her makeup. I know everything I
know about makeup from watching her. I would sit
on her lap, and she would work over my head. When
I got too big for her lap, I was put on a chair to one
side. I remember she had this box of things for me to
play with. They were wonderful things, but I could
only play with them in her dressing room. It was her
way of keeping me there, but out of trouble.

When I was little, I never thought much about our
life being different from anyone else's. I first became
aware of it in little things. For instance, I saw that I
was driven to my school, Greenvale, by the chauffeur,
not by my mother like the other kids. In my lunch

126

box, I had breast-of-chicken sandwiches, the others had peanut butter and jelly. I used to swap. I was never allowed to spend the night at any of my friends' houses, but they were allowed to visit me.

I remember my mother used to have a Rolls Royce, one of those chauffeur-be-damned limousines with an open front and an enclosed back. It was hideous— patent-leather fenders and carriage lights outside—an antique job. Sometimes the normal cars would all be in use, and I'd be driven to school in that thing. I used to hate it! I would hide on the floor, I was so embarrassed. I would have the chauffeur drop me at the entrance, and I would walk up the driveway. I didn't want to be seen in that thing. You know how kids are; they want to be like everyone else.

The best thing was when Mother would take me out of school to go on those fantastic trips on the Sea Cloud. From about seven to nine o'clock, I would have lessons with my governess. Then, unless there was some special schoolwork to be done, the rest of the day I was free to play around the ship or go ashore if we were in port. Mother and Daddy would have their friends on board, but I couldn't have mine; they were all in school. In various places Mother would dig up kids for me to play with, but the crew were my friends. We had terrific fun together. They were always doing things for me. One found a baby kid on an island and brought it back for me to play with.

And then there was my father. He was a jolly person and used to love to play. He was an explorer by nature. He used to love it when he and I would go off exploring on an uninhabited island. When my mother married Joe Davies, the Sea Cloud changed completely. It was no longer for fun and good times; it became transportation between world capitals. They used it to entertain royalty, prime ministers . . . and at my age, that didn't amuse me at all.

127

But when my father and mother were still married, we'd all have such incredible times on that ship. My father loved games. He'd teach me pinochle and Russian bank. Sometimes with him it was like we were two kids and Mother was the adult. Mother would stay below in the mornings; Daddy and I would come up on deck for breakfast along with the other guests.

I remember Mother got very excited about something called the hay diet, and she insisted that my father and I go on it for breakfast and lunch. I forget what it was, but it was pretty awful. We'd eat it, then scoot off to the crew's mess and stuff ourselves with eggs, pancakes, and sausages along with the crew. Mother would say, "See how marvelous you both look. The diet is doing you worlds of good."

I had such a wonderful time. I really loved that boat. It was like a living thing to me. Until I was thirteen, I spent about six months of every year on it.

One of the best trips was to the Galápagos. The animals were so tame; they hadn't ever seen any humans. One of the islands had only fourteen people living on it; others didn't have anyone. You'd land at one of these places and you could get a few feet away from a seal before he'd back up a little bit; you could pick up the marine iguanas. . . . Mother loved all that. She adored animals.

But she could be cold-blooded about them too. Up in the Adirondacks she had a big collection of stuffed animals. On James Island there were enormous flamingos and she decided she wanted one for her collection, so she said to my father, "Ed, go out and shoot me one of those things. I want to have it skinned and stuffed." So we went out and shot one and brought it back.

We had a surgeon on board; we were gone so long we had to have medical people on board. The doctor got out his scalpel and began struggling to remove the *fatty tissue—which was bright orange, by the way, right underneath the pink feathers.*

Mother was watching the doctor's bumbling and finally said, "Oh, for God's sake, give me that knife!" She grabbed the knife and sat down on the deck tailor fashion and proceeded to do a quick, expert job of skinning the bird. I said, "Mom, where did you learn to do that?"

Without looking up, she answered, "From my father, dear, skinning bears in Texas."

I loved it because it was so unlike her. She was always so elegant. In the sun, for instance, she would wear a big hat and be covered with calamine lotion. She had chestnut hair, but a redhead's skin, and she hated to be freckled. She'd always be done up with the calamine stuff and dark glasses. She used to go in the swimming pool at the Bath and Tennis Club that way —and with a hat, too. I used to love to jump in and splash her. It woud make her furious. She liked everything very neat and unruffled.

But here she was sitting on the deck of the Sea Cloud *skinning this bird.*

We had the roast flamingo meat that night for dinner. It was terribly fishy. Mother could be quite adventurous about eating. She loved game; down in the Galápagos we'd catch a lot of turtles and have turtle soup. But then for breakfast once she tried to pass off scrambled turtle eggs on me. I couldn't take them; they were too fishy. Mother said, "Eat them, dear. Those are perfectly good eggs."

I said, "I know what they are."

You see, we had almost no fresh provisions. We'd been at sea fourteen days. And at least the turtle eggs were fresh. We fished a lot and would have wonderful fish chowders and things. We picked up a giant land turtle. Mother wanted it for its shell, but she got so fond of it, she couldn't kill it. It was a friend.

129

In Tahiti we met Zane Grey, who told us the turtle was about 150 years old. I used to ride his back, standing up doing a ballet number. I tried getting him to turn left and right with a kick. That didn't work too well, So I got a stick with a green banana hanging on the end, and I tried to steer him with that. That worked when he was hungry. One day Mother had a green dress on, and the turtle just took the whole back out of her skirt. We gave him to the zoo when we got to Honolulu.

When my mother and father got divorced, it hit me very hard. Mother tried to turn me against my father. That was a big mistake. Kids love their parents, and if you try to get them to believe anything bad about them, it will just hurt you. For a long time that made me down on Mother. But as I got older, I came to understand how Mother felt, how hurt she must have been.

Marjorie Post was an avid collector of photos, clippings, letters, and similar mementoes of her event-filled life. Here, from her albums and those of other family members, is a portfolio of pictures covering a century and ranging from Battle Creek to New York, Palm Beach, Moscow, Belgium, Tahiti, the Galápagos Islands, the Adirondacks, and Washington, D.C.

C. W. Post was as intense about his daughter Marjorie as he was about making his fortune (photo c. 1890).

The Post family home (below) in Springfield, Illinois.

Carrie and Rollin Post (above), Marjorie's paternal grandparents.

C. W. Post's piercing gaze (right) came to hypnotize patients, employees, and the public alike.

A chubby-cheeked Marjorie (opposite) in her boarding house days, ready to face the world. ▶

Ella Merriweather Post, Marjorie's mother, was overshadowed by her dynamic husband.

The Coffee Drinker

a few hours after breakfast—just about the time a business man should be alert.

That's the reaction from the coffee drug—caffeine.

Coffee drinkers can realize how good it feels to be bright, elastic and assertive, when they quit coffee and use well boiled

POSTUM

for the morning beverage.

"There's a Reason"

Postum Cereal Co., Ltd., Battle Creek, Mich., U. S. A.

An ad typical of the barrage that made C. W. Post millions.

Marjorie was eighteen when she married Greenwich socialite Edward Close.

◄ *After her divorce from C. W. Post, Ella (opposite) frequently visited her two granddaughters, Adelaide, and, on her lap, Eleanor (1911 photo).*

Marjorie, during her years as a Greenwich matron, lived the quiet life that Ed Close favored.

The sleeping nursery (opposite left) and the adjoining room (opposite right) with its platoon of dolls. ▶

The Boulders, Marjorie's Greenwich house (above). She would never again live so simply.

The decor of the master bedroom (above) at the Boulders reflects an earlier period and an earlier Marjorie.

Marjorie, with daughters Eleanor and Adelaide, 1913. Within a year she would inherit the booming Postum Company.

Adelaide (center) and Eleanor (right) were attendants at their mother's 1920 wedding to E. F. Hutton.

The trio becomes a quartet with the birth of Nedenia (Dina).

A change of style accompanies Marjorie's emergence from quiet Greenwich to the New York and Palm Beach of the twenties.

*No costume was too elaborate for Marjorie or the masquerade
balls of the twenties. She and Eleanor pose in full regalia in
her Manhattan apartment.*

Marjorie and Dina.

In the Palm Beach spirit of
the twenties Marjorie strikes
a Ziegfeld pose.

When Marjorie's seaside
castle (above) took shape
after four years of construction, Palm Beach was agog.

The opening of Mar-A-Lago
in 1927 marked the begin-
ning of a series of parties
and entertainments. Here
dancers Ruth St. Denis and
Ted Shawn are caught up in
the exuberance.

Marjorie capped her buying and building spree with the world's largest private sailing yacht, the Sea Cloud.

E. F. Hutton's lusty vitality enlivened the voyages on the Sea Cloud but eventually caused trouble in the marriage.

The costume collection grew with stops in Tahiti and other Pacific ports.

Dina and her father, E. F. Hutton, on the deck of the Sea Cloud.

When Dina organized shipboard masquerades she saw to it that everyone—crew and guests alike—threw themselves into the fancy dress spirit. Dina and Marjorie pose in the first row (fourth and fifth from left.).

Dina rides her pet Galápagos tortoise.

Ambassador Joseph Davies poses with his wife and daughter, E. K., and the staff of Spasso House (above), before presenting his credentials at the Kremlin.

Entertainments at the embassy in Moscow in the thirties (right), were strictly of the do-it-yourself variety.

Marjorie Durant, ("Marwee", below left), was Marjorie's first granddaughter. She and Dina (below center) served as attendants at Marjorie's 1935 wedding to Joseph Davies.

A family portrait (above) in Washington, shortly after the return from Belgium. Left from Marjorie: daughters Adelaide (with Melissa on her lap, Ellen at her feet), Eleanor, Dina. Right from Joe: daughters Eleanor, Rahel, and E. K. Marwee stands at the far left; third from left is Millard Tydings, Eleanor Davies's husband. Joe Tydings stands in military uniform at right.

The wicker side panels on the Sea Cloud beds were among the decor's few concessions to rough seas.

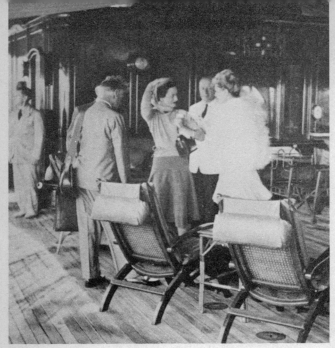

The yacht's carefree mood weathered impressive titles and royal blood. Marjorie and Joe with Belgium's Queen Elizabeth (left), and the Duke and Duchess of Windsor (above and right).

Sailors working the **Sea Cloud's** *deck had to watch out for porcelain and containers of fresh flowers.*

In the Sea Cloud's *dining room Marjorie and Dina await guests.*

Passing the hours at sea with a game of backgammon.

Expeditions on the yacht provided a luxurious counterpoint to the austerity of Moscow.

Fifty-three years after her first wedding, Marjorie married Pittsburgh businessman Herbert May (above) and carried him off to her recently completed Washington estate, Hillwood (below).

French Ambassador Hervé Alphand delights Marjorie with the Legion of Honor and a kiss, 1957.

The main drawing room at Hillwood.

A glass-topped table at Hillwood displays some of Marjorie's collection of Czarist bibelots.

At Dina's wedding to Cliff Robertson in 1967 (l. to r.): Ellen Iverson, Stanley and David Rumbough, Dina, Nina Rumbough, Stefanie Robertson, Cliff, Marjorie, Augustus Riggs, Adelaide.

Marjorie's Merriweather carried such guests as Omar Bradley to the Adirondacks and Palm Beach.

Marwee wades into the publicity waters during her starlet days.

After looking after Mar-A-Lago for Marjorie, Frank Moffat (far left) and Jim Griffin (near left) now oversee the estate for "the only employer with more money," the U.S. government.

Marjorie would sometimes hide in the gallery of Mar-A-Lago's drawing room to see guests' first reaction to the decor.

The living room at Topridge was a mish-mash of stuffed animals and Indian art.

CHAPTER TWELVE

Photographs of Marjorie taken in the mid-thirties show a major change in her image. She no longer wore her hair in a soft bob, but rather in an upsweep. This set off her fine features, yet made her appearance more imposing, more severe. She began wearing large hats of the regal, Queen Mary fashion, and she would appear in public festooned with trailing furs. The look cannot be dismissed as a mere reflection of the day's styles; she was taking on the appurtenances of a grande dame.

It would be difficult to determine if the more ponderous self-view was a result of Joe Davies's entrance into her life or the cause of it. Whether or not he can be blamed for this overall change in her personal style, he is definitely responsible for a major overhauling of her interests and pursuits. Each husband to date had left his stamp on her life. With Close she experienced the life of quiet, suburban parenthood. With Hutton, it was the big-spending, freewheeling good times of self-made millionaires. Now with Davies she would be introduced to the world of statemanship and governmental power-brokers.

Davies was ambitious, but in a far different way from his predecessor. Unlike Hutton, Davies wanted money not for the fun it could buy, but for the power it brought. His ambition had been endorsed at an early age by the Democratic Party who pronounced him "promising." With both political and professional successes behind him, at the time he met Marjorie, Davies saw himself as one of the men destined to run the world.

He had modest beginnings in Wisconsin, where his parents had migrated from Wales. His mother, like the mother of Clyde Griffiths in *An American Tragedy*, had been a practicing evangelist. Davies graduated from the University of Wisconsin law school and threw himself into Democratic politics. He moved up rapidly, taking full advantage of a good mind, good looks, and a quick-smiling affability.

Politically, he was a progressive and became western manager of Woodrow Wilson's 1912 campaign, afterward moving to Washington. In his book *Mission to Moscow* he claims that Wilson offered him the Russian ambassadorship in 1913, a bit of timing that would have pleased Marjorie, since Nicholas and Alexandra were still in power.

Davies had been an active adherent of Wilson's "The New Freedom"—a movement to break up large corporations and restore personal morality to American business. He helped draft antitrust legislation that resulted in the establishment of the Federal Trade Commission, which he briefly (1915-16) headed. His distaste for corporate bigness did not survive his meeting with the General Foods heiress.

Davies remained in Washington practicing law and furthering his political ambitions. He rose in the party concurrently and along the same routes as his good friend, Franklin Delano Roosevelt. With Roosevelt's election to the White House in 1932, Davies shifted from corporate law to representing foreign governments —Peru, Mexico, the Dominican Republic—who would pay him hefty fees to murmur in Roosevelt's ear.

When he met Marjorie Post Hutton, Davies was a rich lawyer and White House insider. She had met Davies on a transatlantic crossing—one reason for not always using your own yacht—and very quickly decided she wanted to marry him. There was one problem. He had three grown daughters and a wife to whom he'd been comfortably married for three decades.

Marjorie handled the nuisance as she had the noise on Fifth Avenue. She didn't exactly demolish Mrs. Davies, but as before, she opened her checkbook and asked, "What do I have to do?" Specifically, she sent her lawyers to call on Mrs. Davies to learn what financial settlement would be necessary to obtain the release of her husband. Around Washington, this cool transaction is portrayed as Marjorie Post's buying Joe Davies from his first wife for $2 million.

Some years later, in recapitulating the Davies marriage, *Time* magazine described the following scene: "In 1935, Joseph E. Davies, distinguished lawyer and socialite, crossed the Atlantic, walked in to his wife's suite in London's Claridge's hotel. Mrs. Davies hurried forward affectionately to greet him, but Joe held her back with a dramatic gesture. 'Emlen,' he intoned to his wife of thirty-three years, 'I want my freedom.'

"She replied, 'Why certainly, Joe.' "

Davies saw the monumental homes and the yacht and the cash surpluses as tools for enhancing his prestige and influence in ruling circles. His goal was the presidency; Marjorie's infatuation was such, she saw no reason why this ambition should not be realized. She never shared this hunger for power, yet his influence was sufficient to shift her attention away from Palm Beach and society nonsense to the more purposeful social action of Washington.

This turned out to be the right milieu for her, even if Davies did not turn out to be the right husband. Assembling ambassadors and statesmen at her table gave more significance to the vintage wines, the bowls of fresh roses, and the gold service. She would never play the power game herself, yet she relished and never quite abandoned the aura of importance these power-players gave to her entertainments.

During her marriage to Davies, the games were real in that he was, for better or worse, a friend of the president's. Barring a specific feud, this automatically made him a "friend" of almost every important man or woman in Washington. When her marriage to Davies ended, Marjorie maintained the stance of a Washington hostess, but with ever diminishing substance in the political implications of that epithet.

Not everyone in Marjorie's world took Davies unreservedly to their bosoms; and several tried to communicate their dislike of her new beau. Minnie Marston had the temerity to complain to Marjorie that she was being seated next to Joe at every dinner party and she was tired of it.

"But, Minnie," Marjorie said, "Joe knows you and likes you and enjoys talking to you." She appeared oblivious to the fact that Joe's likes and dislikes were not what Mrs. Marston was trying to establish. Dina's feelings, perhaps understandably, were negative on first sight, and the two older daughters were no more enthusiastic.

The press had no such reservations about the match. By now Marjorie was a celebrity of a sort the press adored—the big-spending heiress who didn't shy from publicity. Her natural attention-getting facility and Davies's friendship with FDR were all the press needed to bless the marriage with the full Hollywood treatment.

In return, the happy couple played the game by Hollywood rules, right down to the coy denials that they were more than just friends—even while the *Sea Cloud* was being refurbished in Charleston for their wedding trip and the monogram on a great deal of silver and gold was being changed from H to D.

During this period, Marjorie's taste for publicity gave out, and she had a testy exchange with a reporter who had just learned of Joe Davies's divorce. He asked her if the rumors about them were true.

"Which of four or five published rumors?" snapped the beleaguered heiress.

"The one about your marrying Joe Davies."

"Mr. Davies is handling a tax case for me, and that is all. One might be allowed to stay single."

The wedding took place in Marjorie's Fifth Avenue apartment on December 15, 1935. The guests, it was announced, would be limited to family and close friends, but there were enough of them for the party to cost one hundred thousand dollars. Since the select group of invitees included the attorney general and the treasurer of the United States, and most of FDR's top aides, a special train was arranged to bring them up from Washington.

In spite of the rain, a large crowd gathered under the green-and-white marquee that had been set up at the private entrance of her residence on Ninety-second Street. Huddled here were curiosity seekers, hoping for a glimpse of the notables attending the wedding, and reporters, all of whom had been barred from the building. As a concession to the press, a telephone-relay system had been arranged to pass move-by-move descriptions from butler to butler, ending up at the entrance gate where reporters scribbled the developments:

"Mrs. Hutton is being brought down the stairs by her uncle, Mr. Carroll Post of Pasadena, California. . . ."

"Mrs. Hutton is wearing a dress of ivory-colored velvet trimmed in large bands of sable. She is carrying a bouquet of her favorite flower, orchids. . . ."

"Miss Nedenia Hutton is bridesmaid for her mother. Miss Marjorie Durant, Mrs. Hutton's granddaughter, is flower girl . . ." And so on until Marjorie Hutton became Marjorie . . . Davies. The apartment's enormous rooms had been banked with towering palms in front of which stood massive arrangements of lilies, roses and chrysanthemums. The flowers were all pink and white—as was everything else, including the seven-tiered 150-pound wedding cake.

All of this was dutifully recorded in the nation's papers. The *Milwaukee Journal* topped their account with the headline: "THE WATERTOWN BOY AND THE BATTLE CREEK GIRL." (Marjorie was forty-eight, Davies fifty-nine.)

Even after it was all over, the press continued to write about the wedding. The United Press dispatch of December 17, 1935 said:

"Mrs. Post Close Hutton Davies' luxurious 62-room apartment was deserted last night except for her twenty-five servants, the lingering perfume of $4,800 worth of flowers, and the remains of a $7-a-slice wedding cake. The thrice-married Postum and Post-Toasties heiress whose income is estimated by her neighbors at one million dollars a year, was speeding southward with her most recent bridegroom, Joseph E. Davies, toward the yacht anchored in the warm waters of Nassau. . . ."

There was a sour aftermath to the wedding, one that gives an insight into Marjorie's feeling about the Depression. The press picked up on the cost of her wedding cake, three hundred dollars for about forty guests, and set up an editorial blast at such unfeeling extravagance in the face of widespread want.

In her scrapbooks of the period, Marjorie had pasted an editorial from the Oil City (Pennsylvania) *Blizzard*. The writer starts off about the extravagance of the cake, that it took a week to make, that it weighed 150 pounds, that it was all pink, crowned with a temple of love. At the end of the editorial, the writer then shifts his ground and departs from the opinion of his press colleagues:

> *Present-day folk have become used to spending by the lavish outpouring of money by the New Dealers and their fantastic schemes, their boondoggling that has brought forth so many indignant protests. Some of the money has gone for purposes just as wasteful and foolish as this $7-a-slice wedding cake. The only difference is that the taxpayer will eventually have to pay for the cost of boondoggling, while the money spent by Mrs. Davies is hers to spend as she chooses, after Uncle Sam takes a good cut of the income she receives. And then there are taxes to be paid for the materials that went into the cake. So on second thought, the cake doesn't sound as foolish as it first did. The more money that is spent for such cakes, the greater is the public's share in the wealth of the heiress.*

Next to the clipping Marjorie had written, "Not all of the columnists minded. Some straight thinking!"

Another editorial from the San Francisco *News* is pasted into her scrapbook. It winds up, "The Hutton-Davies wedding gave employment to a lot of people, scattered a good many thousands of dollars. It was perhaps the best way of redistributing wealth that they knew or was in their power." There is no comment after this clipping, but Marjorie had inked brackets around the last sentence. Regardless of the soundness of this bit of economic theory, it is obvious that Marjorie believed it was true.

Enough criticism had been leveled at similar extravagances of the rich, so that Marjorie might have anticipated some such fusillade and kept the wedding more modest. But here is evidence of an intensely romantic streak that befuddled her judgment when she was in love. She did not delude herself that she was young. In her album she congratulated herself for having written all her thank-you notes before leaving on her honeymoon, then added, "I didn't think an old-lady bride rated presents." Still, she mooned and gushed over her new husband in a way some sorority girls might have found excessive.

On the honeymoon cruise around the Caribbean (a trip that included Dina and one or two friends) the newlyweds were forever nuzzling, pawing and pecking at each other. Photographs of them taken on this trip —whether on a beach, on the *Sea Cloud*'s deck, or in port—invariably show them engaged in bodily contact of some sort. In her inscriptions, Marjorie alluded to her inability to keep her hands off Joe.

Davies responded in kind. Over a year later when they arrived at the American Embassy in Moscow, the new ambassador and his wife unnerved their diplomatically proper staff with frequent displays of affection. At parties they would cling to each other on the dance floor like high-school sweethearts; Joe Davies might suddenly jump up from a formal dinner, announcing, "I'm going to give my beautiful wife a kiss," and then hop around the table and kiss the cheek of a beaming Marjorie.

Toward the end of her marriage to Ed Hutton, Marjorie finally gave in to the nation's Depression (and her own) and closed down Mar-A-Lago. Her lack of a house did not stop her from carrying her new husband back to dazzle the old gang at Palm Beach. The Davieses were the houseguests of Mrs. Stotesbury at El Mirasol and were feted at a round of highly publicized parties; one dinner dance at the Bath and Tennis Club had a guest list of one hundred. The complete list was printed in several newspapers across the country including the New York *Herald Tribune*.

With his divorce from Marjorie, Ed Hutton had quietly resigned from General Foods. On April 8, 1936, Marjorie was elected to the board of directors of the large corporation, the first woman to be so honored. That she had till now not held any official position in the conglomerate was somewhat less a slight than her exclusion from the board of the Postum Company. With General Foods she was only the major stockholder; she had been outright owner of Postum. She did not linger over such distinctions. In her scrapbooks under the newspaper clippings announcing her election to the board she wrote, "Again back into my Daddy's business."

Marjorie only once tried to use her holdings in the company to get the board to do something they were against, recalls Clarence Francis, a former board chairman. At the time of her own election, she lobbied hard to have Joe Davies named along with her. The board's determination to keep him off matched hers to get him on. They resisted, until it looked like Marjorie would push the issue into an open stock battle; only then did they relent. Francis met with Davies and brought up a procedural point.

"Before we can vote you onto the board," he said, "we must know the number of shares of General Foods stock you hold." Davies replied he didn't know exactly how many shares he had.

Francis said that unless he got the precise figure by noon the next day, they would have to drop his candidacy. Davies never phoned with the information.

"Apparently," says Francis, "he wasn't anxious for anyone to know how much stock he had. He'd only been married to Marjorie a few months, and he didn't want people asking how he'd gotten so much stock so fast."

Rumors at the time put his holdings at 70,000 shares, which would have given him an annual income of $126,000. Since gossips were already talking about the $2 million Marjorie paid the first Mrs. Davies for Joe's release, he was understandably reluctant to give them additional information about the dowry.

According to Marjorie's old friend John Logan, she made a standard practice of fixing a block of General Foods stock on husbands to give them financial independence from her. As years went on, a number of prospective husbands turned down the offer, Logan among them.

Davies was not poor. On one of his corporate cases he was said to have picked up ulcers and a fee of $1 million. And the foreign governments were obviously paying him handsomely to watch over their interests in Washington.

That Davies held no federal post during FDR's first term probably was Davies's choice; he was doing too well outside of government. With his marriage to Marjorie he not only had the wherewithal for a fat campaign contribution, he no longer needed to scramble for those million-dollar fees.

The amount contributed to Roosevelt's 1936 campaign by Marjorie Davies to secure him an ambassadorial post is in dispute. A political writer of the day placed the figure at $17,500 which, if true, means that the icons and Fabergé were not Marjorie's only Russian bargains. Dina Merrill says she always heard the amount was $250,000.

Judging from the size of their campaign contributions in the 1930's, the smaller figure sounds more likely. For a contribution of a quarter of a million, FDR would have let Marjorie replace Eleanor. Dina's figure may be the total amount of political contributions made by the couple at this time. Joe once boasted to a business associate that his political future was not dependent on Roosevelt; he and Marjorie had made substantial contributions to the campaigns of some fifteen senators.

Davies was quick to realize other benefits from his marital coup. In May 1936, when Marjorie was laid up with an infection, he took a group of men on a stag cruise to the Dominican Republic. The group of prominent lawyers and businessmen assembled in Charleston and sailed the *Sea Cloud* off into the Caribbean for good times and leisurely powerbroking.

On another occasion that spring, the *Sea Cloud* was dispatched to Bermuda with one of Davies's daughters and a group of her young friends. In addition to the seventy-two man crew, there were official chaperones, but no Marjorie and Joe. Photographs of the handsome college-age young people lounging on the huge built-in sofa on the yacht's afterdeck offer unmatchable tableaux of got-it-made youth.

Marjorie and Joe Davies could indulge themselves and those close to them for a few months of hedonistic irresponsibility. They knew that they were soon to represent the United States on a high-level diplomatic mission. They would no longer be free to wander the world at will on their yacht or loll about their many estates. They were abandoning the guests they found glamorous, exciting, and amusing to entertain leaden commissars and starchy People's Heroes. Flirtations with history don't come cheap.

CHAPTER THIRTEEN

There is no evidence that Franklin Roosevelt saw the irony in sending one of the richest women in the world to represent the United States to Soviet Russia a mere twenty years after the Revolution. And no one has seriously suggested he pushed Marjorie into their midst with her French furniture, her 2,000 pints of fresh cream, her two tons of frozen foods, and her 350-foot yacht as a way of advertising the rewards of free enterprise. The circumstances of the Davies appointment to Moscow suggest no such ulterior calculations. Davies had first been assigned to Germany, but at the last minute was switched to Russia. Earlier, he had been rumored for France. This does not bespeak any inevitability in Roosevelt's mind about Davies and the Moscow post.

A more likely reason for the assignment was the state of Soviet-American relations in 1936 and Davies's special connections with the president. The United States had recognized the USSR only three years earlier, the last major power to do so. Recognition had been grudgingly granted by Washington in exchange for a number of conditions.

The most substantial of these issues between the two countries—the repayment of outstanding Russian debts to the United States—was left for the first ambassador, William Bullitt, to resolve. In his three years in Moscow, Bullitt had been unsuccessful in getting the Russians to pay up. With that major frustration and a diary full of minor ones, Bullitt left his job anything but sanguine about the Kremlin's good faith and anything but discreet about voicing his disillusion.

Relations were strained, and Roosevelt was anxious to improve them. A renewal of trade with the Russians would be a lift to America's depressed economy. Also, in 1936 Hitler's rise and the growing truculence of Japan made large nations like the United States and the USSR anxious to repair minor differences with more friendly powers.

People close to Davies now claim that his private instructions from Roosevelt were to make the Soviets as appealing as possible to the American public. If Roosevelt couldn't get better relations in substance, he wanted them in appearance. Whatever his other reasons, Roosevelt's diplomatic maneuverability would be far greater if Americans were favorably disposed toward the Soviet Union.

It is possible Roosevelt foresaw that this public-relations assignment would involve considerable distortion. He needed someone outside the normal State Department hierarchy, someone who would report to him directly. His old political chum Joe Davies seemed ideal. A wily lawyer, he would be adept at reprocessing

175

facts. He was ambitious, thus unlikely to be disloyal. He also had an attention-getting wife.

The Soviet Union was ripe for this sort of shift of United States policy. Stalin, consolidating his power, was himself changing from a national to an international outlook. The first Five-Year Plan had ended with decided industrial gains but much confusion and disarray in agriculture; the world was skeptical of the plan's overall claims of success. Collectivization was becoming a reality, but at an awesome cost in sabotage and human lives. In addition to the government-imposed traumas, the Russians had suffered terrible famines that aggravated the hardships of the worldwide Depression. The Soviet Union was in no position to be bellicose or hostile toward the United States.

Still, the USSR was not considered a major diplomatic post in 1936. The plum assignments, from the point of view of importance as well as glamour, were still London and Paris. Only a few farseeing students of contemporary history felt that the Soviet Union was of major international importance. Davies claimed to be one of them, saying his first choice had been Germany (he spoke German) and his second choice Russia.

When Joe and Marjorie Davies sailed from New York on January 5, 1937, the press gave the departure as much attention as the wedding. Davies would be the second United States ambassador to the Soviet Union, but since Bullitt was divorced, Marjorie would be the first ambassador's wife to represent the United States to the Communists. One of Davies's three daughters, Emlen Knight Davies ("EK") took a year off from Vassar to accompany her father and stepmother.

The party stopped in Berlin for some diplomatic briefing, then proceeded by rail eastward. The chargé d'affaires at the US Embassy, Loy Henderson, met the Davieses' train at the Russian border. The new ambassador and his party had been warned about the dangers of eating contaminated food in Russia; when Henderson appeared with a severe stomach distress, Marjorie's fears were intensified.

The international press made much of her arrival with 2,000 pints of cream, followed later by two tons of frozen foods. (She had sent ahead fourteen deep freezers, which were already installed in the embassy cellars. But they did not mention that all embassy personnel were warned against eating dairy products, raw vegetables, rare meat, or products canned in Russia. Ambassador Bullitt had suggested to the new ambassador that they bring some foodstuffs with them. (Actually dairy products, unhealthy or otherwise, were almost unobtainable in Moscow in the mid-thirties. One of the agonies of the collectivization program had been the peasants' slaughtering almost half their livestock rather than yield it to the collectives.)

Joe and Marjorie arrived in Moscow on a bright, cold morning. The streets had a clean layer of snow. The US Embassy, Spasso House, was a large nondescript affair of no great historical distinction. It faced a charming park, at one end of which stood an old church, lovely and dilapidated, that was now occupied by a number of homeless families. Nearby, a crumbling townhouse of a czarist nobleman had been put to similar use.

As American embassies went, Spasso House was in good condition. Bullitt had made some renovations, and Marjorie's advance guard had refined it further, so it was pronounced livable by the new ambassador. The main discomfort was the cold. Temperatures in the large rooms never got above fifty-five degrees, causing Marjorie never to leave her bedroom without a fur coat.

In addition to a functioning building, the embassy had a large and experienced staff. As evidence of how operational it was, the Davieses hosted a dinner party for forty-eight the night they arrived.

Most of the staff that Davies inherited were highly knowledgeable about Russia. Some, like George Kennan and Charles Bohlen, had decided early in their careers that the Soviet Union would be the central diplomatic problem of their time and had made themselves specialists even before the establishment of diplomatic relations. Others had learned much during the few years they had been at the post. It is not hard to imagine a certain antagonism toward Davies, whom they couldn't help but regard as a dilettante and an amateur.

Davies's way of getting acquainted with his staff was to have each for dinner alone with him and Marjorie. One of the most junior members, Elbridge Durbrow, remembers with disgust his evening, during which Davies seemed more intent on showing off his grasp of world affairs to his wife than in hearing anything Durbrow might have had to say. Mrs. Davies sat enthralled at her husband's every pronouncement.

Loy Henderson had an early run-in with Marjorie. The Italian ambassador in Moscow, Augusto Rosso, had married an American who was an old friend of hers. She decided to give the Rossos a big dinner party. In going over the arrangements, she told Henderson of her intention to seat Ambassador Rosso on her right and Madame Rosso to the right of Ambassador Davies. Henderson insisted that it would not be possible. The ranking diplomat present must sit at Mrs. Davies's right, and that would not be Rosso.

"Of all the foolishness," Marjorie said. "All my life I have entertained—in New York, Washington, and Palm Beach—the most influential people in America. I know what you can do and what you cannot!"

"Davies came to my rescue," Henderson adds, chuckling. "He explained to her the importance of protocol. She never gave me any trouble after that. She had been quite nice throughout the whole argument, but it was clear she wasn't used to having subordinates argue with her."

His staff remembers Davies as cocky, bristling with confidence that he could succeed where Bullitt had failed in winning the Russians' friendship, trust—and, finally, the acquiescence to United States' debt claims. His determination to be friend and apologist for the Russians at this critical time in world history made his tour of duty a significant one. And his wife, who was the most devoted disciple of his diplomatic technique, became an active accomplice.

Any examination of Davies's actions as ambassador to the USSR must grapple with two enigmas: To what extent was he being hoodwinked by the Russians, and to what extent did he know he was being hoodwinked, yet played along for reasons of his own?

It is interesting to read Davies's book on that experience today. While his stance in *Mission to Moscow* is that the Russians can become, if trained and treated properly, honorable rivals, even friends—he at least acknowledges that there is a counterargument. He knew that most Russian observers of his day felt either, as he did, that there was a potential for friendship, or that the two countries were irreconcilable enemies. Forty years later, the United States government is still debating the question.

Davies wasted no time launching his policy of putting a good face on the Kremlin's every action. In early briefing sessions, he seized the opportunity to straighten out his staff on what he termed their negative, pessimistic view of things. He also had at his disposal the accumulated knowledge of the American newspaper correspondents in Moscow, all of whom were happy to drop by Spasso House for a steak, some poker, and a chance to give their views to the new United States ambassador.

Davies would prove resistant to these unbiased opinions. When he heard something that did not jibe with his Pollyannaish view of the Kremlin, he would say, "Well, that's very interesting—and I know you fellows have a lot of experience and good sources here. But you see, I have some good sources too, and I think the whole thing can be put in a different light. . . ."

To his staff, it was quickly obvious that he intended to distort his reports to Washington. Davies would read a memo drafted by a junior staff member, say it was fine and ready for Washington, then tack on a final paragraph that reversed the paper's conclusion. Loy Henderson understood that this was being done, at least in part, for Russian eyes.

"We knew the Czech ambassador was a Russian spy; yet Davies always called him over to read dispatches before they went out," he says.

It is surprising Davies bothered. From the outset both Marjorie and Joe Davies knew that Spasso House was bugged. To have a private conversation, they would go out for a walk in the facing park. But most of the time they conversed with the assumption they were being overheard. This may explain Davies's misrepresentations to his government. If you lie for the benefit of eavesdroppers long enough, it may color your view of the truth. In any case, Davies quickly developed the reflex of reporting to Washington that the black smoke he saw curling from Kremlin chimneys was really white.

Some of the younger embassy officers were incensed at this deception. They saw Davies's distortions as only confusing the State Department, with the ultimate effect of worsening relations between the two countries, or worsening the United States advantage in diplomatic dealings. George Kennan was moved to organize a protest against the new ambassador. Others convinced Kennan that in the foreign service there were only two ways to register disapproval of a superior: to resign or seek transfer. That Kennan shortly left Moscow, the only post he wanted and the one he waited years to get, shows the extent of his disaffection.

If Joe Davies saw his role as apologist for the Soviet government, Marjorie Davies saw hers as gracious hostess and triumphant pearl in the capitalist oyster. She quickly moved into high gear with a series of elaborate dinners. In addition to the fresh cream and sirloin steaks, she had brought large crates of her own crystal, china, linens, and silver. When the diplomatic corps of Moscow were ushered in to see her tables ablaze with polished silver and resplendent with fresh flowers brought in by train from Belgium and Holland, they were dazzled, seduced, and reduced to whispering that they had seen nothing like it since czarist days. The international press corps was similarly charmed. These were men and women usually irritated by displays of wealth, but if you haven't seen a steak in two years . . .

As for the Kremlin, they knew that Marjorie was the key to the Davies operation. They were flattered that the American cereal heiress would bring her gold candelabra all the way from Palm Beach, thus treating their capital as if it were a major diplomatic center. They were eager to show that they could "handle" Marjorie the way they could handle trade deficits, crop failures, and the menace of Hitler. Besides, they never said that capitalism couldn't produce a few moguls, only that the price in human exploitation was too high.

Marjorie was eager to make friends, if possible, with the wives of Soviet officialdom. This proved all but impossible; Kremlin wives were rarely seen. The Communists did not consider one of their women important merely because she was married to a high-ranking man. Certain wives mixed freely in the highest circles, but only because of their own accomplishments and position. Madam Molotov was a prominent old Bolshevik who had served as commissar of textiles and was now launching a cosmetics industry. The wife of the People's Commissar for Foreign Affairs, Ivy Litvinov, was an Englishwoman of considerable intellect, a writer and teacher who was rumored to be tutoring Stalin in English. (Later, when her husband, Maxim Litvinov, served as Soviet ambassador in Washington from 1941 to 1943, she would switch roles with Marjorie as a displaced but successful hostess.)

Most wives of Soviet officials were permitted to mix with the foreigners only in rare circumstances at restrained and cautiously programmed events. The few opportunities for friendship that came Marjorie's way, she pursued with vigor. She had considerably more success along those lines than had other diplomatic wives. But even if social congress were more relaxed, it is doubtful that Marjorie would have gotten close to any of the Russian women who were serious, intellectual, and austere.

Once at an official function some Russian women asked Marjorie to tell them the name of the handsome white beads she was wearing around her neck. When she told them that the "beads" were in fact pearls, one of them said, "That is not possible. Pearls cannot be that large." Marjorie preferred to risk losing a Russian friend than to be thought wearing a fake anything. "They *are* pearls!" she insisted firmly.

If Marjorie puzzled the Russians, she scored a sure success with the diplomatic and press corps. This foreign colony was small and insular. They had been primed for the appearance in their midst of the famous millionairess. They knew about Grape-Nuts and Post Toasties, and they knew of her Catherine de' Medici

182

style of living. Most of the foreign diplomats were from down-on-their-luck aristocratic families, a breed quick to condemn as ostentatious anything they themselves coud not afford.

"Whatever feelings they had about her displays of wealth," says United Press correspondent Henry Shapiro, "she overcame with her natural, down-to-earth manner. Everyone liked her."

Shapiro was not so kind about Ambassador Davies. "He was a political man in the American, but not the European, sense. That is, he viewed politics as the means for amassing personal power, of moving up the hierarchy, or winning votes. He didn't think in terms of populations and political systems. He was ignorant. He couldn't talk about history or about Marx the way Kennan and Bohlen could. But he was energetic on the job. He was curious about Soviet industry. He liked to get out and see things. And he was a great host. Very generous. Generous about information, too. And opinions. He had an opinion about everything and was quick to deliver it.

"The Davieses entertained constantly," Shapiro continues. "And they had a lot more Russians to their parties than was customary—not just government people, but writers, actors, dancers. There were no dissidents in those days. Solzhenitsyn wouldn't have lasted five minutes under Stalin. . . ."

Not all of the Davies's entertaining was official. Elbridge Durbrow recalls that there was little for foreigners to do in Moscow; they had to make their own fun. According to Durbrow, they made a lot of it, with Marjorie making more than her share. She had dinners and luncheons constantly—inviting diplomats, journalists, foreigners passing through Moscow—and once gave a costume party for her stepdaughter at which everyone came as the person he or she most admired. (Durbrow's choice was Mae West.)

One of Marjorie's entertainments at Spasso House was a great success, not only with the diplomatic corps but with the Russians as well. At 4:30 in the evening she would show first-run American films. People living in Moscow were starved for the output of Clark Gable, Greta Garbo, Gary Cooper and the rest. The movie events alone made the American Embassy the most popular spot in town. Even Litvinov, accompanied either by his wife or daughter, would frequently turn up for the screenings.

The embassy staff never saw Mrs. Davies in the mornings. She would stay in her room doing her toilette, her exercises, her correspondence. She would often have a massage, and she would read up on Russia. Most ambassadors' wives are out inspecting nurseries and the like by eight. Marjorie did her share of factory tours with official guides, but her mornings were her own, as they would always be.

On one of her tours she got into quite a lively conversation about the new Russian cosmetics industry with Madame Molotov. The Russian woman was impressed with the rich American's grasp of problems of mass production and marketing. She invited Mrs. Davies to have lunch at her dacha a few weeks later. Such an invitation from a highly placed Russian was unheard of; the diplomatic community was agog.

The day of the luncheon, Marjorie and some of the other American women drove out of Moscow to Rublova Woods, a suburban area of luxurious homes. The large Molotov residence was described by Marjorie as sparsely furnished and totally impersonal—no photographs or bric-a-brac. She also noted that the dining room had cyclamen, the flowers "at least three inches each" and eight or ten potted lilacs on the floor "white and lavender—fine big heads and full of flowers." Whoever arranged the party had evidently researched the preferences of their flower-loving guest of honor.

The food was a tableful of hors d'oeuvres, followed by a number of elaborate courses that included three kinds of meat and six kinds of fish. "One was very special" Marjorie wrote, "a snub-nosed little thing about eight inches long—very good, and comes from the Volga River. I had to eat regardless of the Embassy doctor's warning—so I did, *at length*."

The lunch passed amicably, if decorously. Marjorie spoke later of how anxious the Russian women were to show the Americans a good time. ". . . But, oh!" she said, "if only one could speak the language. Through an interpreter it is difficult, to say the least."

That same evening Marjorie was at a dinner seated next to Lord Chilston, the British ambassador. Great Britain had been one of the first countries to acknowledge the Soviet government, and he was dumbstruck at Marjorie's diplomatic coup.

"You Americans are remarkable!" he said. "I have been here seven years and haven't been able to get so much as a toe in their house—and you come and after only a few weeks you have a luncheon given there in your honor. I don't understand it!"

Joe Davies was very frank with the Russians about his pro-capitalist, anti-Communist position. He went to great pains, however, to appear open-minded and to show he did not consider the two systems inimical. When both Marjorie and Joe got into theoretical discussions with the Russians, as sometimes happened, they would confine themselves to requests for clarification of the Communist position. They had no desire to antagonize their hosts with heated polemics.

Marjorie had one such conversation with Madame Krestinsky, the wife of the under secretary of state, on the subject of religion. Madame Krestinsky said that the Soviets were not against religion per se, but only the abuses of religion that had so hurt the Russian people before the Revolution. She went on to brief Marjorie on the ecclesiastical invasion of the Duma and other clerical horrors the Soviets were trying to expunge. Her reasons seemed to be quite a departure from the prevalent popular notion of the Soviet position on religion. Even if it was propaganda, such glimpses into Kremlin thinking were rare in 1937, and the exchange was interesting to Washington.

Although Marjorie was not strongly political, neither was she oblivious to the ideological battleground on which she found herself. Her photo albums have a series of pictures of a Sports Day Demonstration, phalanxes of white-robed, sunburned young men and women, prancing and strutting around Red Square. Clearly impressed by this pageant of Russian youth, she wrote a short essay under the photos:

> *Lenin and Communism declare that it was religion that was the opiate, that dulled the people under the czars and made them insensitive to the wrongs that they suffered. Communism controls public opinion largely through the enthusiasms of youth to whom propaganda is constantly addressed. Probably the most spectacular instance is the Youth Movement. All measures and kinds of sports and competition and regulations are encouraged and featured. These youth parades are inspiring spectacles and should be an example and warning to the democracies.*

Joe Davies, less apprehensive, got carried away by the intellectual stimulation of it all. At one point he gushed to a friend, "My wife and I thank God that Franklin has given us ringside seats to the greatest experiment in the history of man."

CHAPTER FOURTEEN

For all his calculations about sending the Davies spectacular into Moscow, Roosevelt had no inkling that it would be there during one of Russia's darkest, most agonizing periods. If brutality can be measured in terms not of numbers slaughtered —although Stalin could hold his own with anyone here —but in the cold-blooded annihilation of his colleagues, the purge trials of 1937 and 1938 have to be considered one of the most oppressive eras of history.

In December 1934, some two years before the Davieses arrived in Moscow, Stalin's second in command, Sergei Kirov, was assassinated in Leningrad. It is a comment of the complexity of Russian affairs at that time that specialists still disagree as to whether Kirov was a victim of the purges or the cause of them.

Trials in Leningrad in 1935 relating to the Kirov assassination were followed in 1936 by a trial of sixteen alleged conspirators against the government. To some the charges semed trumped up, but no one saw the trials as steps in the wholesale liquidation of an official class. Not until the third trial, which began in Moscow early in 1937 (two weeks after Davies's arrival) did the full fury of Stalin's rampage begin to reveal itself. This was the famous Radek treason trial. Since it signaled the existence of an ongoing purge, it attracted the keen attention of the rest of the world.

The Kremlin encouraged foreign diplomats to attend the trials. Being both an interested diplomat and a lawyer, Joe Davies attended every session. He had the ringside seat that FDR had given him. In *Mission to Moscow* Davies tells of adjourning for beer and sandwiches with the American newspapermen attending the trial; the event takes on the macabre festivity of a public hanging. Adding to the odd horror of the purges was the invisibility of the man behind them. Since Stalin was only head of the party, he could shunt chores like receiving diplomats onto his president and premier. Stalin received few foreigners and seldom appeared in public. It was a rare diplomat who had ever met him; some had never seen him.

Davies studied the trial testimony carefully and sent back to Washington long analyses of the crimes admitted and the statutes violated. Invariably he would conclude, with sad head-shakings, that the Soviets had established their case beyond question.

Looking back, it is hard to understand how any observer could take seriously trials in which dozens of the nation's most prominent leaders stood up in court and calmly confessed to crimes, any one of which would earn them the death penalty. *Why* Stalin was eliminating two-thirds of his leadership was another question, but that he was somehow extracting false confessions from men he wanted to destroy was obvious at the time to most people both on the scene and abroad.

But not to Joe and Marjorie Davies. It is staggering to read Davies's dispatches, with their dogged apologies for Stalin's bloodbath. Laboriously, he recites the Soviet laws that make it a crime to plot the assassination of the country's leader or the overthrow of the government. He cites the dates these laws became effective. He points to the confessions of the accused . . . with expressions of deep regret, he makes the only conclusion possible: They are guilty.

Davies and his wife argued this position all over Moscow. When the complete trial testimony was published, the Davies sent off sixty copies to influential friends in the States. Marjorie sent one to her friend Eleanor Roosevelt with a note saying that on every page of the transcript there was overwhelming evidence of a conspiracy against the Soviet government, which was justified in pursuing the purges. Marjorie also complained of the international press's strong bias against the Kremlin and Stalin.

It is one of the great, if unimportant, ironies of history that at the time when even the most enthusiastic fellow travelers were having second thoughts about the Soviet path to Utopia, when non-Russian Communists were lapsing into unaccustomed silences, two of the most dogged defenders of Stalin's purges were the cereal heiress and her $2-million husband.

At first it appears the Davieses were acting on some sort of big-shot esprit de corps; a more likely reason for their advocacy was their belief that Joe's assignment was to render the Soviets more palatable to the Americans. One has to laugh at the picture of Davies riding into Moscow, beaming with midwestern bonhomie, determined to put a good face on the Kremlin's peccadilloes, only to be stopped dead by one of the more heinous episodes in political history. He may have missed a few beats, but his good-guy, friend-making smile stayed frozen in place.

Davies even went so far as to report to Washington that most of his fellow diplomats in Moscow agreed that the trials were justified. Others there at the time say this was blatantly untrue. One begins to see Davies as a lawyer so programmed to defend his "client"—in this case the Soviet government—he automatically justified every action. Perhaps too he saw that, unable to help the trial victims, he might at least try to profit by siding with those wielding the power.

If Joe and Marjorie averted their eyes from the true nature of the trials, they were unable to ignore some of the attendant horrors. A Davies innovation had been a full-dress dinner party honoring the Red Army. Nothing of the kind had been done before in the diplomatic community. The nation's leading generals all accepted the invitation, and some brought their wives, signaling the dinner's success. Many warm after-dinner toasts saluted the valiant army and Soviet-American friendships as well.

Within nine weeks, Marjorie's dinner partner of the evening, Vice-Marshal Tukhatchevsky, had been condemned for conspiring to overthrow the government. Along with four other generals who had been the Davieses' guests that evening, he was shot.

This was not the only time the purges intruded into the Davieses' wining and dining. They had become friendly with a mysterious Baron Steiger, a man of German origin who held a cultural-liaison post in the Soviet government. One night during the trials, the Davieses accepted Steiger's invitation to join him in the former Royal Box at the opera. Davies's daughter, EK, and some other members of the American party accompanied Steiger afterward to the nightclub at the

Hotel Metropole, though Joe and Marjorie declined the invitation. During supper two men in civilian clothes approached Steiger and tapped him on the shoulder. He excused himself from his guests, went with the men, and was never seen again. (His name later appeared on lists of those executed for treason.)

On many occasions Stalin's iron fist crashed down nerve-wrackingly close to Joe and Marjorie Davies. Among those marked for execution by the trials of 1938 was Litvinov's first assistant, Under Secretary of State Krestinsky, to whom Davies had presented his credentials one year earlier. Another condemned man was a Dr. Pletnov, a physician, who had treated Davies and with whom he had become somewhat friendly. Also executed was the People's Commissar for Trade Rosengoltz, whose country home the Davieses had visited.

In 1938 Davies again attended the trials each day. Now that he knew the principals, the experience was even more excruciating. "It was difficult to look upon the prisoners in the box without shrinking," he wrote. "There these men sat not more than ten feet from me . . . I hope they saw in my eyes the sorrow which I felt in seeing them again under these conditions."

Marjorie has been criticized for frequent absences from Moscow during her husband's tour there. She made a few irrelevant trips to Paris and London, but many of her excursions were in the line of duty. As wife of the ambassador she did all that was expected of her, plus a lot more. It takes not only money and fourteen freezers to entertain as lavishly and frequently as she did; it also takes considerable energy and interest. Just mastering complicated Russian names was not easy, and the diplomatic life allows no mumbling. Given the fifty-five degree temperature in her house, the concealed microphones, and the general atmosphere of terror in Moscow, it is remarkable that she plugged away at the job as hard as she did. What's the use of working so hard to charm a general, only to learn he's been shot a few weeks later?

Among the legends that surround Marjorie's Soviet tour is that she brought the *Sea Cloud* to Russia laden with frozen foods and left with it stuffed with Fabergé and other Russian art. She had already shipped much of the food before the *Sea Cloud* arrived, but in its general outline, the story is not so wrong.

During the first months of their stay in Moscow, the yacht was laid up for repairs and refurbishing, but it finally followed its owner to Russia. The sight of the largest privately owned sailing yacht gliding up the Neva River into Leningrad, just twenty years after the Revolution, must surely have been one of the oddest juxtapositions in history.

Making it even odder was that few Russians knew anything about it. The Communist press did not report such events. Marjorie and her possessions may have had the diplomatic community agog, but the average Russian was unaware of her existence. A certain amount of word of mouth spread around the harbor at Leningrad, but the few people who were told that the magnificent ship belonged to a rich American woman refused to believe it.

The yacht provided Marjorie with an escape from Spasso House and the chilly formality of embassy living. When Joe Davies went off on one of his periodic tours of Soviet industry, she would take the *Sea Cloud* on a cruise around the Baltic. These trips were unlike the footloose wanderings around tropical seas of the Ed Hutton days. She was now the wife of an important United States ambassador, FDR's hand-picked representative in Europe. She now took with her on the cruises diplomats and government officials, entertaining royalty and other VIP's in her ports of call.

Marjorie may have resisted protocol during her first days as a working diplomatic wife, but basically the rigidity appealed to her highly organized approach to everything, and she was soon reveling in it. Rather than carefree outings, the yacht trips out of Leningrad were like state occasions. Loy Henderson and his wife and others from the embassy staff would accompany Marjorie and assist in the logistics. This might mean arranging a stop at Copenhagen to pick up the American baritone Lawrence Tibbett and his wife and untangling the complications of a run over to Sweden where the king was to be entertained at an onboard lunch.

It was at this lunch that Marjorie asked the king if he had enjoyed the fish. He replied that he found it delicious. "It was caught six months ago," Marjorie said.

The king expressed surprise. At his request, she took him below to show him the freezers and explain the freezing process. Since this folksy exchange was picked up by the international press, cynics might suspect a public-relations ploy to promote the new food-preservation process, which she now owned in part. It was nothing of the kind, merely one monarch showing another a new toy.

Even when the *Sea Cloud* wasn't touring, it was used as an escape residence, especially in the summer of 1937 when Dina came to visit. It provided a fine haven from the supposed contagions of Moscow. Unfortunately, the Russians would not permit the yacht to moor in the beautiful expanse of the Neva River in front of the Winter Palace—that would have suited Marjorie fine—but relegated it to the boondocks of the commercial wharf district.

In the album from this period she has pasted a

magazine photograph of the Leningrad docks that shows an enormous locomotive being hoisted from a ship. Underneath, Marjorie has written, "This may be all right, but we never saw anything *half* so interesting the entire time we sat in the Leningrad port."

Still, they were far more comfortable on the *Sea Cloud* than at Spasso House. It was, after all, the family's home as much as anyplace. Days would be spent sightseeing and shopping in Leningrad and the surrounding area. Evenings would bring hearty meals of non-Russian food from the yacht's freezers and perhaps an American film. To vary this painless program, the yacht would occasionally make day runs down the Neva.

Dina tells of one warm summer day when they decided to take the *Sea Cloud* in search of an attractive place for a swim and a picnic. With a Russian pilot aboard, the huge yacht moved down the river toward the sea. After some time they spotted a sandy island that looked ideal. Marjorie ordered the captain to make for land. The Russian pilot, in great excitement, told them they must not. It took a while to learn why he was upset. The island was out-of-bounds because it was not Russia, but Finland. It would take several days of bureaucratic paperwork before permission could be granted to swim on the deserted piece of sand.

Marjorie announced she had never heard anything so silly and they headed for the island where they had a fine picnic. She was quite willing to play the Kremlin's game when she was on Russian soil, but on the *Sea Cloud*, she was the law.

On occasion, Marjorie invited the entire diplomatic corps for a similar day's outing. The ship was set up to entertain hordes of non-sleeping guests. Marjorie's Hollywood friend, Will Hays, kept her supplied with recent American films, and the film showings were scheduled nightly. It was understood that any diplomats or newspaper people who happened to be in Leningrad were welcome. Much has been written about the effectiveness of motion pictures in projecting a favorable image of the United States to the rest of the world. It is doubtful if anyone ever put them to such direct use in making friends as Marjorie and Joe Davies.

A note from her album of the summer of 1937 has an epoch-launching ring. While on board the yacht in Leningrad, she writes: "Larry's sister, Deenie, Mrs. Tyler and I went ashore to the famous Fabergé Shop. The Government had opened it again after twenty years and are there selling the remainders of the state warehouse. We found it very interesting."

She found it interesting enough to buy up most of its contents. An entry a week later says, "Joe and I did a check-up on the articles at Fabergé and, of course, had another field day. We took in the Commission Shop too. Joe bought some more pictures. It's just like peanuts—he can't resist them."

Returning from one of her Baltic cruises, she writes, "Joe arrived looking so well. We were both so happy to be together again. His hands were full of bundles. More Commission Shops. It becomes a habit while living in Russia."

Meanwhile, a grimmer reality was intruding into Marjorie's world of yacht outings and jeweled Easter eggs. The fear of Hitler had reached up the Baltic and into the waters of the Neva. Before that summer was over, war preparations were in increasing evidence. To return from one of its downriver outings, the *Sea Cloud* had to pass through mined waters. The Russians provided the yacht with a convoy of one, or sometimes two, pilot boats. Fearing that a mine would slip by the convoy, Marjorie and her guests would stand on deck to watch for the metal object that could blow the whole show—Chippendale furniture, Sèvres china, deep freezers—right out of the water.

Davies saw an important part of his job as investigating Soviet claims for industrial and agricultural progress. This involved a number of trips out of Moscow without his wife. While the trips may have been useful, he relished the outings, for which he would fill a private railroad car with favorite staff members and convivial journalists. They would roll around the country—playing poker, eating steaks, having parties—and occasionally touring a factory.

In an effort to combine one of these exploratory trips with his wife's enthusiasm for yachting, Davies planned an elaborate trip for the *Sea Cloud* into the Black Sea. Late in the summer of 1937, the yacht was dispatched to Monte Carlo, where the Davieses, including Dina, were to join her. The family assembled on the Riviera and were poised to embark. At the last minute the US Navy forbade them to take the trip. The threat of war was too great. So they consoled themselves with some travel and shopping before returning to Moscow.

In her album, a photograph of Marjorie has been cut off just below the eyes; attention is focused on a dazzling tiara sitting atop her chestnut hair. The caption: "It was here in Vienna that 'Anna' came to live in our family. There is no doubt that Joe spoils me and I love it!" Anna was a piece of Hapsburg jewelry, perhaps the first live-in tiara.

Some tension arose concerning Davies's ambassadorial performance when Secretary of State Cordell Hull reprimanded Davies for his frequent absences from Moscow. Davies countered that the president had requested him to serve as the European eyes and ears of the White House. This announcement must have left the secretary of state wondering what part of the anatomy his European ambassadors represented.

Davies's understanding with Roosevelt was that he would get the German ambassadorship as soon as it was free, sometime within the year. He had, in fact, agreed to serve in Russia only until the Berlin post opened up. By the end of the year, the situation in Germany had become so acute that the promise was voided. Davies, however, held Roosevelt to his pledge to be relieved from Moscow. Members of the staff at Spasso House say there is no possibility that Marjorie would have put in another winter in Moscow. Perhaps she saw little advantage in being the richest woman east of the Rhine if she was going to be cold all the time.

On January 8, 1938, Washington announced that Joseph E. Davies would be transferred to the American Embassy in Brussels. When she heard that Belgium was to be their new home, Marjorie was jubilant. "Thank God," she said. "They've got a king!"

The actual transfer was not to be effected until June. This gave the Davieses a second chance at their Black Sea trip which had grown as important to Marjorie as it was to Catherine the Great. The war scare had shifted from the Mediterranean, so this time the trip came off as planned. On May 15, 1938, the Davieses left Moscow by train, arriving in Odessa two days later. When Marjorie encountered her yacht in the Odessa harbor, she was startled. "It was a definite shock," she reported, "to see the Red flag floating from our yard. Nothing could be more far-fetched, the largest private sailing craft in the world and the Communist flag. We went to the Commission Shop in Odessa and we might as well have been Stalin from the mob gathered. . . ."

It is interesting that the Davieses should have been treated like celebrities in Odessa, but not in Moscow and Leningrad. It is possible that because this was an official trip on the part of the United States ambassador, the local newspapers mentioned their arrival. It is more likely that the *Sea Cloud*, which had been hidden by the Russian authorities in the wharf area of Leningrad, was now gracing the harbor for all Odessa to see. With such an attention-getter, it would not have taken six hours for the Davieses to be known to the city.

Something strange happened to the Davies party that must have had the more superstitious Russian peasants crossing themselves and swimming out to touch the American yacht. Joe Davies's valet made international headlines by winning $120,000 on the Epsom Derby. To many, the yacht was an obscene affront to the world's have-nots; to others, it was a piece of floating economic theory. With this windfall, it surely must have taken on an aura of enchantment that removed it from the world of inflexible reality.

Even those onboard were shaken by this bit of good fortune. When they had recovered from the shock, they found their spirits—and the voyage's—raised considerably. Moscow and its cold were almost behind them, a servant had struck it rich, and the next stop was a sophisticated European monarchy. It was an ebullient ship that glided past the cyprus-covered hills of the Russian Riviera. They stopped at Yalta and at Sochi where Stalin had his winter dacha and where many of the imperial court had maintained villas during czarist days. None of the scenic beauty and historic romance was lost on Marjorie.

The final days in Moscow were filled with sentimental farewells and a bit of high drama. The foreign colony was sorry to see the ambassador go. Whatever staff members, newsmen, and fellow diplomats may have thought of his performance, they had enjoyed partaking of the spectacle of the Davies Moscow turn. And it wasn't just the steaks, the fresh cream, and the American movies. An ambassador can be a skillful diplomat and a commendable representative of his country and still be achingly dull. The Davieses had not been dull. Most of the foreigners, moreover, included Joe and Marjorie in feelings of camaraderie; together they had all gone through a difficult and historic time.

A number of parties were given in their honor, and the Davies reciprocated with a series of gatherings, culminating in a giant reception for the entire diplomatic corps, the press, and more Russians than had ever been invited to a foreign diplomat's house. The other ambassadors were overwhelmed by the sixty or seventy writers, artists, and other nongovernmental Russians whom the Davieses had attracted to their party. At a small ceremony (held at a museum), Madame Molotov presented Marjorie with a pair of porcelain vases, a tribute to "the first Ambassadress of the United States to the Soviet Union."

As a final bit of business, Joe Davies had to make formal farewells to the Kremlin officials with whom he'd dealt—those who had survived the purges. He intended taking his military attaché as interpreter, but the Soviet foreign office reminded him that protocol dictated he come alone. Davies thought nothing of this; it later appeared significant, however.

He called first on President Kalinin with whom he had the customary exchange of compliments and expressions of friendship between the two countries. Next he was escorted to the offices of Premier Molotov. The two had met often, and their greetings were genial. No sooner were they seated than a door opened, and into the room walked Joseph Stalin.

Davies remarked later on how gentle he looked, also

that he was surprisingly small and slightly bent. Stalin seemed intent on an informal, unceremonious chat. They discussed Davies's impressions of Soviet industry. Stalin was gratified that the ambassador had gone to such pains to see what the Communists had accomplished.

It must be remembered that the only account of this conversation we have is Davies's, though there is no doubt that it occurred—the entire diplomatic community talked of nothing else for days. If Davies had hallucinated Stalin, the Kremlin would surely have denied the meeting. But the account is Davies's only and suspiciously self-serving. At times it borders on the "and then I said to Stalin," school of fantasy.

Davies reports, for instance, that after the discussion about industry and a few compliments, he made a diplomatic move to depart. Stalin asked if he had another appointment. When Davies said no, Stalin told him not to be in a hurry, and they talked for two hours. Stalin moved the discussion to the debt issue, still the greatest obstacle to Soviet-American harmony. He made a new proposal on how the issue might be resolved, which Davies promised to relay to his government.

Talk became general. A friendly exchange evolved on the merits of Communism as opposed to democracy. Davies acknowledged Soviet efforts to raise living standards for the average Russian, but claimed the American system did far more for the common man. As Davies warmed to his subject, he shifted from conversing with Stalin to lecturing him.

The ambassador felt Stalin should know of government efforts in the United States to reduce the disparity between rich and poor. He asked if the Russian leader had any idea what percent of Mrs. Davies's annual income went to her government in taxes. Stalin did not. More than seventy-two percent, that's how much. Having missed that one, Stalin was given another chance.

Did he have any idea how much of Mrs. Davies's entire estate would go to the government when she died? More than eighty percent!

At the time of this discussion, Stalin had much on his mind: faltering Five-Year plans, peasant sabotage, currency shortages, the Nazi menace—and the blood of his old comrades still moist on his hands. It is irresistible to think that for a moment he was asked to shift his attention from these epic woes and focus on the tax problems of Marjorie Merriweather Post.

Foreign Minister Litvinov gave the Davieses a farewell dinner in an old mansion used by the Soviet foreign office for official parties. Nothing was stinted to make the event an all-out, full-dress festivity. Over the linen, silver, and china of the old regime, warm toasts were exchanged.

Davies spoke of the many events in the two countries' histories that should lead to strong Soviet-American friendship. He pointed to Russia's refusal to assist the British during the American Revolution, Russia's eastward expansion, America's westward. In a paroxysm of comradeship, he rejoiced in both countries having rid themselves of kings. This was an unfortunate diplomatic gaffe. Among those listening to Davies was the Belgian ambassador, representative of the king who would shortly be receiving Davies's credentials.

Marjorie was the belle of the evening. She wore a white dress and, in a subtle nod to the Russians, no jewelry. It was a mild spring evening, and the gardens of the old house had been illuminated with colored lights and arranged with clusters of furniture. Guests could stroll the winding paths, then sit for a while in leafy alcoves and gazebos.

Foreign Minister Litvinov and Marjorie started off the dancing after dinner for which a twelve-piece orchestra played the latest European songs. An hour-long concert of Russian artists was followed by another supper. With Marjorie the most popular lady on the floor, dancing went on till after three in the morning. The Davies drove home as dawn broke over the Kremlin.

They had done it. They had fulfilled a difficult post in a way that brought credit to their country. And while there had been much clenching of teeth by Russian experts, Davies's performance seemed to have gratified both Roosevelt and Stalin. The harshest assessment has Davies taken in by the Russians, allowing himself to be hoodwinked. Madame Litvinov later referred to Davies as a "naive fool." If indeed it had been her husband's job as foreign minister to deceive Davies for a year, it was graceless of her to point out how easy it had been.

Davies put a detailed account of his tour into *Mission to Moscow*, a fact-filled compendium of dispatches back to Washington, diary entries, letters, and after-the-fact reflections. Published in 1941, it became a best-seller in a wartime America curious about her new and mysterious allies, the Russians.

As for Marjorie, she not only had charmed the Russians and other diplomats, but the press corps as well. She had seen to it that they all benefited by her presence in Moscow. The staff at Spasso House never found her anything but gracious and considerate. And even those most antagonistic toward the wealthy— from Communist newspaper reporters to Russian peasants—were inevitably disarmed by her easy friendliness. She had developed a real interest in the Soviet Union, its history, and its current turmoil; and she would take with her a lasting affection for the Russian people.

It is tempting to think of her Russian tour as an exotic diversion in a life that had grown stale from too much pleasure. But few people in her financial bracket ever put themselves out to the degree she did by going to Moscow. For all the luxuries she brought in her luggage, her stay was filled with discomforts, tedious duties, boring officials, and endless encounters with people with whom she had no language in common— and little else either.

One of Marjorie's critics compared her unfavorably with other diplomatic wives, women who had grown up in the foreign service and who could intelligently discuss the work. In a sense, this was a tribute. Marjorie knew in advance the drawbacks, yet she entered this alien world, made the greater effort her inexperience required, and, to a large degree, succeeded.

She would return to the United States with greatly enhanced prestige. The newspapers wrote favorably about the Russian tour, and they had been on the cover of *Time*. As she concluded her middle years and headed into grande-damehood, she could always say she had done *something*. It set her apart from sister grande dames who generally win the title merely by being grand long enough. Marjorie had earned her stripes. Now she was off to Belgium to see the king. Back at Spasso House there was a little grumbling that she had taken her fourteen deep freezers with her.

DINA (II):

For years after my parents were divorced, I hoped something would happen and they'd get back together again. There was some disagreement between them about money. I think my father used some funds from a joint account to cover losses at the time of the Crash. Mother threatened to force him to pay it back. I don't think she was serious; she just wanted to use it as leverage in getting other concessions, like reducing his visitation rights with me. I don't know if he promised her he'd leave a certain amount to me in his will.

I wanted them to stop arguing and patch it up. Things in my life turned grim after they separated. I didn't like Joe Davies. The first time I met him he was wearing a black cape, just like a villain. He put his arm around me and said, "Ah, Dina, you look so like your beautiful mother. . . ." You don't say that sort of stuff to a kid.

When Mother went with Joe Davies to Moscow, she wouldn't let me come with them. She had heard about unsanitary conditions, and she was afraid I would catch some disease. She let me come to Leningrad, though. I'd stay on the Sea Cloud and only eat our own food.

It was fascinating being in Leningrad then. We would take marvelous excursions down the river or visit the palaces.

When Mother and Davies were transferred to Belgium, I went and lived with them there. The embassy in Brussels was beautiful. Mother gave me a budget and let me furnish my own room. Davies was also minister to Luxembourg. I can remember just before the Second World War broke out, we would visit Luxembourg and take drives out to the border and look at the German entrenchments. We could see the soldiers walking around.

I was never sent to boarding school until Mother went to Russia and it was absolutely necessary. My niece Marwee and I practically grew up together at Hillwood. My sisters were grown by the time I came along. Sometimes it was like having three mothers.

Even though Marwee was wild, Mother adored her. She always stood up for her. I remember years later when Marwee was getting married for the second time Mother said to me, "Isn't it wonderful Marwee is going to marry the physics professor?"

"He's not a physics professor, Ma," I said, "he's a physical-education instructor in a high school."

"He is not," Mother snapped. "You are always putting her down. She's marrying a physics professor."

It was wartime when I was coming-out age, so I never had a big party like my sisters. My father wanted me to run around with those social North Shore kids. I never could figure out why; I wasn't interested. Later, when I had boyfriends, I much preferred actors to those socialite types.

I knew all along I wanted to be an actress, but Mother was never very enthusiastic about this. She was very theatrical herself, and I think if she'd come along in a different era, she would have gone on the stage. As for my acting, I don't think she believed very strongly in careers for women. She brought me up to be a wife and mother.

But she did believe every woman should have a way of supporting herself. She used to brag that if anything happened, she could support herself in several ways. She could be a hairdresser, and she was a damn good manicurist. She made me take typing and shorthand— which I hated. I'd say to her, "Ma, I'm going to earn my own living, but not that way."

My father wanted me to go to law school and run for Congress. Mother wanted me to go to the University of Wisconsin. She was from the Midwest, and she wanted me to experience it too. I went, but it was a disaster. I hated it. I pleaded with her to let me quit, but she said I had to stick it out one year. I stayed away from classes for three weeks, then told Mother what I'd done and that no one had missed me. She got my point and let me come home.

I went right to New York and entered acting school. I got work as a Vogue model to pay the rent. I was determined to do it on my own. Mother didn't think the acting would work out, but she felt I had to find out for myself. After working for a year, I fell in love, got married, and gave up acting for eight years.

One of my first professional acting jobs was at the end of World War II, when Moss Hart hired me for an USO tour of the South Pacific. Mother was frantic at the idea of my going into war zones; she was sure

I'd be shot. But I knew how to get around that. I appealed to her patriotism. She was very patriotic. I told her she had no sons to give to her country, so the least she could do was let her daughter entertain the troops. She gave in.

But she had me tracked all over the Pacific. She got all these admirals and generals she knew to make sure I was all right and that we were being treated properly. Moss Hart began to sense something funny. He came to me and said, "What is all this red-carpet treatment we're getting. Do you know someone?"

I said, "It isn't me, Moss."

Even today I try to keep my acting career separate from all that. I know it's inevitable that my name will be linked with hers, that people will know my mother was Marjorie Merriweather Post and my father was E. F. Hutton. But I never mention it when I write those biographies of myself that go into theater programs. I don't think it has any place in a professional biography.

I suppose, in a sense, I'm still crouching on the floor of that limousine. . . .

CHAPTER FIFTEEN

C. W. Post was proof that merely having money and an enthusiasm for art does not make you a collector. On his trips to Europe, he bought extensively so that his Battle Creek hotel would have Great Works of Art; for the most part, the lobby of a small midwestern hotel is where the stuff belonged.

His daughter's interest in acquiring important and valuable objects began when she moved from Greenwich to Manhattan. It was then that she was first able to spend money without having her father looking over her shoulder. Then, too, the grandeur of her Fifth Avenue mansion required serious furnishings; she set a standard hard to live up to with the acquisition of some excellent French furniture of the eighteenth century and museum-quality tapestries.

Her daughter Eleanor takes credit for giving Marjorie her first piece of art: a Pajou statue for which Eleanor saved three-months' allowance. In 1931, when Eleanor had come into her own money, she gave her mother a Christmas gift of the last great Fabergé Easter egg that had been made in 1914 as a present from Czar Nicholas II to his mother.

During the twenties, Marjorie had acquired some important items—Marie Antoinette's jewels, the Hapsburg lace. (It was almost as though she needed the reassurance of prior royal ownership before she felt sure an object was "good.") Later, with the building of Mar-A-Lago, her taste was at its most diffuse. The building contains a mélange of things acquired here and there—Mrs. Horace Havermeyer's fifteenth-century Moorish tiles, the patio pebbles from a Long Island beach—and copies of things that had impressed her on her travels, like the Thousand Wing Venetian ceiling and the Delft bedroom. Her acquisitions during this time did not make her a collector, just a woman with a lot of money who took a vague pleasure in owning good things.

Her arrival in the USSR when the Soviet government was selling off czarist treasures is one of the more opportune bits of timing in the history of art-works preservation. This happy coincidence had the effect of focusing Marjorie's acquisitive instinct and putting these important artifacts in the hands of one person—a person who would build a museum around them—rather than have them scattered on coffee tables and mantels around the world.

Some people familiar with the Russian art she collected say that her buying spree was prompted by her friend, the renowned art dealer Lord Duveen, who told Marjorie of the upcoming sale and advised her to buy everything she could get her hands on. The explanation seems to spring from the circumstantial fact that she knew Duveen and that admirers of her collection resist the thought she did it on her own. But Marjorie's own diaries give a picture of more accidental stumbling on the treasure-filled Commission Shops.

The Communists claimed to be selling the items in celebration of their twenty years of rule, calling attention to the czars' extinction. A more cynical view is that they were motivated by a need for hard currency. Either way, in 1937, the year the Davieses arrived in Moscow, enormous amounts of Russian fine arts were put up for sale—centuries old icons, jeweled bibelots of the czars, exquisitely wrought chalices selling for the equivalent of five cents the gram weight of silver, gold chalices slightly more—with workmanship thrown in for free. The world was still in an economic depression; not everyone had money to snap up diamond-encrusted cigarette boxes and ruby and emerald brooches, even at the Kremlin's bargain prices. Marjorie not only had the time and money for some major shopping expeditions, but she had found in the Russian art objects her true enthusiasm.

In the introduction to one of the books she later issued to catalog the collection, Marjorie refers to the incredible use of bright colors in all their art—paintings, porcelains, Fabergé pieces. Elsewhere she refers to her fondness for "this gay Russian art." There is no doubt that she had an affinity for the Russian esthetic, that her enthusiasm was not based merely on its low-priced availability.

According to her friend Nettie Major, Marjorie bought her most important Russian art, not at the Commission Shops in Moscow, but outside Russia on the open market. Henry Shapiro concurs in this. "The Russians saw her coming," he said. "They didn't put out any of the really good stuff for her to pick over. They took the best things for themselves."

This is disputable. True, some of the best things

were acquired elsewhere. The exquisite Orlov tea set, for instance, she found in an antique shop in Vichy while taking the cure. Also in her foreword to her Fabergé catalog, she mentions receiving a pink Fabergé clock for her birthday in March 1938, and of going to the Bolshoi Opera that night unable to think of anything but the exquisite clock. This would have been at the end of the Davies tour. It is hard to think she would be preoccupied with one piece of Fabergé if the *Sea Cloud* were anchored in Leningrad loaded to the gunwales with the stuff. But what about that "field day" she and Joe had enjoyed in the Fabergé shop in 1937?

The answer lies in between. Yes, she did get some very good objects in Russia through the Commission Shops and the government storehouses; and she did buy some of the most outstanding pieces later when her interest in Russian art had solidified and she realized she was on her way to owning the most important such collection outside the Soviet Union. Then, too, her announced enthusiasm solved the problem for her children and rich friends at Christmas and birthdays. What do you give the woman who has everything? You give her a piece of Fabergé.

By the time she arrived in Brussels in the summer of 1938, Marjorie already had enough Russian art to fill the vitrines and to top off the commodes of the palatial old mansion that was the American Embassy. The imposing building that had been the town residence of the Marquis d'Assche was built in the elegant French style of the eighteenth century. The place needed work, but it had the makings of a beautiful and princely residence. Adding to her delight at the move was the mansion's location in a city that had ample veal, cream, and fresh flowers—and a king who was eager to meet the American cereal heiress. This was more like it.

Marjorie brought much of her household staff from the United States. This was fine for getting the squabs cooked properly, but it presented a problem in that none of the servants spoke French. Marjorie's daughter Eleanor, who was now married and living in Paris, would come up to Brussels on weekends and use her fluent French to help her mother and the staff get settled.

The ultimate punctuation of the Davies's Communist experience was the splendid ceremony surrounding the ambassador's presentation of his credentials to King Leopold of Belgium, an occasion of almost extinct pomp. To start it off, the king sent his gold-encrusted royal coach for Davies, complete with a plumed and sworded 40-man horseguard, who clattered and flashed Davies's carriage through the streets of Brussels to the Royal Palace.

A short time later a luncheon was given for the Davieses and the king and queen at the rural chateau of Colmar-Berg. Marjorie writes how both Dina and EK were in a dither about meeting a king and queen, how they couldn't take their eyes off the footmen in royal-blue knickers, scarlet coats, white wigs, and gloves. Marjorie's reaction, as recorded in her diary, is only slightly less breathless.

The embassy wasn't completely spruced up until September 1938. Marjorie was just hitting her stride as a major European hostess when her husband decided the Nazi storm had gathered sufficiently to warrant sending her back home. Space was booked for Marjorie and Dina to sail for America in October 1938.

Marjorie wrote in her diary: "We sail October 1st on the *Duchess of York,* our minds much at peace now that Munich has been settled and the world can breathe again." Underneath in a different ink she has written: "Little did we know what 1939 would bring!"

She stayed in America only a short time; in November she headed back to Europe on the *Queen Mary*. Nancy Randolph, in her New York *Daily News* column, was nice enough to miss Marjorie at the opening of the opera: "Mrs. Joseph E. Davies is one of the most conspicuous absentees on this year's list. Mrs. Davies could usually be depended on to be one of the most elaborately dressed women at opening nights. Her costume of blue and silver lamé and swirling white fox that she wore last year was a particularly memorable one."

With an embassy under renovation and the increasing threats of war, Marjorie had only a brief taste of normal diplomatic life, and most of that was on the *Sea Cloud*. She stayed in Brussels the winter of 1938-39, then returned home for the summer in July 1939. In September, Hitler invaded Poland.

After the war Davies would talk about the *Sea Cloud*'s jaunts out of Ostend on the eve of World War II. They sailed around Belgian waters, he said, "Entertaining diplomats, discussing matters, chinning on the afterdeck. It afforded the best kind of opportunity for getting real confidences from one's diplomatic associates. When you sat back on that afterdeck and looked up at all those square-rigged sails billowing out . . . golly, what a sight!"

Davies's train of thought seems to imply that it would be churlish of any diplomat to withhold secrets from the man who commanded such an expanse of sailcloth.

Hitler saw to it that Marjorie was not to preside over the most lavish embassy in Europe; during the war the Davies settled in Washington where they bought an estate, Tregaron, on Embassy Row. Davies was named Special Assistant to the Secretary of State in charge of Emergency Problems and Policies. Marjorie set about becoming a Capital hostess to be reckoned with, but never with the naked determination of a Perle Mesta or Gwen Cafritz, which may be the reason she achieved a more solid niche for herself in the Washington party hall of fame. Or maybe it was because she had more money than the other two.

Both Joe and Marjorie threw themselves into wartime activities. Before Belgium fell to the Germans, Joe returned once more at FDR's request, occasioning the only time Dina remembers seeing her mother break down emotionally. "She cried and cried," Dina recalls. "She was afraid Joe would be shot."

Hearing this, Dina's niece Marwee adds, "Ten years later she was afraid he wouldn't be."

Shortly after the Davieses return to the States, they were at a charity dinner at Palm Beach's Everglades Club. A prominent dowager, a woman who had known Marjorie since they were both young brides together at the Breakers, spotted the couple looking alone and friendless. She went over to speak to them.

Marjorie insisted the woman join them, and they regaled her with stories about their Russian experience. When the woman expressed polite interest, Marjorie said, "Would you like to see our scrapbooks?" She said she would, thinking that after dinner at Mar-A-Lago some night she might be invited to browse through them. Not at all. The next morning, she found one of Marjorie's butlers standing before her with a stack of albums.

She went through the books and found them very interesting, but she was taken aback by the photos Marjorie had inscribed to Joe and vice versa—all with passionate declarations and testimonials. "To my dearest treasure, my life began when first we met," etc.

"It's all right to have photos with that stuff written on them," the woman snapped, "but you don't send them over with the butler for others to read."

A rather significant character slipped into Marjorie's

214

world early in the World War II years. A somewhat mannish young typist, Margaret Voigt, was enlisted to help Joe Davies and his ghost writer draft *Mission to Moscow*. Davies was working on the book aboard the *Sea Cloud* in Florida and the word went out that he needed a typist. A crewman, Frank Voigt, suggested his wife, Margaret.

She proved so efficient and hardworking that Davies took her back to Washington with him. Margaret Voigt became the single most significant individual in the last twenty years of Marjorie's life. As with most people who started with nothing and rose to positions of influence, she had many admirers and many enemies. The latter group accused her of being a master at intrigue, especially talented at discrediting people and at poisoning relationships that had lasted many years. She made short work of Marjorie's then secretary, and within a year Margaret Voigt had the job. As Marjorie grew older, she increasingly felt the need to turn over the details of her rococo life to someone else. Margaret Voigt was in position and ready. With her advent a period of intrigue and backstairs politicking began that would have lifted the eyebrows of Cesare Borgia.

In November 1941, just one month before the United States entered the war, Marjorie was concerned enough about the plight of the Russians to overcome a horror of public speaking and address a two-thousand member meeting of the Council on Soviet Relations. The theme of her talk was the pressing need for United States military aid to the Soviet Union. Her appeal took a curious feminist turn. Her speech, as reported in *The New York Times,* stressed that the status of women in Russia, Britain, and the United States was "higher, freer and broader, with greater rights, privileges and duties than in any other country . . . To none in this world is the outcome of this war more vital than to women. If the Nazi totalitarian system should dominate our world, the status of women would be too horrible to contemplate. It would be reduced to that of breeder and hausfrau for an ordained super-male in a world dominated by a so-called Nordic master race. Under such conditions, idealism, freedom, self-respect and opportunity for women would find no place."

The newspapers of these years are sprinkled with other reports of Marjorie's war efforts, often on behalf of Russia. On one occasion she lent her Russian art collection for a New York show to benefit Soviet War Relief. She presented an exhibit of American nursery items to be displayed in Moscow in exchange for a similar exhibit of Russian items.

Back in Washington, Marjorie hurled herself into the more routine war work of American women with leisure. While rolling bandages at the Red Cross she made a remark to the woman working next to her that has become a permanent part of Washington lore. Surely it takes some sort of prize for a succinct evocation of an altogether unearthly existence.

"Tell me, what time is it, dear?" she asked. "They forgot to wind my watch this morning."

It is heart-warming to note that at a time when families all over America were losing their cook or cleaning woman to defense work and high wages, "they" had not deserted Marjorie.

CHAPTER SIXTEEN

Marjorie's marriage to Joe Davies came apart in an unpredictable and unpleasant way. Contributing to the deterioration was his career disappointment. Throughout the forties he had ridden the crest of the fame *Mission to Moscow* had brought him. A film version was made, and the book impressed the public consciousness enough to earn a parody of its prolix prose style by Edmund Wilson. Many people who don't know the name of the present United States ambassador to the Soviet Union, know that for a short time during the thirties it was Joseph E. Davies.

After the war President Truman sent Davies back to the USSR on a diplomatic errand. He flew into his former post with *Mission to Moscow* painted on the side of his plane (in English and Russian), compounding this bad taste by bringing a print of the movie. He screened it for the non-plussed commissars, who failed to recognize either themselves or their country. Davies was later part of the team Truman brought with him to the Potsdam Conference. After a lifetime circling the centers of influence, Davies probably came closest to true power at Potsdam.

For all these honors, he was merely playing out the accumulated chips of Russian expertise. He never again had a major post, and no one but his daughters spoke of his presidential qualifications. He would still have lunch with columnist Drew Pearson and bend the ear of White House insiders with his view of the world situation, but gradually his influence faded.

It is easy to ridicule Davies, if only because he was the husband of a very rich woman. Enough stigma has always been attached to this role to keep many men from auditioning for it. Marjorie never seemed aware of this. It was an oversight that perhaps brought her more unhappiness than anything else in her life.

It is a sad comment on human nature that all of Davies's accomplishments in the diplomatic world were overshadowed by his wife's fortune, even at the moment of his greatest success. As his career waned, her fortune did not. The disparity was a growing source of friction.

Before seeing Davies at his lowest ebb, we should review his credits. Whatever misrepresentation he may have made from Moscow, no one suggests he did it for reasons other than his conception of his country's best interests. He pursued the job with diligence and enthusiasm. And his conciliatory view of Russian intentions is not so outlandish today as it appeared during the worst days of the Cold War. In recent years, increasing numbers of historians have suggested that perhaps the Cold War was not as unavoidable as Truman and Churchill led us to believe.

Other of Davies's appraisals that were once in conflict with the majority have subsequently proved correct. When Hitler invaded the Soviet Union, Roosevelt, Churchill, and George Marshall all believed that the Russians would collapse quickly. Davies was alone among knowledgeable observers to state publicly that the Russians would be the first to stop Hitler. His perspicacity required some backbone; a pro-Russian bias was not the easiest stance to maintain in Palm Beach.

The principal reason Davies had so many detractors is that he appeared to be an opportunist and a poseur. Comments range from Elbridge Durbrow's "the most dishonest man I ever worked for" to Marwee's "just a fourteen-carat phony." Marjorie herself said at the time of her divorce that she had known "Joe was an actor two weeks after our wedding."

She also knew he was something else. Early in their marriage, he asked for, and received, her agreement to lease the *Sea Cloud* to him for a dollar a year. He wanted to be able to refer to it to reporters and others as "my yacht." Perhaps she swallowed this as good public relations for public figures, but she must have blanched when he told reporters how he built the yacht in 1931. When Marjorie commissioned the yacht, she didn't even know Davies.

Marjorie's remark about Davies being an actor is particularly interesting in light of an observation she made to a close friend that she had been happier with Davies than with any of her other husbands. Surely the excitement of diplomatic life had something to do with this tribute, but in addition, Davies, more than the others, had been singlemindedly devoted to her. If she knew he was an actor, perhaps she required no more than the performance of a good husband. The authenticity of the underlying emotions may have been less important to her than the authenticity of one of her Louis XVI chairs.

A bit of philosophy she once gave Marwee was surprising both for its candor and its content. "Who cares *why* the men want to marry you?" she said. "How important are these motivations? The main thing is that they treat you right."

This may have been the disillusionment of an eighty-year-old still looking for a husband. It does not necessarily mean she was so indifferent to her husband's character when she was young. If she knew that Davies was, as the French say, "interested," she also knew that he had treated her better than any of her other husbands. The purity of Close's and Hutton's feelings for her, and later May's, perhaps grew less important when measured against the unhappiness they caused her.

Davies became a worse problem than any of the others, but it was discord of a different order. He became increasingly obsessed with his wife. His obsession grew as he felt dependent on her for both his prominence and his ducal standard of living. When he became impotent, his possessiveness and jealousy bordered on insanity.

Jealousy is always ugly and unbalancing, but it takes a most grotesque form when the sufferer is in his seventies and the object is sixty. His age certainly did not impair the intensity of his feelings. Every time Marjorie showed the slightest friendliness to any man other than an old friend, she earned an is-that-your-new-boyfriend attack. Soon it reached the point that if she danced with another man at a party, she would hear about it for a week.

One such flare-up occurred in public and got into the press. At a war-bond rally in New York's Madison Square Garden, Marjorie was stirred by the speech of industrialist Henry J. Kaiser. Afterward, Kaiser passed in front of the Davies box and Marjorie leaned down to tell him his speech had been one of the best she'd ever heard.

Kaiser, feeling expansive after his ovation, replied, "Those are beautiful words from a beautiful woman."

This exchange was sufficient to convince Davies that Kaiser had been selected for his replacement and was probably already on active duty. Newspapers quoted Marjorie as saying, "I was kept up half the night wrangling over this . . . that I was making a pass at Henry Kaiser." To a close friend she said, "As God is my judge, I never saw Henry Kaiser before or after that moment."

Yet, the marriage endured. The *Sea Cloud,* which had been conscripted into wartime duty, was returned to civilian status. The Davieses had leased it to the government for a dollar a year (its highest charter fee to date), and it had distinguished itself first as a weather ship, then as a sub-chaser, winning a citation for sinking two German submarines and for an assist in the sinking of a third.

To get it back in shape for luxury yachting, it was refurbished at a cost of $3,145,188, the work starting in 1946 and progressing in stages until 1950. The masts had been taken down for its war service, and for a time the Davieses used the ship without sails. Eventually, however, it was fully restored to its square-rigged magnificence—using over eight miles of Manila rope in the process.

Dina, who has spoken of the *Sea Cloud* as being like a person to her, mentioned how her mother regretted not having a son to send out to fight for his country. And while neither Dina nor her mother ever made this parallel, Marjorie must have felt something of a parent's anguish when she sent the *Sea Cloud* into combat. In any case, her first sight of her ship after the war was a moment of high emotion. Except for some chipping of a marble fireplace where ship's officers had misdirected darts, the yacht was in excellent shape.

After some time, when the final touches were completed and the sails restored, Marjorie described in her album watching her ship approach Palm Beach:

"*Sea Cloud* in full sail came over the horizon as we watched from the eighth floor of Whitehall [a former Palm Beach hotel]. It's the first time Joe and I have seen her made out in full sail and not been on board. What a picture she is! We watched, excited and fascinated, until she was out of sight beyond the Breakers. Joe said, 'Well, dear, there goes your baby.' "

With her yacht back to full glory, Marjorie got down to some serious social cruising. Preparations were intense. A New York newspaper mentioned the *Sea Cloud*'s taking on $24,000 worth of food, gratuitously adding, "That's a lot of groceries." Whether or not Marjorie had any motive of reestablishing herself as a major figure on the American society landscape, the *Sea Cloud*'s postwar wandering up and down the East Coast had that effect.

The yacht tied up at Alexandria, Virginia (the deepest water close to Washington), where, among other parties, Marjorie hosted an onboard lunch for Mamie Eisenhower. She sailed up to Glen Cove, Long Island, for another round of parties for old North Shore friends. A dance for Dina's friends brought 400 young people on board. The New York papers made a fuss over the arrival on the *Sea Cloud* of the Soviet delegate to the UN, Andrei Gromyko and his wife, who joined Joe and Marjorie for dinner and a film.

On Long Island, return dinners were given them by the John R. Drexels and Mrs. Cornelius Vanderbilt. The Davieses touched down at Newport and the coast of Maine for more partying and social flag-raising, then sailed down to Nassau where the local press got so excited at the visit they referred to Marjorie as "the former Barbara Hutton."

During the at-sea portion of those *Sea Cloud* days,

there were always guests. Family and friends were picked up here and dropped off there—with the same logistical precision that marked all of Marjorie's operations. Away from socially dense spots like Long Island and Newport, the pace became relaxed to the point of indolence.

Gliding around the bright seas of the Caribbean or South Atlantic, guests would be treated to free-form days of rare luxury. Crisply uniformed crew members provided snap-to execution of the silliest whims. Marjorie's memos to the crew and galley staff contained precise instructions about dietary restrictions or preferences of her guests; allergies were noted in considering fresh flowers in staterooms; and when it came time for guests to depart, the ship's crew and radio facilities were put to use to arrange the guest's travel plans down to the most minute details.

Onboard the *Sea Cloud* as well as at Topridge, Mar-A-Lago, and Hillwood, fleet admirals and corporation presidents were boggled by Marjorie's organizational genius. Even her father, C. W. Post, who was a dynamo of efficiency himself, had been impressed. "If Marjorie were left on a desert island," he once said, "she would organize the grains of sand." As she got older—and richer—this quirk grew to legendary proportions.

In a sense, this concentration on monumental good times that marked the late forties and early fifties was an echo of the twenties—also a postwar period—and took the appearance of a million-dollar sigh of relief that the world was once again safe enough for the very rich to play in.

Marwee suggests that all her grandmother wanted in return for the good times she showered on people, was to be appreciated. A note pasted in one of the *Sea Cloud* scrapbooks from this period bears out her theory. It is handwritten by Mrs. Paul McNutt on stationery engraved *On board the SEA CLOUD:*

> *Dearest Marjorie,*
>
> *I am having such a good time, I can hardly stand it.*
>
> > *Kathleen*

Underneath the note, Marjorie scrawled, "This came with my breakfast tray! Bless her!"

All of the socializing and high-seas fun came to a climax of sorts when the Davieses invited the Duke and Duchess of Windsor to join them on a Caribbean cruise. The Duchess was quick to accept, and even though she addressed her future hostess as "Mrs. Davies," she wasn't shy about indicating the destination they favored. She said that she and the Duke "have never had such a thrilling invitation! I can't think of anything the Duke and myself would rather do than have a trip with you and Mr. Davies on the *Sea Cloud.* Nassau, of course, would be charming, but we must be frank and say we are tempted by your suggestion of Cuba as we have never been there. . . ."

The cruise for the Windsors was to a king's taste. Writing about it in her album, Marjorie presents a vivid picture of *la vie Sea Cloud:*

> *"I think today has been the most beautiful one at sea I have ever seen. All sails were up, a smooth sea, cool and sunny. We were all on deck early. The men sat reading and happy, the sailors mending the sails which were split in the high winds. This ship is marvelously equipped to handle any emergency. We played some bridge, knitted and loafed. In the afternoon we passed quite near the tip of Cuba where there were enormous mountains and cliffs, seemingly uninhabited. We could detect*

no signs of life through the binoculars. We passed one ship, a freighter, otherwise no sign of anything."

On another trip, the Davies gave a dinner onboard for Rafael Trujillo, who reciprocated the next night by offering a concert by the National Symphony Orchestra in Marjorie's honor. At a ceremony after the concert, Trujillo bestowed on his guest the Dominican Republic's highest order, a decoration that put Marjorie squarely in the midst of an exclusive band of heroes.

Perhaps such attentions aggravated Joe Davies's behavior, which grew stranger. A woman who would later become a close friend of Marjorie's was the wife of an official of the American consulate in Caracas when the *Sea Cloud* called. As was customary when Davies was aboard, their approach was announced in advance, and parties were arranged at the United States Embassy. The embassy staff knocked themselves out for the short-order dinner reception only to have Joe Davies arrive without his wife. She had remained onboard, he told them, with a headache.

Twenty years later the woman felt she knew Mrs. Post well enough to mention the incident, saying how unfortunate it was that Marjorie had not felt well enough to attend the party.

"What party?" Marjorie asked angrily. "I remember that day very well, and Joe never told me anything about a party. He told me he was going ashore to do some shopping. You say it was a dinner? How perfectly dreadful! What was that woman's name? I'll write her a note right now. . . ."

Such duplicity was typical of Davies's later behavior. Marjorie's marriage to Joe Davies lasted twenty years. For ten of those years he was an adored husband, and for ten he was a problem that had to be coped with, planned around, and finally, avoided.

There was a sad glimpse of the final stages in the diaries of columnist Drew Pearson, who described a dinner given in 1954 for Marjorie by three hundred former houseguests at Topridge. He wrote, "It was obvious to almost everyone there that Marjorie would like nothing better than to see (Davies) on his way. This is her fourth husband and gossip has it she has already picked out the fifth." Pearson, who here gives her an extra marriage, described the seventy-five-year-old Davies as looking "on his last legs."

As buffer against Davies' eccentricities, there were continual parties and houseguests, as well as the constant presence of intimates like Margaret Voigt and the numerous staff to inhibit his more frightening outbursts. As he grew senile, his jealousy grew worse. On several occasions he attacked Marjorie physically. Marwee recalls nights at Hillwood when her grandmother asked her to sit sentry duty in the bathroom separating Marjorie's bedroom from her husband's. Marwee would remain there until she was certain Davies was asleep.

On more than one occasion Margaret Voigt said to her employer, "That man is going to kill you yet." Voigt, the consummate palace schemer, was perfectly capable of playing on Marjorie's fears to lessen Davies's influence and increase her own. Still, the evidence is abundant that Davies's last years were anything but benign and that Marjorie did feel physically menaced by him.

One summer, to avoid Davies, Marjorie leased Sutton Place, the magnificent English manor later purchased by J. Paul Getty. Her plan was to invite her daughters with their families. Then with her family ensconced she could have a round of glittering house parties for her European friends. Margaret Voigt did some quick figuring and said the house parties would not be possible.

"Whyever not?" Marjorie wanted to know.

"Because," Voigt replied, "with your daughters, their husbands, their children and their governesses, you have run out of bedrooms."

Schedules were worked out with Marjorie's usual exactitude, and she had both her families and her houseguests. Eleanor remembers the summer in the English manor as a great success for all of them, so much so that the house was leased for the following summer and the entire experience was repeated.

Despite periodic contretemps, Marjorie and her three daughters were close; the English summer was a period of particular calm in their relations. Dina had forgiven her mother for divorcing Ed Hutton, Marjorie had forgiven Eleanor about Preston Sturges, and so on.

The three daughters had settled into diverse existences—they saw each other infrequently—so the summer in Sutton Place was a rare and relaxed reunion. At night they would sit up late talking and comparing lives. This went on until one night their mother discovered them. Marjorie was horrified.

"What are you doing up so late? You'll get bags under your eyes! Wrinkles! Go to bed at once!"

Her daughters pointed out that they were grown women with families and households of their own, households where they could go to bed whenever they pleased. Marjorie was not going to stand by and watch her daughters' faces fall. She insisted they go to bed. It was hopeless; they made a show of going to bed, then reassembled later in a more secluded corner of the vast mansion to continue their seminar on marriage and children.

A number of years later, Marjorie was invited to have lunch with Getty at Sutton Place. She and her party were appalled to be served a tough, stringy piece of bully beef. Getty was served a bowl of dry cereal. The Post group assumed Getty's stomach had given out. Being on a stringent diet, he had perhaps lost touch with normal appetites and had let his kitchen deteriorate.

They were even more appalled to see the majordomo remove Getty's bowl and put a large sizzling steak in front of him. As Marjorie and Getty chatted about the problems of running the mansion, she and the others watched in wonder and envy as he wolfed down the juicy meat.

The Sutton Place interludes reminded Marjorie that life was far more enjoyable without the constant presence of an irascible and unbalanced old man. She decided on a divorce. As her lawyers looked into legal problems of untangling her life from his, they discovered something new about Davies: a larcenous streak that predated their marital difficulties. Various highly prized objects—a particularly valuable portrait of Catherine the Great, for example—turned out to be in Davies's name. The final blow fell when she learned he had also put in his name Tregaron, the twenty-nine-acre estate that had been her principal residence for sixteen years and upon which she had lavished much money and attention.

In the foreword to *Mission to Moscow* Davies, in a burst of enthusiasm for the capitalist system, writes that it "permits to each of us an opportunity to acquire property according to our respective abilities. . . ." He got to keep the estate.

Usually Marjorie was philosophical about such trifles, but this snatching of her home from under her was so infuriating, that she resolved to build herself a Washington estate twice as splendid as Tregaron. She also went back one night, accompanied by gardeners, and dug up all of Tregaron's azalea bushes that she had worked so hard to establish.

MARWEE (I):

I think they first knew I was going to be trouble when I cut my dog's tail off. It was an accident, of course, but it was my first big caper. Forty years ago. I mean, I was always a ratty little girl. I'd kick guests in the shins, swear at Adelaide, the usual stuff—but it was that dog's tail business that really made them wonder about me.

I decided to give my dog a trim . . . cut his hair. When I got going I thought he'd look better with his tail a little shorter, and I snipped off a few inches. I didn't know it was bone in there. I thought it was hair. Christ, it was horrible. Blood all over the place, the dog screaming his head off. I tried to bandage him up, clean up the blood, but they found out. The dog was rushed to the vet. I told them a door had been slammed *on his tail. But Adelaide called me in later and told me the vet said it couldn't have happened that way. The tail had been severed, not crushed. I was cooked. And Adelaide's the biggest dog lover in the world. There was hell to pay. I was always getting in trouble like that, always living on the brink of disaster.*

One reason I got so close to my grandmother, she never did the heavy punishing. If I was bad in front of Grandma, she'd never dress me down. She didn't have to; she'd just look at me with those steely gray eyes— they went right through you. That's all she had to do. I was in awe of her. She was the only one I feared. Of course it didn't take me long to figure out what was what. My grandmother ran the show. When my mother and father broke up, we went to live with Grandma at Hillwood on Long Island. There was another house on the property right next to her house. We lived in there but would go over and have dinner with Grandma. I used to hate the formality—the big dining room, the butlers—but I was impressed.

Grandma ran it all. My mother, Deenie, myself . . . we looked to her. So I've always keyed off of her all my life—not my mother, her. Later, when I was sent to live with my father in California, she sent money to take care of me. So she's always been like my mother.

I was always out of step. I never remember being in step. Deenie and I had night-and-day bodyguards that never let us out of their sight. Even in the playground at school the bodyguards would be lurking around. Someone once asked me if that was fun for us. Goddammit, it killed everything. It took every bit of freedom away. We couldn't run around like the others. I remember one time, I made a break for it. I plotted it out like a theft. There was a cop at the gate of Hillwood in a little box. The box is still there. I was riding my bike on the grounds and as I went past the gate, I shot out, made that right turn on 25A, and pedaled as fast as I could for freedom by myself. I barely made it to the intersection when—my God—I was besieged. They were all over me.

I resented the formality of those meals and not being able to be casual. As a result, I don't have a dining room today. We eat in the kitchen. But even though I didn't like the life my grandmother forced on me, I looked up to her like a queen. She never let her hair down with us. Play with us? I didn't think of her in those terms. She never disciplined me. I didn't require discipline from her. I didn't screw up around her. I felt the power.

I should hate Dina. Grandma always threw her up to me. She'd say, "What's the matter with you? You're in school every day, yet you have to go to summer school every year. I take Deenie out of school, take her on the Sea Cloud, she gets about three months of school, yet she gets straight A's. I can't understand it."

But I'll tell you something about that Dina. I wouldn't say Deenie did the same things I did, not to the same degree . . . but she wasn't quite as pure as what my grandmother believed. She could do it and get away with it. There was something about her. And I just got caught every time. She had to cover my tracks a few times. She's the most adjusted lady—nothing fazes her—she's completely together, without being a total bore, I mean. I always adored her.

I lived at Hillwood until I was eleven. It's C. W. Post College now. They have a philosophy class in my bedroom. I'm going to be a guest speaker. Ha!

Once when I was about fourteen, I asked my grandmother for one of Charlie Munn's greyhounds. My father, Tim Durant, had gotten my grandmother to invest in a business Charlie was starting, the betting machines for the racetrack—the Totalizer Company. Grandma wasn't into racing or gambling—she didn't approve—but she loved to make money, so she backed *it, and she made millions. Anyhow, I told her I would love one of Charlie Munn's dogs, and she said she would arrange it. I picked out this beautiful black dog, Beau. I loved that dog, He was trained to attack anything that moved, and when he finished off the white poodle that belonged to my father's girlfriend, I had to get rid of him. Once one of those dogs has been trained to follow his killer instinct, there's no way you can break him.*

I was being sent out to my father on the West Coast, and Grandma still had me under tight security in those days—a guard or somebody had to be with me all the time. Grandma had a secretary named Mrs. Woolsey. She preceded Mrs. Voigt. Well, everything went fine until we had to change trains in Chicago, and that's when it hit the fan.

I wanted to go back to the baggage car to see if Beau was all right. Woolsey said for me to meet her at one place, I thought she said another. I'm not sure how it happened, but all of a sudden Woolsey and Beau had taken off in the train for the West Coast, and I was still standing in the Chicago station. There I was with no money, no dog . . . nothing.

I told my story to a conductor in the station. He said, "Do you have nerve?" I said yes. He told me there was a troop train pulling out in a few minutes that got to Omaha, Nebraska, before the other train did. It didn't make any stops. He said if I snuck on that train, I could catch up with Woolsey and Beau.

Meanwhile Woolsey shot off a telegram to my grandmother and—my God—she called out the marines. I got on the troop train and told my story to some soldiers. They hid me in the john until the dum-de-dum-dum went through the car, and I got a free ride. The soldiers made a mascot out of me. They made me stand up on the seat and tell the whole car what had

232

happened. When Woolsey found me in Omaha, she all but died.

God, my grandmother loved that story. She told it again and again.

I was always getting in trouble. I got kicked out of one school for shoplifting a cheap ring. I got kicked out of Mount Vernon in the tenth grade for cheating. I was then dating this guy who was a paratrooper. It was during the war. One night I had him and some of his friends over to Grandma's house in Washington for a party. Things got a little high-spirited and a vase got broken. I don't know what it was, but it was worth a goddamn fortune. Boy was my grandmother mad!

The thing that really capped it was when my paratrooper friend went up for a jump. My friends and I, we all followed his plane in cars. When he jumped, he judged the wind wrong, and his chute got caught in some electrical wires. He just hung there, spinning around. Christ it was funny. We started razzing him, and he cussed us back. Just then Jimmy, Grandma's chauffeur, drove up—I can't remember how that happened, somebody phoned back to the house or something—and he saw the whole thing and told my grandmother. That did it. My grandmother called up Mount Vernon and had me expelled.

I was sent up to a hospital in Connecticut for psychological tests. I was so mad at being sent to this hospital, I put down wrong answers on all the tests. Sometimes I'd just reverse the order of the answers. Then I'd go around and switch the charts on the doors of the rooms. People with broken legs were getting barium enemas. It was a mess. They really loved me up there.

My grandmother took me to lunch in New York to tell me that she had to wash her hands of me. It was the Louis XVI Restaurant, very elegant. She said she was sorry, but the family had decided I was causing everyone too much grief. After lunch I was being put on a train to California to live with my father. She was not having anything more to do with me. I figured I was finished.

Do you know what happened? The Duchess of Windsor is there having lunch and comes over to speak with my grandmother. She joins us for coffee. She asks me a few questions, and I start telling her about myself—about school, about swimming. When I go to the ladies room she tells my grandmother what a wonderful wholesome girl I am, how fresh and American, how she wished she had a young relative like me. I don't know whether my grandmother had told her about the trouble I was giving them, but whether she did or not, she got back nothing but compliments for me.

And do you know what? That coffee chat saved my goddamned neck. The Duchess turned my grandmother around. I was back in with Grandma, I was back in the will—everything. On the way to the train Grandma took a completely different line with me. "Well, Marwee," she said, "we all make mistakes . . . you're still very young. . . ."

You know, years later Grandma was giving a big charity dinner at Mar-A-Lago and got sick at the last moment. She asked me to act as hostess in her place. And who shows up? The Duke and Duchess of Windsor. That was the same party when Grandma asked to see the Duke, and he was escorted into her suite. He stood there and looked around and said, "I never thought I'd get to see the inside of Marjorie's bedroom."

Anyhow, when I greeted the Duchess I said, "Duchess, you don't remember this, but one time years ago you saved my life."

The Duchess said, "I remember it very well; it was at the Louis XVI Restaurant in New York."

CHAPTER SEVENTEEN

In January of 1955 Marjorie changed her plans about going to Europe and went instead to Sun Valley, Idaho, where she was granted a divorce. Explaining her failed marriage to reporters, she said. "The Ambassador had a funny lack of basic straight thinking that was awfully hard to live with." This analysis would be hard to surpass as a succinct summary of two people, any two people, not getting along.

A less measured remark she made later offers a more telling glimpse of the low regard in which she now held Davies. She had become a board member and major supporter of the National Symphony. At a board meeting the conductor, Howard Mitchell, presented an idea for a series of concerts aimed at the young people who swarm to Washington. Mitchell felt there was a prime opportunity to implant interest in the arts in youthful, fertile soil. The plan, he said, would cost one hundred thousand dollars above the regular budget.

Marjorie excused herself from the meeting and phoned her financial manager, Meyer Handleman, in New York to check on her finances. She returned and announced quietly that she would underwrite the Music for Young America series. Later when a friend complimented her on this munificence, Marjorie brushed it aside. "I had just divorced the ambassador," she said, "so I was in funds for the moment."

At the time of her divorce, *Time* magazine referred to the sixty-eight-year-old heiress as being "as well preserved as a frozen peach." Preserved or not, she was far from ready to settle down to quiet old-ladyhood. She immediately started ripping apart the new house she had bought and rebuilding it into the most elaborate showplace in Washington, a city of elaborate showplaces. She wanted a place to serve in the long run as a museum for her collections. Perhaps she wanted it, in the short run, to signal her triumph over the men who had tried exploiting her. She named the new place Hillwood.

Some Post well-wishers must have felt relief at this unimaginative reemployment of her Long Island estate's name. In naming things, the family had a weakness for disastrous inspiration. As far as large possessions were concerned, it wasn't too bad. The Boulders, Topridge, and Hillwood for estates and *Sea Cloud* for a yacht are inoffensive; but Mar-A-Lago begins to fight the tongue, and Hogarcito is downright ugly.

It was in the nicknames that things went to pieces. Deenie, for Nedenia, makes sense, but it is too close to teenie-weenie for comfort. Marwee may be all right for a five-year-old granddaughter who can't pronounce

Marjorie; at forty-nine, it would seem to be time to use the adult pronunciation. Perhaps in revenge, Marwee differentiated Ed Hutton from her grandmother's other husbands by calling him Deenie-Daddy. At the first Hillwood, Marjorie built a scaled-down cottage as a playhouse for Dina and Marwee called the Deenwee.

For reasons of vanity, Marjorie forbade her grandchildren to call her Grandmother or any diminutives thereof. Her grandchildren settled on Mummy-da. When *great*grandchildren came along, Mummy-da permitted them to call her Grandmother, thus neatly eschewing a generation. So it goes with Post names.

Along with her new Washington home, she took an apartment in New York's Ambassador East and finally sold her gargantuan Fifth Avenue apartment, perhaps moved by a *New York Times* article that spoke of the city's largest apartment sitting unused for years. It was a period of setting things straight.

As work proceeded on Hillwood, Marjorie supervised every detail of the estate's design—both of the house and the elaborate gardens, which would include a formal rose garden in the French style, a Japanese garden tricked out with ponds, waterfalls, and footbridges, a dog cemetery, and exquisitely manicured woodland walks.

Marwee points out a detail of her grandmother's remodeling that shows her foresight and practicality. "I was in her Hillwood bedroom hundreds of times, but I never knew about the small bathroom concealed right behind her bed. It had been part of the earlier house. Instead of having it taken out when she put in her new dressing room and bath, she said to the builder, 'Leave it there! Someday I may not be able to make it all the way to my regular bath. It will be useful to have that nearby.' Anybody else would have said, 'Rip it out!'"

An escort of Marjorie's in those days was Washingtonian John Logan, who did much hand-holding, as a friend and as a lawyer, during the ordeal of renovating Hillwood. "Marjorie was a very intimate person," Logan recalls. "She liked to have someone with her at all times, someone she could discuss the details of her life with. And she never wasted a minute. I remember she used to carry a swatch book around with her in her limousine. When she was being driven someplace, she could use the time selecting fabrics for the new house. She did most of her own decorating, and she always wanted someone at hand to give her a second opinion."

Logan tells of an incident in connection with the building of Hillwood that shows Marjorie's imperious, damn-the-cost side. For several days she hadn't been to check on progress of the house; in her absence the roof had gone up. She stood looking at the new roof with the construction superintendent, then said, "It's three feet too low."

The builder sputtered, "But Mrs. Post, that is the height given on the drawings."

"I didn't ask you what height was given on the drawings," she said icily, "I said it was three feet too low."

"Mrs. Post! It would cost a hundred and sixty thousand dollars to change the height of that roof now."

"I didn't ask you how much it would cost to change it. I said it is *three feet too low*." With that, she spun on her heel and walked away.

After two years, the house was finished, and Marjorie moved in. The year was 1957, and she was seventy years old. She would die in this house in 1973, but in those sixteen years she would entertain constantly at Hillwood, Mar-A-Lago, and Topridge; she would buy the largest plane owned by a private individual; and she would consolidate her reputation as the most lavish hostess of her time. Her philanthropy would accelerate, and she would make complex plans for giving away her empire after her death.

She still had one marriage to go—and more scandal and unpleasantness than she had endured in her first seventy years.

Hillwood had been designed with the idea that it would one day be a museum for the Post collection of Russian and French art objects. A large drawing room, built at one end of the mansion, was proportioned to accommodate two priceless Beauvais tapestries woven to designs of François Boucher. The room provides the setting for two sofas and twelve chairs which had been made for Louis XVI and Marie Antoinette to give as a gift to Prince Henry of Prussia. Vitrines on either side of the fireplace contain sets of Sèvres china—pink on one side, turquoise on the other.

Over the mantle is an exceptionally fine portrait of the Empress Eugenie by Winterhalter. The painting troubles purists, however; it is of a different period than the room's eighteenth-century theme. If the picture gives connoisseurs trouble, a Wurlitzer grand piano at the room's far end, in faked-up eighteenth-century French style, gives them stomach cramps. Consuelo Vanderbilt Balsam, an authority on the room's dominant period, asked Richard Howland, the Smithsonian Institution's overseer of the Hillwood project, if he couldn't "get her to get rid of that monstrosity." He couldn't.

Hillwood has many ingenious solutions to the problem posed by a house that is to be a museum without appearing to be a museum. The most interesting objects —jeweled bibelots of the czars, imperial porcelains, tooled silver, and gold chalices—are displayed in illuminated showcases in foyers that connect the main rooms. To get from the entrance hall to the drawing room, for instance, you must pass through one of these display rooms. This makes a perusal of the collection inevitable as you move around the house.

The most artful devices are small shelflike panels that slide out from the display cases about waist high. Under glass on these panels, printed legends describe the objects in the case above. Visitors can read about what they are seeing, slide the panel back into its slot, and the museum feeling vanishes.

The house contains much of historic interest. Among the highlights are a large collection of imperial Russian portraits; large quantities of Russian porcelains, icons, and chalices; small jeweled objects, many of them by Fabergé, that had belonged to Catherine II and various Romanovs; and a fine collection of eighteenth-century French furniture.

Despite the effort at authenticity in the settings and the furnishings, Hillwood has an aura of stage set. Heightening this feeling are the abrupt transitions between new and old. A door concealed in oak paneling from an English manor leads into a small service room where little red indicator lights twinkle on a lighting control panel. To step from the library of an English manor house to a technological control center is like wandering through the sound stage of a sumptuous and costly costume film.

Nowhere is the space-age technology more apparent than in Hillwood's vast, shiny kitchens. Hotel lengths of stainless steel, complicated intercom and servant-signaling devices give these service rooms the look of needing, not butlers and cooks, but scientists, technicians, and stage managers.

The pantry has a fine sample of Marjorie's genius for organization. Small glass doors reveal one plate and one cup and saucer from a dinner service. This is not where the china is actually stored, but serves

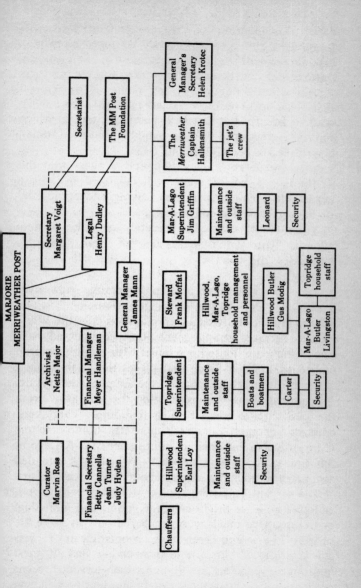

241

rather as a filing system to remind majordomos what is available; the complete service is stored elsewhere.

While the staff might have needed this aide-mémoire, Marjorie did not. People who worked for her for years were constantly dazzled by her computerlike knowledge of the location of every last tea cup—not only in which residence, but in which basement, and in which cabinet. She was not only an acquirer, but a custodian as well, and a fiercely zealous one.

After one large Hillwood dinner, a guest who did not know his hostess very well, thanked her for a memorable evening as he was leaving and apologized for having broken a coffee cup.

"Good God!" she said, completely losing her hostess aplomb, "you didn't break one of Franz Joseph's demitasses, did you?"

Hillwood has an impressive view over Rock Creek Park to the Washington Monument, which it faces in a carefully balanced plan—as does the White House. Terraces on the meticulously manicured park side of the main house have tables with brightly colored umbrellas, another touch that places the establishment closer to Beverly Hills than to the English countryside.

Scattered about the grounds on the side away from the park are a number of outbuildings: caretakers' cottages, garages, servants' quarters, bomb shelters (Marjorie also had shelters built under Mar-A-Lago at this time), and a Russian dacha, which was intended as a party room and a place to house more Russian art.

The servants' quarters are like dormitories in a well-endowed college: bright common rooms and individual bedrooms. Two maids were employed only to make the servants' beds and keep their rooms clean. It was characteristic of Marjorie to pamper her staff. If guest bedrooms needed air conditioning, then servants' rooms got it too; if paint in the servants quarters grew dingy, it would be painted just as quickly as dingy paint anywhere else. At Mar-A-Lago Marjorie allocated a portion of her incredibly expensive beachfront for a servants' beach, thus giving the Mar-A-Lago staff an advantage over many Palm Beach millionaires.

Frank Moffat, for years the majordomo at Topridge and Mar-A-Lago, says Marjorie was quite different from her fellow plutocrats in this regard. "Most of them give their servants any sort of hole for a room, then never want to see them again, never want to know anything about them. Mrs. Post was constantly looking out for the well-being of her staff. And if any of us had a specific problem, she wanted to know about it and she'd do something about it."

In the basement of the servants' quarters at Hillwood, offices were set up to care for Marjorie's collections. She hired art historian Marvin Ross as curator, plus a staff to help him compile the beautiful color picture books of her Russian collections. An art library was part of these offices.

The Hillwood staff was broken down into three categories. There was the executive staff, which included people like Marvin Ross, Margaret Voigt, and James Mann, her general manager. The second group was the financial staff—four people in a downtown Washington office who handled payroll, bill-paying, etc. The third category was domestic staff, including indoor servants, gardeners, chauffeurs, and security men.

Key staff people had an overall organizational chart showing the chain of command for the entire Post operation. At the top was Marjorie Merriweather Post. From her, lines of power flowed to Margaret Voigt, Meyer Handleman in New York, her lawyers, and her general manager. The next echelon was the top man at each of her three estates and the captain of her airplane. Lines trailed down from them through household staffs, to maintenance men, to security staffs, to special positions like the boatmen at Topridge. Complex as the chart is, it by no means covers everyone who worked for her.

In her incredible fastidiousness about details, Marjorie was unlike other proprietors of vast property. In wealthy intown neighborhoods—Washington's Georgetown, for instance—it is not unusual to see affluent people living in relatively small houses that are polished and scrubbed down to the last door hinge by two or three domestic servants. People with large establishments, however, generally develop a more casual attitude toward meticulous maintenance. The English country houses with their falling plaster and cracked windowpanes would be the *ne plus ultra* of this school.

But Marjorie brought a ship captain's fanaticism to her huge houses and rolling acreages. For example, the great lengths of intricately wrought iron grillwork at Mar-A-Lago, even though painted, were coated with a mixture of oil and wax as protection against ocean air. Afer a time the coating loses its effectiveness, but before a new protective coat can be applied, the old must be removed with a solvent. It is an incredibly tedious and painstaking process, and Marjorie had several men working full time doing nothing else.

The large patio encircled by Mar-A-Lago's cloister is made of rounded stones found on a Long Island beach. Ocean-smoothed rocks would not seem to require much maintenance. None the less, each winter before opening Mar-A-Lago, Marjorie had the stones scrubbed down with lye, and after they were lightened in this way, a coat of varnish was applied to restore their shine.

Wherever she was, Marjorie would stroll around the property once a day. Jim Griffin, Mar-A-Lago's superintendent, said these walks were usually followed by a phone call to him, or perhaps a memo. Mrs. Post had noticed a dead twig on one of the lime trees; there was a brown spot on the lawn near the fourth tee; a few gardenia plants needed water. Some employees would find such scrutiny unbearable. Griffin is the sort who relished it.

"She really cared about her properties," he said. "She noticed everything, and if something needed to be done, she would say to go ahead and do it and not to worry about the cost. Some of these people down here at Palm Beach—they have plenty of money—but they let these beautiful houses fall to ruin. That wasn't Mrs. Post."

With Hillwood open and ready for dinners for fifty and Mar-A-Lago and Topridge in peak operating order, the gay divorcée of seventy got down to the two-fisted entertaining for which she would be remembered. She became Washington's top hostess and, in the process, the most renowned hostess of her time. But for all that, she was never fully accepted by "old" Washington society.

This seeming paradox throws light on both Marjorie and on American concepts of society. Her preeminence was unarguable in terms of frequency and lavishness of entertaining; she became the best-known Capital hostess to the American public. Adding to her social clout was a growing reputation as a philanthropist and patron of the arts.

But for old society, she had several disadvantages. She was not a native Washingtonian—an accident of birth that homegrown bluebloods, who like to think of themselves as sophisticated, find hard to forgive. Marjorie was also rich beyond the bounds of good taste—that is to say, she was richer than most old Washingtonians. She did not excel in areas they deemed important: political acumen, intellectual conversation, or VIP head-hunting. And, finally, old society was dubious because of her ostentatious lifestyle. Her houses were too big, her servants too numerous, her parties too lavish, and her art collection meretricious in that it was longer on impressive lineage than it was on esthetics.

Perhaps another subtle obstacle to her full-fledged top-society status was her speaking voice. Marjorie had lived in the East since she was fifteen, but despite several tries with voice coaches, she had never lost her nasal midwestern drawl. Whereas accent has never been the implacable class designator in the United States that it is in England, it might be more of an influence than generally believed.

The coolness of top Washington society toward Marjorie should not be overstated. She was in the best clubs, she could get whomever she wanted to attend her parties, and she was invited to most important functions. But there was a small but doughty inner corps who accepted her invitations, yet refused to think of her as one of their own. Their attitude was manifest in small but highly symbolic ways—most notably in their refusal to admit Marjorie to a subscription-party series called the Dancing Class. Some members of the group were so incensed at her exclusion, they broke away and formed another series around her. Although considerable pressure had been applied by Marjorie's friends, the good ladies of the Dancing Class were adamant.

"It wasn't an issue," one of the ladies said after many years. "She didn't apply . . . one didn't do that. She wasn't put forward by anyone. That wasn't done, either. She just moved in different circles. We didn't know her."

The lady finally broke down and outlined the ineffable machinations that transformed Marjorie Post from the world's oldest and richest outsider to an insider in good standing.

"One night at one of the parties, her daughter Dina came up to me—Dina was married to Stanley Rumbough then and was a member. She told me how she'd enjoyed the dance, then said, 'These dances are such fun. I know my mother would enjoy them so . . .'"

"I told Dina I'd see what I could do."

"About that time I happened to have been invited to a dinner party by a young bachelor. It couldn't have been simpler . . . two card tables of dinner guests. The other woman at my table was Marjorie Post. I liked her enormously, she was so down to earth, such fun, no silly airs. We took her in, and I became good friends with her."

The lady was not going to let the story end on a note of full equality. "But one thing about Marjorie, she just didn't know the difference between people. She would invite my husband and me to Topridge along with the most *dreadful* group. She simply didn't know the difference."

A woman who had known Marjorie slightly for many years said, "Marjorie was never very smart about her social climbing. With her fortune, it would have been easy to reach the top. She only had to set her sights on the right organizations, the right charities, the right dinner guests. But she lacked the finesse."

The woman, like many people, missed the point, and her criticism is an inadvertent compliment. Marjorie would have liked to join the Dancing Class—if only because so many of her friends were members and it was an embarrassment not to be included. But achieving top social status, in the *haut bourgeois* sense of the expression, was never her goal.

Rich parvenus could always reach the heights. In the twenties and thirties when Marjorie was first trying her wings, Elsa Maxwell and others were making careers of instructing freshly minted millionaires how it was done and whom it was done with. But this would have involved relinquishing more of her sovereignty than Marjorie was prepared to relinquish. She would play the game as long as she could remain in charge. She knew what she liked to do, and she knew whom she liked at her parties. If this earned her social position, fine. If it didn't, the hell with it.

Few Americans have ever had her set-up for large scale entertaining. At times she would use it to pursue various enthusiasms—titles during the twenties, diplomats and statesmen during the Davies years—but basically she entertained whomever she liked. (She didn't care if they were rich or poor, powerful or insignificant, American or foreign, Jewish or Gentile, Protestant or Catholic.)

She prided herself on liking natural, unaffected people, and she felt she could recognize such people on sight. As long as acquaintances fit her definition of "nice," they were the people she wanted to entertain— as they'd never been entertained before.

Those watching her massive party-giving from the sidelines would note among her guests ambassadors and other prominent people and assume she was doggedly building a social power base; they overlooked the armies of invitees who could not advance her social position one millimeter. For Marjorie the fairy-godmother role was enough. She was not seeking to alter or enhance herself by means of dazzling guest lists; she was quite content with herself.

The same attitude prevailed in her collecting. When Marjorie first came into her fortune, she could easily have thrown herself into the hands of experts, and up to a point she did. But she wasn't tyrannized by them. Those who snorted that Marjorie had no taste were the purists who were shocked by her deviations from accepted practice: the grand piano in the eighteenth-century drawing room, for instance, or the architectural mishmash of Mar-A-Lago. They could console themselves that, while she had more money than they did, they knew better, by God.

Marjorie adhered to rules just so long as they pleased her. When they did not, she did what she wanted. This was true of her taste in art, house-building, her decorating, her entertaining, her friend-ships. It is an attitude that dismays members of the upper-middle class whose meager store of status has been amassed by an assiduous memorizing of the dos and don'ts.

Marjorie's indifference to such dos and don'ts might have disqualified her from the top society of Washington, a city that didn't exist two hundred years earlier. It put her, however, squarely in the ranks of Catherine the Great of Russia, the French Louises XIV through XVI, Ludwig II of Bavaria, and a handful of other monarchs who knew who they were.

CHAPTER EIGHTEEN

One of the people who fit Marjorie's definition of nice was Herbert A. May, a prominent Pittsburgh businessman, who for many years had been a top executive of the Westinghouse Corporation. He was a widower with three sons by his first marriage and an adopted daughter. He frequently socialized in Washington and Palm Beach. In Pittsburgh, he was a popular member of the exclusive Rolling Rock Club. May was tall, handsome and had a self-assured, outgoing manner that most people responded to quickly. Marjorie decided he was so nice, she married him.

At the time of their wedding in June 1958 Marjorie was seventy-one, May sixty-five; according to information given to reporters, apparently by someone embarrassed by May's comparative youth, "he would be sixty-six within a month of the wedding."

The wedding was a festive event with Dina's husband, Stanley Rumbough, giving away his mother-in-law. (Years later when Rumbough was asked if there were any things he didn't like about Mrs. Post, he replied, "Of course there were, but you won't hear them from me. I loved her.") Joe Davies died a week after the announcement of the marriage.

Rumors at the time of the wedding had May heavily in debt. This talk may have started with a scene at a lunch party shortly after the wedding. May's sister, angry at her brother and in her cups, blurted out, "Herb May, you were one jump ahead of the sheriff until Marjorie bailed you out!" Marjorie was growing deaf and did not hear this, but everyone else at the table did. Close friends of May's say that if he was in debt, it was not in any great amount. The question was moot. She settled a trust fund of several million dollars on her new husband; he would draw the interest for his lifetime.

Unlike her former husband, May was immediately liked by everyone—family, friends, servants. He took to his new status with relish and brought about a relaxation of Marjorie's efficient but stiff empire. He got her to loosen up about liquor; dinner guests were allowed a second drink, and each cabin at Topridge was equipped with a bar. This change alone would earn Herb May the love of many in Marjorie's circle.

Mar-A-Lago was reopened and put to quick use by May, who threw a stag luncheon for Saudi Arabia's King ibn-Saud. (Marjorie watched some of the proceedings from behind a curtain.) May also inaugurated an annual lunch at Mar-A-Lago for two hundred top industrialists, an event he hoped would become an unofficial convention of American business power. He staged these events not from any apparent personal ambition, but rather because these were the people who stimulated and interested him. It was all done in a more easygoing way then Joe Davies's grim-jawed empire-building.

For some time Marjorie had realized that the *Sea Cloud* was too great an extravagance even for her. In the twenties she could hire a crew member for seventy-five dollars a month. In the 1950s the salary would have to be ten times that. There was something, too, in laborsaving devices being antithetical to a sailing yacht. But having made her decision to sell, Marjorie found few people in the market for a 350-foot yacht that needed seventy-two men to operate it. There was no way to recover her costs: Over the years she had spent, in addition to the purchase price, between $5 and $7 million on furnishings, maintenance, and frequent refurbishings—not including the operating costs of salaries, fuel, insurance, port fees, etc. Even at the give-away price of $1 million stripped, or $1,200,000 furnished, she had no takers.

The problem gnawed at Marjorie, who rarely worried about money matters. At that time she was active in Christian Science. The group met on Wednesday evenings in Georgetown to "testify"; individuals would stand up and tell the others of some problem Science had helped them through. The problems were generally illness, fights with the boss , marital friction. When it was Marjorie's turn, the group was stunned to hear her talk about the difficulty of selling her yacht.

Finally a deal was worked out with her old friend Rafael Trujillo. He would present her with a new forty-four-passenger Viscount propjet in exchange for the yacht. The purchase price for a new Viscount was about a million dollars. Science had seen her through.

Now with her own plane she stepped up her traveling, not that she was now relieved of the nuisance of buying plane tickets. She continued to fly to Europe by commercial airline, which made better time, taking with her Mrs. Voigt and whomever she was traveling with. She would send ahead the plane (named the *Merriweather*) for duty around the Continent. Pilots and the servants needed on the plane could bring their wives and families with them; while Marjorie was idling at the Ritz in Paris or at London's Connaught, they could have an all-expense vacation anywhere they chose, until it was time to airlift her someplace else.

She had three full-time pilots on her payroll. Three increased the chances of always having two well rested. While one was flying, another would be standing by in case the first had a heart attack. The third could sleep. Her traveling style on the ground was every bit as grand as in the air or at sea. In London, she would take a half-floor of the Connaught, making sure that three Rolls Royces with drivers were on constant call. Her travel, like everything else in her life, was controlled by a series of memos that she and Mrs. Voigt issued to all concerned personnel. The following memo excerpt, for example, itemized a trip that would take place in two months:

> *Wed. June 26 1:00: Merriweather leaves Nice, France for Vienna, Austria . . . Lunch on board . . . Flying time . . . two hours, 30 minutes.*
> *3:30: Merriweather due in Vienna (Time Change?) Hotel Sacher. Note: Full American Express coverage . . . two cars and small baggage van on arrival . . . Limousine to remain at Mrs. Post's disposal with English-speaking, reliable chauffeur during her stay, and courier . . .*

When the entourage arrived at the last stop abroad, the *Merriweather* would be sent directly back to the States for a thorough going-over before Marjorie needed it to fly her to the Adirondacks. The European jaunts were not that frequent. The plane was mainly used to fly guests to Topridge and to Mar-A-Lago.

Despite the enormous expense of maintaining the plane and keeping it in the air, Marjorie could be off-hand about its use. An old friend from Washington visited her at Palm Beach. He learned that he and Eva, Marjorie's personal maid, were to be the only passengers on the *Merriweather* that day. He phoned his hostess and suggested it would be far less expensive if they were to fly by commercial airline. Marjorie wouldn't hear of it. She had established her style, and there were to be no deviations.

She was also quick to offer the *Merriweather* in personal emergencies, rushing one friend to a special hospital, another to a dying relative's bedside. The reason had to be a good one, however. The governor of Florida once asked her if he could borrow the plane to bring some friends down from Washington for a visit. Even though the request made her furious, she still phoned a mutual friend to ask how she could gracefully refuse the governor's request.

The trouble in her marriage to Herb May came soon and from an unexpected quarter. Although he had been comfortably married for years, throughout most of his adult life May had evinced a distinct preference for members of his own sex and had never been shy about acting on this preference. In the marriage of a sixty-six-year-old man to a seventy-one-year-old woman, the matter might seem moot, but this was not the case. Some months after the wedding May lamented to a friend, "My God, she wants to do it every night!"

In his later years, May had grown increasingly indiscreet about his leaning. Many Washingtonians knew of it. "I knew what he liked," said one of Marjorie's old friends. "Before she married him, she asked me what I thought. I wasn't going to get into the middle of *that*. You only end up an enemy of both."

Marjorie was not particularly broadminded; neither was she very sophisticated about this subject. When a close friend of hers became involved in a homosexual arrest, Marjorie remarked, "You know, I think when he had those monkey-gland injections . . . something may have gone wrong."

Her daughters later chided their mother for her naiveté. Marwee jumped in with: "Grandma, don't you try on a pair of shoes before buying them?" Marwee answered her own question: "Not her. She sends the chauffeur to buy them for her." The analogy grows confused.

For a while, the trouble in the nuptial chamber didn't seriously threaten the marriage. The couple seemed happy enough and threw themselves headlong into Washington socializing and house parties at Topridge and Mar-A-Lago. But May grew increasingly reckless. Standing next to his hard-of-hearing wife at a dance in Washington, May would see a handsome young man go by, and turn to a like-minded friend, saying, "How do I meet *that*?"

In Palm Beach May had a swimming pool installed on Mar-A-Lago's beachfront and began throwing all-male parties around it. Since Marjorie rarely visited this part of the estate, she was unaware of such frolics. The servants knew of them but closed their eyes. Marjorie found out only because of another scandal.

The staff in Marjorie's various establishments was plagued with the factions and infighting always prevalent in large households. The situation grew worse as Marjorie got older and less interested in what was going on around her, and as she delegated more and more authority to Mrs. Voigt and others. It was perhaps also aggravated by the anachronism of domestic work, which increasingly attracted misfits and others maladapted, for one reason or another, to contemporary life.

In Marjorie's later years the backstairs were less and less under her control. With the enormous amount of purchasing for her estates, the opportunities were rife for servants to take kickbacks from various suppliers. At best, the kickback is a gray crime not far removed from a legitimate commission. Still, it is money that should be going—in the form of discounts—to the one who signs the checks; if anyone else gets it, it is stealing.

The practice was now threatening to get out of hand. At one point, the manager of a Florida supermarket chain refused to do further business with Mar-A-Lago saying, "We expected it to some degree, but it was getting ridiculous." Ironically, it was Joe Davies who had warned Marjorie that there would always be servant hanky-panky and that she should expect to write off about sixty thousand dollars a year for this. She preferred not seeing such things.

Herb May was less cavalier. When he learned what was going on, he was appalled. He dropped hints to Margaret Voigt and others at the center of the Post operation that he was going to do something about it. Voigt had always worked against any man who threatened to get too close to her mistress, and Herb May was threatening to rock the boat in a most disagreeable way. May's own record for rectitude, though, was not exactly sterling. A plot was hatched.

Photographs of May naked with young boys were obtained and taken to one of Marjorie's lawyers who took them to Topridge and put them before her. Now well into her seventies, Marjorie had a horror, not only of scandal, but of confrontation and change. She had a great affection for May and was an innocent about sexual deviation, knowing only that it wasn't nice. Her entire life had been devoted to screening out the unpleasant or offensive, even to the point of telling her majordomo when she detected a hint of body odor from one of her servants. She had spent millions keeping her world beauty-filled and odor-free.

In addition to the unpleasant information in the photos, the picture expedition apprised her of an added disaster: Her entire staff knew of May's delinquency and, most likely, all of her friends did too. For the romantic, theatrical Marjorie Post—who had always had one eye on the figure she was cutting—the humiliation was too much.

If she hated confrontation, she didn't shrink from it when necessary. With her lawyer, she went directly to May's room and presented him with the photos. May denied the accusations and insisted the photographs were faked composites. The matter was dropped.

In this sordid drama, it is difficult to know who was a conspirator and who was simply playing out a scenario the conspirators had set into motion. The lawyer was probably doing his job as an old friend and employee. Perhaps Voigt was too.

But the next development was uglier still. Marjorie was informed a book was about to be published exposing a number of people in high places who were leading double lives of one sort or another. A chapter would be devoted to Herbert A. May, the husband of the famous Marjorie Merriweather Post and enthusiastic homosexual.

This was too much. Marjorie gave instructions to buy off the author and to start divorce proceedings against May. The scandalous book may have actually been an extortion plot. When asked if she had ever seen the manuscript, Marjorie replied, "I couldn't bear to." No one else has seen it either.

Although Marjorie had good reason to feel she had been duped by May, her feelings toward him remained warm and sympathetic. Until his death several years later, she maintained an apartment for him in Ft. Lauderdale. One houseguest at Mar-A-Lago asked if Marjorie would object to the guest's paying May a visit; she was delighted at the guest's thoughtfulness. Still, after the divorce was final, she had her name legally changed to her maiden name—Marjorie Merriweather Post—and would be known for the rest of her life as Mrs. Post.

Less sinister actions too, by Margaret Voigt, caused concern among Marjorie's friends and family. The personal secretary had cornered the decision-making for an alarming amount of Marjorie's life. Margaret handled everything.

Marjorie even turned over to her secretary responsibility for swelling out the guest lists for dinner parties, making her a talent scout among Washington's continuing flow of distinguished newcomers. Dinners at Hillwood were peopled more and more with guests known to Margaret Voigt but not to Marjorie. More substantial people considered Mrs. Voigt the paid secretary; it would not have occurred to them to invite her to dinner or to call her anything but "Mrs. Voigt" (as Marjorie always did), but social climbers courted her, trying to get on a chummy, first-name basis. Stanley Rumbough spoke of the parties at Mar-A-Lago at this period of Voigt's rule: "There were lots of people there whom Ed Hutton wouldn't have allowed in the house."

Anyone who entertained as many guests as often as Marjorie, was bound to have some unlikely arrivals. At one of her Palm Beach square dances, she pointed to a particularly good-looking young woman and asked her companion who she was.

"Why, Marjorie," the friend replied, "you should be

honored. That's Snow White; she's the most famous call girl in New York."

"Good Grief," Marjorie said with only slight surprise. "How did she get here?"

The friend explained that the girl was the house-guest of friends of Marjorie's.

Except for such tag-alongs, the guest list's basic outline had always been dictated by the hostess. Now the guest lists were made up more frequently with Voigt's people. The secretary got so carried away with her invitation-bestowing power, she reminded the few old friends of Marjorie's what was what. Once when the hostess was old and quite deaf, she retired early from one of her parties. As John and Polly Logan were leaving they asked Mrs. Voigt to tell Marjorie what a good party it had been and how grateful they were to her.

Margaret Voigt replied sweetly, "It won't be necessary. I make up the guest list."

At times when Marjorie was not feeling well, even her own daughters could not get past Voigt to talk to their mother. They began to suspect that Marjorie was "indisposed" to suit Margaret Voigt's convenience or strategy.

Dina Merrill became aware of the havoc Voigt was raising with tradespeople in Washington and Palm Beach. She would hear her on the phone bullying and haranguing them, using Mrs. Post's name. This particularly upset Dina who could see Voigt destroying her mother's long-standing reputation for graciousness. She told Marjorie how Voigt was undoing the goodwill of a lifetime and pleaded with her mother to get rid of her.

Marjorie never liked interference in her life; she was particularly adamant where Margaret Voigt was concerned. "You run your house, Dina," she said, "and I'll run mine."

MARWEE (II):

Out in California with my father, things didn't turn out much better for me than they had with Adelaide. I couldn't get along with him either. Christ, the fights we used to have! Then I sort of signed off out there by getting kicked out of Carmel High School three days before graduation. So I was sent back to my grandmother and Mount Vernon.

She was urging me to get married. She had been married at eighteen. My mother had been married at eighteen. She probably figured marriage would calm me down. I was going with this guy at the time. I said, "Grandma, I can never marry Charlie. He snores so loud I'd never get any sleep."

She was building Hillwood and she said, "That's no problem. I'll build a snoring room for you."

I said, "What's that?"

..She said, "It's a little room off your bedroom where you can go to get away from a snorer—or where you put the snorer so you can sleep." And she built it. That room at the top of the stairs at Hillwood; there's a small bedroom connected to it. I'm the only one who had her own room at Hillwood.

When I was finally about to graduate and be on my own at last, my grandmother pleaded with me to stay on and live with her. She said she would give me my own car and driver, I could come and go as I pleased, anything that I wanted. She was so lonely, she said, and it would mean so much to her. Without thinking I said, "Grandma. You've got a choice. I'll tell you what I'll give you just as fast. My right arm." I really meant it too. She understood and never held it against me. But I always felt guilty.

Once during the Second World War my grandmother telephoned me. "Dearie, I think it would be very nice for your country," she said, "if you would go into the army, you know the women's auxiliary, the WACS . . ."

I said, "Grandma, I'm going to tell you something. If there's a mainland invasion, you're going to have to catch me. I had a hard enough time in a girl's private school; in the army I couldn't last a minute. Imagine me with them dodos." She wanted me to do a service for this country. She loved this country.

My grandmother was so great to me. Sometimes I'd be driving with her in her car and she'd have the chauffeur stop at a shoe store she liked. We'd go in and she'd buy me six pairs of shoes.

She'd make me come to her dinner parties as I got older. I'd have to talk with all those stuffed shirts. I remember once I came back late from somewhere and she was having a big dinner party and I found myself sitting next to Harry Truman. My mind was on a million other things, and I looked at him and said to myself, "Okay, Harry . . . Hell-lo," and I started to talk to him about the state of schools in America today. You see, I learned this trick. I didn't know enough to talk about their subjects—those big shots—besides they were sick of their subjects. I would talk about what I knew about. And it worked.

I'm the only one in the family who got along with Joe Davies. I forced myself to. I looked at it this way. Either I get along with him and get to see my grandmother or I put the high-nooner on him—you know, the stare—and I don't get in the house. Adelaide and Eleanor didn't come around much when he was married to Grandma; Dina almost never did. So I compromised. It wasn't that hard, I suppose. He was just a phony—just a fourteen-carat phony. Other than that he was charming.

One time we were having lunch at the old Tregaron. My grandmother had given me an ultimatum. She said, "Look, you've been thrown out of every school in the country. None of them can put up with you," she said, "so now you either have to go to work, find a career, or get married." She gave me the big three. I tried being an ice skater. I figured I only had to learn nine steps to be a showgirl, because I was tall. But I ended up being a swimmer and swam for Los Angeles for five years. Okay, I came back East, and the three of us were sitting at lunch, and Davies said to me—I'll never forget this—"Marwee, you won't tell anyone you're a swimmer, will you? It's not ladylike."

My grandmother came to my rescue. "Now, Joe," she said, "that's entirely wrong. The child is working as hard as she can to get in the Olympics. There's nothing disgraceful about that. She should be praised for it."

She was proud of my swimming. She used to pit me against those guys over at the Bath and Tennis, and

I'd say, "Grandma, make it a distance if you want me to win." Because you know a guy can outsprint you, even if he's not trained. But on a distance, I'd get them every time.

One time we had the nationals in Palm Beach at the Biltmore, and I brought some of my swimmers over to meet my grandmother at the Bath and Tennis. I'd been hyping my friends on what a beautiful, with-it human being my grandmother was.

We came through the tunnel and around by the cabanas. I took one look in the pool, and I spot her and I go, "Oh, my God." I tell the girls, "Let's skip it, she must be eating." There she was, I swear to God, in the water with gloves on, a hat, the whole thing— a two-piece bathing suit with long sleeves, a high neck, dark glasses. I took one look at that and I said, "Forget it." She had a redhead's complexion and was terrified of getting a sunburn, so she'd wait till the old-ladies' time at the pool—twelve-thirty to one-thirty they didn't allow any kids—and she'd go in like that and paddle around by herself.

I really liked that Herb May. He was a real gentleman and the nicest husband of the bunch. You know, he had those three sons and a daughter, maybe the daughter was adopted, I don't remember; but then he turned gay later in life. And that was before people accepted it. You know, it's not that big a deal nowadays—unless you're married to one and you like to screw. He was masculine—I don't mean super macho —but he was smooth. He brought my grandmother's operation back to reality. He saw to it guests got plenty to drink.

We were so different, my grandmother and I. I use to wonder if she had any idea of what my life was like. After my trouble at Southern California, I transferred to the University of Miami until things cooled off. I rented an apartment out on Phoenetia Avenue and was *living with a football player who I met the day I registered.*

I had a little poodle named Monique and two geese I'd picked up to make pets out of. My landlady was getting fed up. Then to top it off, two guys I knew, two swimmers, had gone on some sort of treasure hunt in the Caribbean. They'd been ripped off and they landed in Miami broke. They accosted me in the administration building. What could I do? I didn't have the money to send them home, so I had to take them in. Now, the football player and I were sleeping in a Murphy bed, these two guys were sleeping on my floor . . . the two geese, the dog—my landlady blew her top.

She tried to call my grandmother, but Grandma wasn't at Mar-A-Lago and Junior (Jim Griffin) intercepted the call. He was sent down by the office to move us. Oh, God, it was comical. By then the geese had had goslings. We were out on our ass.

I found this little house for sale in Coral Gables— two stories with a guest house. They wanted six thousand. I had about two thousand dollars, so I called up Handleman, Grandma's business manager in New York, and asked if I could have four thousand against my trust to buy this house. I was going to stay on the second floor, then rent out the bottom and the guest house. Somehow the message got mistranslated, and it came out that I wanted to buy a "horse." He turned me down cold. So I took my money and went out to the track—my mother had a trainer named Downey Bonsell—and we plunked the whole roll down on a horse of his named Pot Pourri, and didn't he win in a photo? I went right back and bought the house. The University of Miami football players helped me clean it up. It was the nicest place you could imagine. Over- grown, there were those big banana things. You had to get a machete to get to it. There were a lot of domestic cats that had gone kind of wild; they hung around and ate the rats. I loved it.

Well, my grandmother heard about it and decided to pay me a surprise visit. Jimmy, her chauffeur, drove her down. I wasn't there. Jimmy told me the sight of her in white gloves, a big hat, going through that house —with the cats, the geese, the dog—it was a spectacle. But you know, she thought it was a pretty damn good idea. She really liked the little place. We had taken empty egg cartons and sprayed them gray and covered the walls with them, and we had a white shag rug. It was really cute.

When I left—this shows how ruthless I am—I sold the place to the football player and made a two-thousand-dollar profit. But then he had the use of me for two years.

We really had a neat time those days. The football player was overweight; I had a jeep and I used to run his ass off. He took me up to Scranton, Pennsylvania, to meet his family. There were sixteen of them. His mother was dead or there would have been twenty-one.

I left Scranton and went ahead to Washington to spend a few days with my grandmother. He was going to pick me up, and we were going to drive back to Florida together. I said to him, "Listen, when you come to Hillwood, don't come to the front door, come to the back door." You see, if those people had seen him— if she had seen him—it would have been curtains. He looked like a truckdriver; he was a truckdriver. She never would have accepted him. Never.

He said "Skip it." Boy, was he mad.

Grandma was always trying to fix me up with these jerks, never anyone my type. I remember one super-eligible bachelor in Washington. She had great hopes for him and me. He would take me out and sing light opera, and I'd say, "Jeesus! Will you shut up?" Did I do a number on him one time!

We're at this super-elegant party at the Shoreham with Huey Long, the senator, and all these important people. And my date is going on about Mrs. Post this and Mrs. Post that—hype, hype, hype—until I got sick of it. I stood up and said, "Listen, I cannot go under this alias any longer. I'm one of Mrs. Post's maids, and I'm proud of it. I come from very fine people and just because I work for a living, I can't see why you can't take me for what I am and if you can't, there's no reason to take me out any more. I just can't take it!"

And I started to cry. I tell you, people got up from around the table, they came over and held my hand and said, "Don't you worry, you're a very nice person. . . . Don't think about it."

He yelled, "That's not true! She's lying!"

And I said, "Please. No more! Let me be me." The more he tried to say I was lying, the louder I cried. I never had to go out with him anymore.

She was always trying to fix me up with those creeps. It was miserable. I just did it to please her.

One big strain I had with my grandmother was over Porfirio Rubirosa. I met him at a party, and he was really after me. My girlfriend says to me, "You know who that is? He's supposed to be the greatest lover in the whole world!"

And I says, "No kiddin'? Hell-lo."

We left together, and he brought me back to Mar-A-Lago. Grandmother found out the next day. She called me in and gave me hell. "Under no circumstances do I ever want you to ever talk to that man again, Marwee, let alone see him." She hated him because of what he did to Barbara (Hutton). She was trying to protect me. So I had to sneak around to see him. I really liked him, but I didn't want to sleep with him; he was out of my class. Like an amateur playing with a pro.

Another time my grandmother almost washed her

hands of me was when I got arrested for being in a fistfight with the manager of a supermarket in LA. I saw him hit my dog—I didn't know my dog had just peed on his prize fruit display—and I saw red. The cops came, and I had to go before a judge. I was working in pictures then, and the papers had a big headline: "STARLET ARRESTED FOR FIGHTING IN STORE." My grandmother stayed mad at me quite a while after that.

My grandmother laughed at some of my escapades and screw-ups, but others would have upset her a lot. I never could have told her about my affairs, for instance. When I'd pull one of my stunts, she'd make it clear to me she was angry, but behind my back she used to laugh like hell. She once told me she thought I was the smartest one in the family. That's a laugh. Maybe I do have a head for business—CW without the brains. But she thought I had horse sense and that I'd land on my feet. Adelaide once told me that when they had me evaluated by the psychiatrist, his conclusion was that I was the type of person that couldn't be contained or regimented, that if I were let go, chances were I'd land on my feet.

Let me give you an idea of how naive my grandmother was about my life. When I got married to Ronnie Waller, it was the first time in history a woman gave birth to a twelve-pound baby after a six-month pregnancy. But Grandma never suspected a thing. I'd been living with him for months.

One morning a couple of days before the wedding, she calls me into her suite in the DC hotel where she was living while Hillwood was being built. She sat me down and said she wanted to explain to me about rupturing of the hymen. I mean, can you believe it? Here's Wendy inside me going BONG, BONG, BONG, and I say, "Shut up, Wendy, we're trying to explain

267

something." And later when I'm going down the aisle, Wendy's going BONG, BONG, BONG . . . .

I told my grandmother I wouldn't get married if Adelaide's name appeared on the invitation. So this is how it read: "Mrs. Marjorie Post Davies requests the pleasure of your company at the wedding of her grand-daughter Marjorie Post Durant. . . ." And then going down the aisle I gave Adelaide the high-nooner glare. I would have given her the finger, except I was holding a bouquet of flowers.

I got so loaded at that wedding. Afterward we got into this big limousine to go to Lady Lewis's house in Georgetown where we were going to spend our wedding night. Two cop cars drove with us, their lights swirling and sirens blaring. I said to Ronnie I bet I'm the first person on this earth to have a police escort to get a piece of ass. When we got to the house, my grand-mother had a gold bucket with iced champagne by the bed.

Boy, could my grandmother be extravagant at times. When she came out to see where Ronnie and I were living in California, she took one look at my bedroom —I'm not the neatest—and she said, "Dearie, you don't have enough room for your clothes. I'm going to build you a closet."

I said, "But, Grandma, it's just a rented place. It's temporary."

"That doesn't make any difference," she said. "You must be comfortable while you're here."

She knows this builder—the guy who built the Bel Air Hotel, for God's sake—and doesn't she have him build a room onto that house? It must have been twelve by twelve. The owner of the house made a bedroom out of it later.

I pleaded with my grandmother to make me independent. It was down at the Homestead, when

I was married to Ronnie. I said, "Grandma, if you ever want me to have anything and you think Adelaide's going to set me up, forget it. If you're going to do anything, you have to do it now." So she set me up with a half million then. Later she made me one of the beneficiaries, along with my mother and two aunts, of a trust that had been set up for Joe Davies to be used in his lifetime. When I got my share it was about thirty thousand a year.

When I found out the trustees made more from that trust fund than I did, I blew my top. It was all screwed up by one of the guys who was advising my grandmother on money matters. I set out to get him sacked. It was easy. I wanted to invest in some schemes a guy I know out here in California was launching, real-estate deals.

I called this guy in New York to ask his advice. I had a tape recorder going. He was telling me how California real estate wasn't worth anything. He spouted all this rotten advice. He tried to make dates with me. And behind my back he was telling my grandmother I was a curse.

Anyhow, in a short time the California guy's plan paid off. If I'd been allowed to invest with him the way I wanted, I can't tell you what I'd be worth now. I played the tape for my grandmother, and she fired the guy. She hated making a big change like that. The worry of it gave her a stomach attack, but she fired him.

Then I got tied up with Barbara Hutton. Dina put me onto that problem. She has been living out here—first at the Beverly Hills Hotel, now at the Beverly Wilshire. She's in a pretty bad way . . . and broke, too. It's no surprise, the way she was giving away those hundred-thousand-dollar bracelets to maids and nurses.

My grandmother loved her, and Barbara loved my grandmother. I can remember at the end when my grandmother was sliding into her senility, and she said to me, "Call Barbara in Marrakesh!" I'd have to put in the call, and when it would come through, she'd forget what she wanted to say.

Barbara used to visit Grandmother often. She'd come down to Mar-A-Lago when there weren't a lot of guests around. She just liked being there with Grandmother. When Grandmother came out to LA and was staying at the Bel Air, Barbara had her room filled with huge orchid plants. My grandmother said, "Good grief, I'm only going to be here a few days. What am I going to do with these?"

I said to her, "Don't forget your old buddy here." So she told me to help myself. A lot of them are still growing around my house.

Later I started going over and visiting with Barbara at her hotel. She took a liking to me. Some days I'd spend five or six hours with her. She'd have her mattress on the floor and the entire floor covered with sheets. You'd have to take your shoes off when you went in. I don't know what it was all about.

Like my grandmother, she had this thing about royalty. She was married to that Oriental prince, and she calls herself Princess Barbara. But we'd have fun. Once she got talking about pearls. She had one of her jewel cases brought to her; she pulled out this jeweled flower as big as your fist and gave it to me! If I'm lying, I'm dying. It was a daisy with pearls for the petals, emerald leaves, and a diamond in the center—at least four carats.

I took it, but before I left, I gave it back. I told my grandmother I just didn't feel right about taking it. My grandmother said, "Marwee, you're a damn fool. She will just give it to someone else." But you got to live with yourself, right?

If Grandma had given it to me, that would have been different. That time I stopped Grandma from getting married for the fifth time, she was so grateful to me she gave me this incredible necklace—pale yellow sapphires and amethysts, with earrings and a ring to match. But it had been designated for Dina, and, did that cause trouble.

One night at Mar-A-Lago I mentioned that Grandma had given it to me. Dina was furious. "You have to give it back," she said. "That's mine."

I said, "If you want that jewelry, you're going to have to dive for it, Dina. Before I'll give it to you, I'll throw it off the end of the pier." I figure a present like that is like a will. If you leave somebody something, then change your mind and leave it to someone else, the last action is the one that counts. Right? There was some tension between Deenie and me about that for a while, but it's okay now. She's forgotten about it.

The thing about Grandma, when she'd do all these things for people, she didn't want anything in return. All Grandma wanted was that you appreciated her. One time I didn't get a birthday present from her, and I asked her why not. She said, "There's no point in giving you anything. You don't appreciate it."

I asked why she said that.

"I gave you a nice present last year," she said, "but I never got any thank-you note from you."

I usually wrote, but that time it slipped my mind —and she pounced. No present.

As I got older, I really did start to appreciate her. After I got out into the world and saw what a goddam jungle it was, I saw what a beautiful life she let me have by her generosity. I started writing her love letters—Herb May got me into it—I used to write her once a month. A lot of it was telling her little things

271

that had happened, things that might interest her. But I always told her how much I loved her, how much her love meant to me—and on and on—that life wouldn't be worth living without her. It was like writing to a lover. She was a lover, except for the sex; she was romantic, exciting, she had a flare about things. But best of all was her enthusiasm for life. Every time I came back to visit her, I was excited—to see the house, the beautiful things.

I think I appreciated Grandma more than the rest of them. See, not only my mother, but my father kicked me out, too. I was living in the homes of the help, sleeping on their floors. I'd sneak back at night and steal food and take it back up to where I was living. I knew the other side. I knew what it was to eat with the poor people and not be able to contribute. I knew what it was to be down and out, and I didn't like it.

I also knew what it was to put up with a bunch of crap to get money. My grandmother didn't force you into that position. Even if you didn't live with her or do exactly what she wanted, she was still good to you, took care of you. She saw to it you had all the money you needed, not just close relatives like me, she did it for a lot of people. And all she wanted was to be appreciated.

CHAPTER NINETEEN

"**M**rs. Post wondered if you would be free to come up to Topridge the weekend of the twenty-fourth?" Mrs. Voigt's voice was cheerful but businesslike.

"You are free? That's wonderful."

A few days later the prospective guest would receive a follow-up letter from James Mann, Marjorie's general manager. In it would be the departure time for the *Merriweather*, which took off from Page Airways, the private wing of Washington's National Airport. Mann's letter also was precise about the return time—in case anyone harbored notions of a prolonged visit.

Guests would not know who their fellow guests were until they assembled at the airport. The number could be anywhere from eight to eighteen. A steward would circulate among the guests taking coats and luggage. Schedules were precise, and the wait would be brief. At the last minute a chauffeur would arrive with large boxes of orchids and other fresh flowers from Hillwood's greenhouses to decorate Topridge.

The main cabin of the plane would always have a large vase of fresh flowers. Guests would relax in swivel easy chairs as stewards served drinks and refreshments. On occasion the plane would stop at an airport in the New York area to pick up other guests. As the *Merriweather* touched down at the Saranac Lake airport, several chauffeur-driven Cadillacs would move slowly out onto the airfield. Passengers would get directly into the limousines without having to pass through the airport or to wait for luggage, which followed in other cars.

A half hour's drive brought the convoy to Marjorie's boat dock where a large blue Chris Craft (also known as the *Merriweather*) took on all the guests for the run across Upper St. Regis Lake to the Topridge dock. As they approached, they could see Marjorie, looking crisp in a bright-colored dress fitted snugly to her slim waist. Standing beside her would be Frank Moffat, her chief steward, Margaret Voigt, and one or two men to assist in the disembarking.

After an exchange of greetings, the older guests got into a cable car that pulled them to the top of the hogback where the camp's buildings were situated. Younger guests walked up a paved path.

At the top, one had a view of three lakes: Upper St. Regis, which they had just left, and two additional lakes on the other side of the ridge. Marjorie's acreage encompassed the second two lakes, which she kept well stocked with trout.

Everyone was ushered into the main hall at Topridge, a vast lobby crammed with an important collection of Eskimo and Indian art—totems, canoes hanging from beams, stuffed animals, carved Indians. (Two servants worked constantly keeping these objects dusted and cleaned.) In front of an open fire Marjorie served the new arrivals tea while suitcases were placed in cabins, unpacked, and all the clothes whisked away for pressing.

Moffat would circulate among the guests, giving out cabin assignments. Single people would have a cabin of their own; married couples would have the option of separate bedrooms. The sitting rooms and bedrooms of each cabin had wood-burning fireplaces which were supplied with kindling and birch logs. In a small workshop on the property, a man sat all day, planing the kindling into its artistically curled shapes.

Each cabin had a directory of the camp's forty-eight telephones with instructions on how to summon forth any service desired—boatman, tennis pro, masseur, stenographer—and listed rules and schedules: numbers to phone if you planned to miss a meal, which dinners would be black tie, arranging breakfast in bed. Cabins had fully stocked bars, and each bathroom—always one to each bedroom in the two-bedroom cabins—was also fully stocked with medicines and cosmetics.

A warning bell sounded for meals. Fifteen minutes later, the meal bell rang. This was no casual reminder. A male guest who had been out fishing showed up for lunch as dessert was being served.

"Marjorie," he said beaming, "I just caught the most beautiful trout, and I'm going to have it cooked for your dinner!"

"Why, Henry," Marjorie replied, "that's the nicest thing I ever heard. Now sit down and eat your lunch." Then she turned aside to the butler and said, "Just serve him dessert."

As long as guests showed up on time, her concern with what they ate bordered on the fanatic. For a house-party lunch one day Marjorie had had fresh fish flown up from New York. She took one bite, then rapped on her glass. "Don't any of you eat the fish!" she commanded. "It is not good." Others who had already tasted it thought it was fine, but Marjorie detected something amiss, so her twenty guests sat glumly as the butlers removed the fish and something else was prepared.

The kitchens at Topridge, which would have delighted a Swiss hotel manager, were not set up for short orders or fast schedule changes. Meals were planned with care and on precise timetables; guests were expected to observe these timetables. More adventurous guests figured out how to raid the refrigerators at night; some even learned where the cookies were stored. (At Mar-A-Lago the two night watchmen who sat in the kitchens became adept at whipping up sandwiches for hungry guests.)

The first night at Topridge—in later years invariably Thursday—there would be square dancing after dinner. The dances were held in the dacha, a playhouse decorated with people's art from Russia. On these occasions Marjorie usually dressed in a black velvet skirt with Indian embroidery, a white blouse, and Navajo jewelry. Black-suited butlers and footman stood on duty while Marjorie's guests allemande'd-left and do-si-do'd under the flushed and chubby faces of happy Russian peasants bringing in the harvest.

Also on hand were eight or ten professional dancers to teach the steps and to see to it that everyone got into the fun—including stiff ambassadors and self-important cabinet members. These square dances, which she also held in her other residences, became such a Washington tradition they were borrowed by Lindsay and Crouse and given to Sally Adams (Perle Mesta) in the musical *Call Me Madam*. Had any other Washington hostess held a square dance it would have been *lèse majesté*.

At the Topridge square dances, drinks were not served until the dancing was finished. Marjorie did not want the squares and other configurations disrupted with a lot of drunken cabinet officers charging around. There was nothing to keep guests from ducking back to their cabins for a quick snort—or for that matter, drinking in their cabins from one meal to the next; guests visibly under the influence, however, were never asked back.

Soon after the dancing ended, Marjorie took leave of her guests, encouraging them to continue the party. With Moffat leading her way with a flashlight, she would walk back to her cabin, which was protected by a guardhouse where guards were posted around the clock. There were guards all over the estate. Guests who took walks in the woods reported being stopped and asked if they needed help finding their way back.

Marjorie had first brought guards into her life at the time of the Lindbergh kidnapping when Dina was a child. She later came to realize that if she was going to live a life of conspicuous grandeur, she was obliged to provide security for herself and her guests. Mar-A-Lago would generally call for a security staff of fourteen when she was in residence; at Topridge the number was greater.

Marjorie traveled with large quantities of jewelry, even taking it with her to the Adirondack woods for Topridge's black-tie dinners. On slow summer afternoons, she would sometimes invite close women friends back to her cabin after lunch to see the jewelry and perhaps try it on.

On being shown "a particularly fine emerald," a friend once asked how Marjorie could ascertain its quality. She replied that her father had warned her she would be very rich, but that she would not be able to trust anyone; she would have to gain her own expertise in judging the quality of the costly things she wanted to buy. She then explained to the woman exactly what constituted the emerald's quality in the terminology of an experienced gemologist.

Mornings at Topridge, valets would come into the cabins, light fires, and pick up any clothing that needed pressing. Women were encouraged to breakfast in bed, making the dining-room version more of a stag affair. Guests were free to choose between any of a large number of daytime activities—hunting, fishing, tennis, swimming, hiking, bird walks, boating—or loafing in their cabins.

At least once during the four-day weekends, a "carry" would be announced for the following day. This was a picnic excursion by Adirondack canoe, the rare and valuable longboats of highly polished wood that hung in the main boathouse. Guests who signed up would assemble on the dock at 9:00 A.M. and be taken by speedboat to the staging area where the canoes would be waiting. This two-boat system allowed adjusting the canoe portion of the trip to a non-tedious duration.

The trips usually involved portages from one lake to another or a hike through woods to arrive at the designated picnic spot. For these overland segments, guests were asked to carry some object—a frying pan, a cooler, a camp stool; there were more than enough attendants for this, but it was to lure guests into the roughing-it spirit of the "carry."

Once at the picnic spot, the assortment of butlers, boatman, and woodmen would fly into action setting up tables, building fires, and frying steaks. A feature of these outdoor banquets was Adirondack pie, a construction of pancakes cemented together with maple sugar, smothered in hot maple syrup, then sliced like a cake.

In later years Marjorie herself never went on carries, but she took a keen interest in her guests' reaction to them. She asked Richard Pearson, a Washington bachelor and Topridge regular, if he had enjoyed that day's carry. He said he had enjoyed it very much.

"I'm glad to hear that," Marjorie said. "You've been on a good number of them, and I'm glad to know you haven't grown bored by them."

"Not at all," Pearson replied. Thinking he should elaborate on his good time, he then added, "And I particularly enjoyed the Adirondack pie."

Pearson describes what happened next. "She pushed her chair back from the table, her eyes as big as saucers. 'Dick,' she said, 'I wish when you talk with me you would tell the truth. I happen to know you did not have the pie today. The servants forgot the ingredients. Why did you tell me that you did?'"

Other efforts were made to vary the meals and make them more festive. Sometimes a large raft was assembled by placing a platform across a number of canoes. This was then floated out into the middle of the lake, where butlers would serve dinner as the sun was setting, the different courses arriving by boat. One night during the visit there would be a first-run movie to which Marjorie would invite her neighbors from around the lake.

Considerable thought went into anticipating guests' needs. Large stores of cigarettes, pipe tobacco, cigars, magazines, and many other items were kept on hand, but if a guest required anything Topridge couldn't provide—one ran out of flashbulbs, for instance—a servant was dispatched by boat and limousine for the journey into the shops of Saranac Lake.

In the words of Mar-A-Lago superintendent Jim Griffin, "If you were Mrs. Post's guest, you were king. She couldn't do enough for you." But it was at Topridge where she most became the supremely benevolent but aloof hostess. If Topridge guests wanted to see Marjorie outside of scheduled mealtimes, they had to make an appointment through Mrs. Voigt. As Marjorie's deafness worsened, it became impossible to have a word with her at meals that wasn't heard by everyone. Yet for a private conversation, everyone, even family, had to arrange it through her secretary.

Although her hearing was going, her eyesight remained excellent, perhaps becoming more acute with the failing of the other sense. If one of her guests at the far end of a table for twenty-four seemed to be bored and forcing conversation, she would notice (and suspect too many cocktails).

Throughout all of the house-party rituals, Marjorie maintained a strong sense of theater, a sense of being "on." Her grandson David Rumbough was one of her favorites and spent several summers with her at Topridge. With few people around his own age, he grew bored. He asked his grandmother if he might get a job on the staff. She didn't see why not and sent him to see Frank Moffat. A large black-tie dinner was coming up, and Moffat decided to try Rumbough out as a footman.

One guest at a dinner party knew that David had asked for a job and spotted him among the other footmen. Watching Marjorie, however, the guest concluded she didn't notice her grandson; she paid no attention to him through a complicated meal that involved some minor faltering on David's part.

At the end of these large Topridge dinners, the procedure was for the staff to line up on either side of the dining room doors as the hostess made her exit. As she passed her grandson, she turned quickly and kissed him on the cheek, then moved majestically out of the room.

Behind the amazing organization of Marjorie's house parties—at Topridge, Mar-A-Lago, and to a lesser degree in Washington—was a barrage of memos. Marjorie lived by memos, or rather, she ruled by them. A daily memo to the staff gave the most detailed instructions about menus, dietary peculiarities of guests, special events like middle-of-the-lake dinners or carries, where flowers were to be placed, fires lit, and on and on.

At Mar-A-Lago where the entertaining was more formal and the comings and goings less regular, the memos became even more detailed and complicated. They would list who was arriving each day, how they were arriving, and whether or not they had to be picked up, which suite they were to have, where pre-lunch cocktails would be served, etc.

Memos were circulated to the guests telling them the events of the day, the dress requirements if unusual, if they were all being entertained outside of Mar-A-Lago or, if they were dining at home, who the outside guests would be. The memos were full of special asides. A memo sent (during the winter of 1968) to female house guests noted: "If you are planning to wear a floral tiara to the ball, let us know without delay so that one can be ordered for you."

Guests for Topridge house parties in the late sixties might have been Senators Fulbright and Jackson, Soviet Ambassador Dobrynin, the Stewart Udalls, Mrs. Edgar Bergen. But for the most part, guest lists were comprised of names unknown to most of us. They might have been recognized around social Washington with kindly approval but no great interest.

Visits to Topridge went on in this manner until 1972, the year before Marjorie's death. At Mar-A-Lago, social operations continued right up to her final physical collapse. Few guests were in a position to reciprocate this sort of hospitality, so elaborate schemes sprang up to show gratitude. Sometimes a large group of Topridge alumni got together and gave a dinner dance in Marjorie's honor, and at her eightieth birthday party guests chipped in to buy her a pair of museum-quality ormolu candelabra. The most cloying gesture was a garden path installed at Hillwood. On stone markers bronze plaques were affixed with the names of the donors; the whole affair went by the name of Friendship Walk.

Of all the many remarkable aspects of a visit to one of the Post pleasure grounds, the feature that lingers longest in most minds was her astounding attention to all details that touched on a guest's comfort and happiness—her relentless thinking-through of every action and the possible ramifications for each of her visitors.

An old but casual friend, Edward Howe, remembers a return trip from the Adirondacks aboard the *Merriweather*. The other passengers had all gotten off in New York, and he proceeded on to Washington alone. During the flight, one of the pilots came back and apologized that they were putting in at Friendship Airport in Baltimore. The plane needed some work, and it had to be done there. Howe said he understood but wondered how he would get from Friendship to his home in the Washington suburbs at that hour of the night. As he stepped off the plane a uniformed chauffeur approached him from the dark.

"Mr. Howe," he said, "your car is waiting."

CHAPTER TWENTY

When Marjorie Merriweather Post was eighty and quite deaf, she fell in love with a Washington lawyer with a loud voice named Fred Korth. During the Kennedy Administration, Korth had been Secretary of the Navy until a conflict-of-interest charge precipitated his resignation. He was popular and successful, and Marjorie wanted very much to marry him. Korth was highly attentive to her but was twenty years younger. Gossip said he had another lady friend on the side.

Marjorie's good friends, John and Polly Logan, had a winter home on St. Croix. Polly Logan invited Marjorie, as she invited many people in a casual way, to come for a visit. Marjorie almost never made visits anymore, so Polly Logan was surprised to receive a phone call from Margaret Voigt asking what dates would be convenient for Mrs. Post's visit to St. Croix. A time was set for the middle of the winter.

Marjorie then got on the phone. "Let's see," she said, "we'll fill up the *Merriweather*. There'll be Fred Korth and the Dudleys—and maybe the Wolkowskys—and, of course, we'll need rooms for Mrs. Voigt and Eva and the pilots. . . ."

The Logans had only a small guest house, so John Logan approached the manager of a large hotel on the harbor. He knew that all the main hotels would be booked solid that time of year, but the noise of the harbor made this hotel less popular, and noise of any sort was not likely to bother Marjorie.

The manager said the time Logan wanted was his peak season. He couldn't give him a room, let alone an entire floor. Pressure was applied; the importance of Marjorie Merriweather Post was evoked. The manager agreed to clear a floor, provided Logan would take it for two full weeks. Even though the party was staying only a few days, Logan agreed.

When the Logans' St. Croix friends heard that the legendary Marjorie Merriweather Post was coming for a visit, they vied with each other to give her parties. Dates were cleared with command headquarters in Washington for a round of lunches, dinners, and dances.

On the agreed day, the *Merriweather* touched down on St. Croix. Marjorie loved her rooms overlooking the pretty harbor. She also loved the Logans' charming house where a dinner dance had been arranged for the first night. Marjorie looked radiant. It was a beautiful, starry night. The Caribbean looked black and iridescent. On a dance floor by the Logans' pool, Marjorie Post and Fred Korth danced and danced.

But then something went awry. Marjorie sent word that she was indisposed and would be unable to attend the luncheon planned for her the next day. The same message arrived for the dinner party that night. In the next few days, Marjorie did not attend any of the entertainments planned in her honor. As a hostess on a large scale, she was always a considerate guest. Clearly something was very wrong.

When the visit was up, Marjorie and her party boarded her plane and flew home. The explanation for her unusual behavior came much later. She had planned her St. Croix idyll to climax her romance with Korth. In the excitement of the elaborate visit, in the warmth of the many parties and tributes, in the exotic tropical setting—he would agree to marry. They would fly off, leaving their hosts and other friends too thrilled by the happy drama to object to the lapse in manners.

That first night after the dance, Marjorie was made to understand that Korth would not marry her. The cumbersome plan, the large plane filled with adoring entourage, the tropical island, had all come to one thing: rejection. Her pain and humiliation were such, she could not see anyone. Like her father, Marjorie reacted to emotional stress with acute stomach disorders. In St. Croix she was unable to keep food down.

Toward the end of her life, Marjorie remarked to a friend that her only regret was that she'd never found the right man to go through her old age with. On another occasion she said that she had succeeded at everything she'd undertaken—except matrimony. Talking about her second daughter, she once said "Eleanor's like me. She always marries stinkers."

If anyone had the right to be disillusioned with the institution of marriage, Marjorie did. Beside her own mistakes, her daughters were racking up a good score; two marriages for Dina, three for Adelaide, five for

Eleanor. Yet Marjorie, always brimming with love and optimism, worked at four marriages for a period of almost sixty years. Married for the first time at eighteen, she was seventy-seven when she divorced May and was by no means ready to resign herself to singleness.

The vigor of her conjugal instinct in old age became a subject of increasing alarm to her family, mainly because of the staggering cost. Marjorie would have none of the prenuptial legal agreements that have always protected the rich against matrimonial muggings. When she fancied herself in love, her famous generosity broke through the most minimal cautionary instincts. Even when she was young and desirable her marriages had cost her millions; at eighty she was eager to open her heart and her portfolio.

Of the daughters, the most concerned about this was Adelaide, perhaps because she was geographically nearest. Or maybe being the oldest, she thought it fell to her to take her mother in hand. Most families go through painful periods when parents are forced to relinquish some of their sovereignty to their children. But sovereignty is what Marjorie was all about. She had no intention of abdicating to Adelaide or anyone else. Attempts to interfere in her life caused considerable bad feeling.

In Marjorie's case, the parent-child power struggle was complicated by her tight hold on the economic reins. Her daughters were all financially independent; she had seen to it. Still, she could alter their economic fortunes drastically until she breathed her last. It is harder for young people to treat the old with the usual condescension when that old person can bestow or withdraw millions.

To the degree finances played a part at all in Marjorie's old-age drama, they were probably more of an element in her own refusal to be grounded. There is little doubt that while they disliked seeing their mother squander money, Adelaide and the other daughters were more concerned about her happiness and well-being. For an eighty-year-old woman to marry a man decades younger than herself is not an auspicious recipe for joy.

Relations were so strained over this, that when Marjorie began flirting with another bridegroom number five, the daughters were powerless to do anything about it. In desperation they appealed to Marwee, who was at the moment in particularly high regard with her grandmother. When Marjorie was away from her new romance for a rest at White Sulphur Springs, Marwee was flown down on some pretext to pay a visit. Her assignment was to talk Marjorie out of marrying.

"Grandma," Marwee began, "I think it's wonderful you're thinking of marrying that guy. He seems like a terrific man, and I'm sure he'll give up his other women as soon as he marries you. . . ."

"What other women?" Marjorie asked, her eyes narrowing.

"Oh, you know. Those ladies he's been seeing in Washington."

"WHO?"

"Oh, Jane Bedford, Pam Pancoast, Alice . . ." said Marwee, thinking up names as fast as she could.

Obvious as the ploy was, it was the shake Marjorie needed. She broke off the friendship, and Marwee returned to Washington a heroine to her aunts and, briefly, to her mother. To what degree Marjorie understood Marwee's "service" is not known, but she knew it was a service. When she arrived back in Washington, she presented Marwee with the disputed necklace of yellow sapphires and amethysts with matching earrings and ring. A husband would have cost far more.

With all of her romanticism, Marjorie was under no illusions that she was going to live forever. Her long and fruitless attempts to save her hearing had been a cruel lesson that all the money in the world cannot forestall certain natural inevitabilities. She also knew that her Christian Science, her good eating and sleeping habits, her daily exercise, could keep her looking remarkably trim and youthful, but they could not make her immortal. More and more of her time was taken up with deciding the disposition of her empire.

The money was a simple mater. After a number of bequests to longtime servants, a few friends and various charities, the bulk of the estate would be split evenly among her three daughters. The disposition of her homes caused her more concern. She had lavished so much time, money, and personal creative effort on these homes that she was determined not to let them be demolished.

She had always intended that Hillwood become a museum. At first she planned to leave it to the National Trust for Historic Preservation, but when her friend Richard Howland left that organization for the Smithsonian, she willed it to them.

Some of her possessions, most notably her historic jewelry collection, were given directly to the Smithsonian with the understanding that, at her death, the jewels would join her other belongings on display at Hillwood. She set aside $10 million in a trust for the Smithsonian to cover Hillwood's operating costs.

Mar-A-Lago was far more of a problem. At first it was to be given to the state of Florida. Then the state changed its mind and said that it didn't want Mar-A-Lago. An enormous effort, involving lawyers and influential friends, was made to persuade the US government to accept it; there was some talk about its being used as a winter presidential residence or a place where visiting heads of state and other dignitaries could rest after long jet flights.

President Nixon flew up from Key Biscayne to look

it over; he was enthralled. Perhaps because San Clemente's Spanish-mission style was already beginning to look plebeian to his increasingly imperial self-view, he pushed through congressional acceptance of Mar-A-Lago for the National Park Service.

Topridge was first to be given to C. W. Post College, later to the state of New York. In each situation, cash and persuasion, both in large quantities, were required to get anyone to accept the properties. Before embarking on these giveaway ideas, Marjorie had first checked to see if any of her daughters—either singly or together—wanted to keep up any of the estates. All were quick to decline.

A project dear to Marjorie in her later years was the biography she had commissioned of her father entitled, "C. W. Post—The Man and the Hour." The author was her friend Nettie Leitch Major, who painstakingly researched and distilled C. W. Post's variegated and productive life. The book devotes a fat chapter to Marjorie's life, depicting her as embodying the most praiseworthy characteristics of Jacqueline Bouvier and St. Francis of Assissi. She is rarely referred to by name, but rather with such epithets as "this gracious lady" and "the lovely benefactress."

Mrs. Major says that Herb May urged her to trowel on the adulation, but we can't escape the fact that Marjorie read, approved, and paid for this self-addressed valentine. The expensively published book was sent to hundreds of Marjorie's friends, most of whom prized it more as a token of inner-circledom than as a literary or historical entity.

This eulogy to Marjorie comes at the end of the text and is quickly followed by an appendix that would shake the most faithful Marjorie admirer. The bulk of the book traces the Post lineage back seventy-five years to a cast-iron stove in Battle Creek. The genealogy in the appendix pushes the bloodline back an additional thousand years to Rurik, the Viking, Robert the Strong, and so many other historical headmen that you begin to see the genes of King Arthur, Kubla Kahn, and John the Baptist, all devolving on one inconspicuous birth in Springfield, Illinois. Marjorie's penchant for royalty made her susceptible to flattering suggestions about her own ancestry—but in this appendix more than anywhere else in her life, she seems to have broken free of the most minimal restraint. Eric the Bold indeed.

Marjorie also spent these years garnering honors. She received decorations from a number of foreign governments and tributes from the many organizations she supported. Her biggest philanthropy was probably the National Symphony, which she subsidized over the years to the extent of $2 million. An anonymous gift of one hundred and fifty thousand dollars to the National Cultural Center, later the Kennedy Center, was traced to her. She was the principal benefactor of C. W. Post College and Mount Vernon College for women (where she attended to such details as crisply clean uniforms for dormitory maids and chauffeur-driven limousines for students who wanted to go into downtown Washington).

She financed a nursing home in Springfield, Illinois, in the original Post home where both her father and she had been born. She flew to Battle Creek to dedicate an athletic field she had presented in memory of her father. She gave substantial amounts each year to the Boy Scouts and more modest amounts to a wide number of routine fund-raising drives. Her private charities to needy friends and acquaintances totaled a considerable annual outlay. With all of this, she always stood ready to undertake a new charity, despite a remark made once when feeling besieged by worthy causes:

"By God, there is a bottom to my pocketbook even if no one thinks there is!"

       An odd disagreement sprang up between Dina and her mother over Marjorie's will. Dina, from her own money, had set up her children with capital; she later came to regard the move as unwise. The money had been intended to provide them with lifelong security, but in her son David's case, had served only to fuel his wild streak. At the time of his death at twenty-three he had gone through almost all of his inheritance.

One of his follies had been the purchase of a spectacular house in Denver called Shangri-La. To launch his new digs, David had thrown a party that brought the *jeunesse dorée* jetting in from great distances. The party featured two rock bands, free-flowing champagne, and everything else it takes to keep the spoiled young rich happy for twelve to sixteen hours.

Dina had flown in for the party and is said to have wandered around looking stunned. David's house was too grand, the party too extravagant, the crowd too dissolute. Dina had always been hardworking, disciplined, and frugal. She saw in her son something alien and frightening.

When it became apparent David might soon be out of money, he grew anxious over his future. Unfortunately, the anxiety was not channeled into a constructive plan—only into greater escapades, many involving physical danger. Some observers feel that his death-defying pranks were impelled by a despair over what was to become of him.

His parents were determined not to soothe his anxiety with a fresh supply of money. Dina particularly was indignant. He was, she said, about to have to go to work in a gas station. When asked if she would have

let this happen, she said, "You're damn right I would."
Then as an afterthought, "And so would mother."

Dina was wrong. Her mother turned out to be a less
stern molder of youthful character. In her will Marjorie
stated that Dina had requested David and Dina's other
children be excluded from any bequests. Marjorie then
added: "While I respect my daughter's point of view,
after all, they are my grandchildren and I wish to have
them provided for as provided herein."

Dina claims that her mother misunderstood. She had
meant that her children would have enough money and
her mother should save taxes by skipping a generation.
Whatever her intentions, Dina is definite about one part
of the will business. "I don't think mother should have
mentioned it so publicly."

No one would ever know whether or not too much
money would have ruined David Rumbough. In the
summer of 1973 he pushed his speedboat too fast in
Gardiners Bay and was thrown from it. The boat, rigged
to circle when the controls were unmanned, turned and
ran over Rumbough, killing him instantly. Strangely,
the body disappeared. For several days the search went
on, with Cliff Robertson helping the searchers in his
own plane.

Marjorie was in very bad condition at the time of
the accident. She would die six days later without ever
knowing of her favorite grandson's death.

One aspect of the provision-making with
which she busied herself over her last few years came
as a great surprise and disappointment to a number of
people. Bequests to longtime servants were small. Many
on Marjorie's staff had devoted most of their adult life
to her. Such people had reason to expect their employer
to provide for their old age. But the largest bequest,
$50,000, was left only to a few close retainers, Jim
Griffin and Margaret Voigt among them. Frank Moffat

was left $40,000. There were many who got $10,000, some $5,000—and some others with a reasonable claim received nothing at all. Even more shocked were those employees who were already retired and living on pensions. When Marjorie died on September 11, 1973, the pensions stopped.

It is an enigma how a woman who had been so remarkably generous to her employees when she was alive—who was constantly concerned about their well-being—could be so indifferent to their fate after her death. Perhaps Marjorie had simply lost awareness of the value of money; she might have known the price of a Cartier pin, but perhaps she still assumed you could buy a nice little house for three thousand dollars. If she had these misconceptions, it is equally possible her lawyers had no interest in correcting them.

Another more bizarre possibility suggests itself. Unreasonable as the notion is, it gains some credence by Marjorie's own reference when speaking of various charities she supported, of doing what she would "while I am here." By making life a condition of continued magnanimity, she might have seen the terms of the will as her protest against death itself.

In 1965 when *Life* magazine was still very much a part of the American consciousness, it ran an eighteen-page color spread on the world of Marjorie Merriweather Post. Alfred Eisenstaedt took the photographs, and few people who saw them ever forgot them, including many with no interest in either the rich or their possessions. There were pictures of Marjorie at Hillwood; Marjorie playing golf on the nine-hole course at Mar-A-Lago; shots of the Russian collection; the main sitting rooms at Mar-A-Lago and Topridge; an aerial view of Topridge; inside the prop-jet; boating on Upper St. Regis Lake; onboard the cable car; her French bedroom at Hillwood with Marie Antoinette's desk.

One photograph in particular stands out. It shows Marjorie in a pale-blue evening dress with pale-blue jewels checking her dinner table just before a formal party at Hillwood. She is inspecting the tablecloth (made of three meticulously sewn together pieces of antique lace), the arrangement of silver, crystal, and flowers—her head butler stands by nervously. The caption explains that flowers and candelabra are centered by means of a concealed overhead spotlight; then measuring sticks are used to place the settings and to assure such details as equal overhang of the lace cloth on both sides of the table. The *Life* caption concludes: "At 8:30, when the French ambassador led the 26 other guests into the French Regency paneled dining room, it seemed a shame to disturb such sheer symmetry by eating."

In her last years, Marjorie slowed her pace somewhat. She traveled mostly between her three establishments, occasionally stopping off in New York for some shopping. Harry Winston recalls her jewelry-purchasing procedure.

"I would show her a number of things; she might show interest in a particular piece, but maybe not. We never discussed price. Later, her man Handleman would phone me, and we would meet for serious price negotiations over a particular item."

If she was a bit reserved in her judgments with Harry Winston, she never had any inward doubts about what she liked. Once in Paris she was shopping in Hermès with a granddaughter who liked a particular jeweled pin. Marjorie looked at it and said, "Get a bigger one. That size looks constipated."

She maintained a full social life, most of it under her own roofs. Particularly memorable were the spring garden parties. Guests would come up the drive, which would be ablaze with azaleas in many shades of red and pink. Attendants would take their cars at the entrance. Entering the main hall, the guests would find it banked with potted calla lilies and cineraria, or some knockout floral display. They would pass the vitrines stuffed with Russian treasures on their way into the main dining room where Marjorie received them, surrounded by Marie Antoinette's furniture. They would then move out onto the south lawn, where a red-jacketed orchestra pumped Viennese waltzes and footmen dashed about with trays of hot hors d'oeuvres and cold cocktails.

Marjorie's private existence was every bit as sybaritic and ritualized. Her first contact with the world, rather with *her* world, was the arrival each day of her breakfast tray. The time she rang for it varied, but the kitchen staff was on duty at 8 A.M. A footman would bring her the wooden tray covered with embroidered linen and decorated with a small vase of delicate flowers. The meal was always the same: hot cereal, scrambled eggs and bacon, toast and marmalade, tea with vegetable sugar. She never drank coffee and at lunch and dinner would drink Postum.

She spent her mornings as always in her room going over paperwork, making plans with Mrs. Voigt, and doing her toilette with Eva. Lunch might bring a few close friends or business associates—someone from the Smithsonian to discuss Hillwood's future, fellow board members of the National Symphony, the president of Mount Vernon College. Such small groups would often have their meals in the orchid-filled pavilion off the main dining room.

In the afternoon she might take a walk around her gardens. This would be pleasure mixed with an all-business inspection. Or she might drive out on some errand or visit. Frank Moffat commented on Marjorie's growing reluctance to be away from her domains.

"Even when she was still quite well, she'd go out saying she'd be gone an hour or so; then she'd be back in twenty minutes."

A young Brazilian who worked as footman the last four years of her life considers the experience the greatest of his life. "We all liked working there," he said. "It paid well, and the work was easy. And we were treated so well. Our quarters were pleasant—we had maids to make our beds every day—and the food we were served was excellent.

"I was one of six footmen. My main job was to wait on tables, but I sometimes polished silver. When serving meals, we would work in teams, usually a newer footman along with a more experienced one. We all knew exactly how Mrs. Post liked things done; there was a definite routine about everything. Everyone took pride in their work. We cleaned those things as if they were our own.

"In the mornings we wore gray suits. Mrs. Post was very particular about the cut and if our suits were neatly pressed. At noon we would have our lunch, then change into black suits to serve cocktails to Mrs. Post's luncheon guests. Many days there toward the end, we were put on half days, which meant that after lunch we were free for the rest of the day. We all had our own cars and could come and go as we pleased.

"Mrs. Post was wonderful, very pleasant to everyone. Of course, she wasn't a regular person like you or me—she was special."

Toward the end she still had occasional large parties. A dinner for two hundred was threatened when she fell ill at the last minute. The dining marquees were already up on Hillwood's lawns, the extra help hired, and the food prepared, so Marjorie decided to let the party go on without her. As the guests assembled for cocktails on the terrace, the Washington Monument catching the late rays of the sun over the trees of Rock Creek Park, Marjorie had her bed wheeled to an upstairs window from which she waved greetings to her guests.

It would seem a shame to disturb such a life by dying.

MARWEE (III):

When Grandma started to be invalided, I went to see her at Hillwood where she was under Adelaide's control. When I walked into her bedroom, she didn't say hello, she just looked at me and said, "Get me out of here!" She was desperate.

I phoned Jimmy Griffin and said he had to get Mar-A-Lago opened right away. He told me it would take six weeks. I said, "Look, Junior, if you won't open it fast, I'll go to California and get some of my football players and we'll have that place open in five days." He called me back and said he would be ready whenever we got there.

Grandma was in a bad way. She was stone-deaf and turning senile. She had had a series of these little mini-strokes. They were giving her cortisone, and it made her unpredictable. She lost control, and she got mean. She really slapped Dina one time. Damn near knocked her to the ground. Dina took it like a champ. Once Grandma got furious with one of her nurses and she screamed at me, "Hit her, Marwee, hit her!" So I went through the MGM bit and pretended to belt this nurse. I don't know how good an act we pulled, but it satisfied Grandma. Those poor nurses were doing the best they could.

One time I was trying to get her slipper on. Her foot was kicking; I thought she was having a twitch. Then I realized she was trying to kick me. You didn't try to physically restrain her. You learn what plays and what doesn't. You humor her and get the hell out of the way. It was her frustration at her situation, I'm sure of it.

It was very difficult when she would come to the table. She couldn't hear anything. She had a pad in front of her, and we would write her notes. But that could aggravate her. If her mind wasn't clicking, she'd just shove the note away. More than once I saw her get up and leave the table when one of us handed her a note.

Sometimes I'd be eating with her alone in that enormous dining room and she would just stare ahead for fifteen minutes—not eating, not doing anything. We'd just sit there in complete silence, those big Italian murals looming up over us, and sometimes a butler would remove a plate or fill a glass.

Deenie was there a lot, and that was a terrific help. Grandma had her ups and downs. Deenie and I got the whole program going. We arranged movies, brought people to see her. We put that little bird feeder outside her window. We took her for walks in the garden. We were trying to get her interest back, to get her sense of humor going. She was coming along.

I'd get up early and go sit with her in the mornings.

After lunch, I'd stay with her all afternoon and stay while she had her dinner. By seven o'clock she'd be through for the day. Then Deenie and I would have our friends for dinner.

Other than the fact Grandma was dying, I had the time of my life that year. I never enjoyed Mar-A-Lago more. With Grandma laid up, Dina and I had the whole operation at our disposal. We could do whatever we wanted. We didn't have Voigt telling us we couldn't do something, or Grandma saying something wasn't protocol. We had dinners almost every night—none of those bullshit people—just the people we liked. It occurred to me the Merriweather was just sitting there with round-the-clock pilots. I said to Deenie, "Listen, Babe, this may be our last chance at stardom. Let's get that damn plane and get it on!" We'd go off on trips to the islands—sometimes just for the day, other times we'd spend the night. We'd take friends, Deenie's kids. I'd dive, and Cliff and Deenie went shelling. We'd have them fix us picnics. It was great.

We had one big dinner party—about forty people —all our friends. Moffat went all out, the way he did for Grandma. We called it the Last Tango. And you know, it was? It was the last party at Mar-A-Lago.

A strange thing happened at the end. The servants took over. After all those years, the servants finally had their day at bat. Even Mrs. Voigt got edged out. With Grandma not communicating, not dictating any letters, Voigt had no function. She was reduced to nothing. It was as simple as that. The other servants were really cruel to Voigt. I never liked her, but if you were a human being, you had to feel sorry for her.

Grandma's personal maid, Eva, came into power, and she fought to keep everyone away from Grandma. It was a constant struggle. I couldn't handle it. I'm *not a daughter. I didn't have the authority. Deenie saved the day.*

Adelaide and Eleanor showed up. It was very moving when Eleanor arrived from Paris. Grandma and Eleanor fell into each other's arms; they both cried. I'm sure it was the first time they ever let themselves go with each other. They had been close enough, as mothers and daughters go, but there had never been top communication. At times I used to think Grandma was jealous of Eleanor's knowledge about art and antiques. Then, they'd had so many ups and downs about all their husbands. But that scene at Mar-A-Lago, it was like their finally coming together after all the years.

Adelaide and Eleanor wanted Grandma back at Hillwood. They said she'd get better care, but I think it was because it was easier for Adelaide to be near her. And Hillwood was Grandma's seat; it was her monument, so Adelaide probably figured it was a more suitable place for her to die. Florida was so much better for her—the weather, the people around—it was more of a family atmosphere, not that gloomy, heavy museum. I told Adelaide that if she took Grandma back to Hillwood, she wouldn't last two months. She lasted three.

Grandma had a lot of doctors. She had been crazy about one of them for years. She was really kind of in love with him. One time he's standing over her, and she's lying there—eighty-six years old, senile, going to die in a few months—she looks up at him and says, "I love you, Harold. Will you marry me?" He was married, but that didn't stop her . . . or anyone else, for that matter.

And he says, "Oh, now, Marjorie, I couldn't do that."

I got that jerk out in the hall and I pushed him up

against the wall. I said, "You dumb bastard. That old lady's going to die. She's going to die soon. You just pissed on the last bit of life she had."

He should have said, "Of course, I'll marry you, Marjorie, but first you must get better. You must learn to walk, to eat, to go to the bathroom, and then we'll talk about it."

It's never going to happen, but why kill the last bit of hope she has?

        An interesting thing happened when a new doctor came on the case. He had me and Deenie, Adelaide, and Eleanor all together, and he was asking us about Grandma. He wanted some background on her personality, that sort of thing. He asked us if she was affectionate. In one breath Deenie and I said, "Yes," and Adelaide and Eleanor said, "No." It was an embarrassing moment, but it said a lot about everything.

        One night Eva came running into my room. "Mrs. Dye, Mrs. Dye," she's crying, "please come right away." I raced in and saw that Grandma was gone. Out. I grabbed her, and I started to shake her. I slapped her face. I never thought I could do that to my grandmother.

I yelled at her, "You can't leave! Deenie's in Aspen. Eleanor's in upper Florida. You can't go yet! I'm here alone. You can't leave!"

Jesus, I was getting red. She had lost pulse. The nurses were standing there, Junior was there.

And just like she left, she came back. She grabbed me. I had this gold-chain necklace on. She got a death grip on it, her eyes sticking out. She was strangling me, and I couldn't break her hold. She was conscious, but like in a lock. I'm motioning to Junior to get her off me. Then the intensive-care unit got there.

302

They carried her to the unit and put her in, her head near the driver, her feet toward the door. Eva is sitting beside her with two cute young interns, two blond boys in those white jackets. Now mind you, she's as good as dead. She looks at me, rolls her eyes toward the two guys. She'd done it a lot of times to me when there were good-looking men around. She looks up at them and gives them a wink. As God is my judge, I cracked up. I said, "Hey, fellows, whether you know it or not, you got a date for tonight." They got bright red.

Here she's near dead, and she's cruising.

It wasn't always so funny. One time she got away from Eva, the nurses—don't ask me how—and everyone was going crazy. Finally they found her in that huge kitchen at Mar-A-Lago. She had climbed up and was sitting on top of the big center table.

Adelaide finally had her way, and they took her back up to Hillwood and the damndest thing happened. Grandma stopped eating, just like her father had. She would sit in her wheel chair by the window, and Gus would spoon food into her mouth. She'd chew it, then spit it out into a little gold bowl Gus held up to her. I'm convinced she never wanted to be an invalid. She had had enough. It was only a short time then.

EPILOGUE

Shortly after the death of Marjorie Merriweather Post, a drop in the stock market nearly halved the paper value of her estate. Inheritance taxes, which are computed at the time of death, threatened to consume her fortune. The Internal Revenue Service granted some time for the stocks to recover, and, to a degree, they have. Some estimates say that Marjorie's three daughters, who divide the residual estate, will each get $50 million. A lawyer close to the situation says, "There will be no residual estate."

The fifty-thousand-dollar bequest to Margaret Voigt came as a surprise to many who thought the secretary would be enriched by her employer's will. Voigt never felt the disappointment; while visiting in Canada shortly before Marjorie's death, she died suddenly of a heart attack. When her safe deposit box in Washington was opened, it was found to contain over a quarter of a million dollars in securities. It was said that she had more money in Canada.

Not everyone would feel stinted by the will. Fred Korth, Henry Dudley, and the other trustees could make as much as $2 million apiece.

Regardless of the estate's eventual outcome, Marjorie's children and grandchildren will continue to live out their days under the general heading of "well off." Trust funds set up by C. W. Post, and others established by Marjorie have seen to that. Adelaide, now widowed, leads the life of a country gentlewoman in Maryland, where she raises horses and has become a national authority on dog breeding.

Eleanor, married five times, has been married since 1954 to conductor Leon Barzin. They live in a Paris townhouse exquisitely furnished with a curatorial eye that Marjorie always aspired to but never achieved. The Barzins have a country place outside Paris and an apartment in Switzerland. Eleanor's only child is Antal Miklas Post de Békessy. (His father, known as the writer Hans Habe, wrote a novel about a beautiful heiress and her overbearing mother, *Katherine*.)

Dina Merrill and her husband Cliff Robertson lead the glamorous lives of working film actors, with some additional glamour thrown in by the Post connection. The Robertsons' main base is Manhattan, where they keep an apartment overlooking the East River; their summer place sprawls over the sand dunes of eastern Long Island.

They have one child, a daughter, and Dina has two surviving children by Stanley Rumbough.

Marwee has settled somewhat boisterously into a Santa Monica beach house with so many art objects spirited from her grandmother that Jim Griffin and Frank Moffat refer to the place as Mar-A-Lago West.

(Marwee boasts that, in order to get a favorite marble bust out of Mar-A-Lago she had to forge a note in her grandmother's hand.) Marwee also has a horse ranch outside Los Angeles.

Sharing the beach compound with Marwee is her second husband Peter Dye, four of her five children, a housekeeper, a handyman, three dogs, a rooster, a Dual-Ghia roadster (a souvenir of her days running around with Frank Sinatra and his Rat Pack) and a live-in Los Angeles Ram. The last is a tenant of the house next door, which Marwee bought and converted into apartments. This house's main room, which faces a pool and the beach, has been transformed into a playroom-cum-gymnasium where Marwee and her tenants lift weights, shoot pool, and watch color tv. Marwee has never lost her passion for football or the men who play it.

Marwee's two half sisters, Adelaide's daughters Ellen Iverson and Melissa Cantacuzene, lead far more conservative lives. Both are quietly married with children. Like their mother, they live proper, tweedy existences in the environs of Washington, DC. To sum up their interests, they categorize themselves as "the horse daughter" and "the dog daughter."

It is in a sense of tribute to the solid-citizen normalcy of Marjorie's progeny to say that her more extraordinary legacy to the world was her possessions. Here the picture is less tranquil. In spite of the arduous legal arrangements for preserving her estates and keeping her collections intact, fixed plans began unraveling shortly after Marjorie's death.

The Smithsonian Institution, which had helped set the amount of the endowment for running Hillwood as a museum, decided the $10 million left for this purpose was insufficient and moved to return the property to the family. Contributing to the Smithsonian's loss of enthusiasm was a strict enforcement of a provision of the will that forbade any sort of entertaining in the house. Museum people are a party-oriented bunch, and Hillwood is the kind of party setting that would make any curator happy he had chosen the museum field. Marjorie anticipated this urge to play richman's bluff on her premises and forbade so much as a cup of tea to be brewed there.

The Smithsonian returned Hillwood to the Post estate, that is to say, to the family. Under the aegis of Adelaide Riggs, the only Post daughter in the area, it is being operated as an independent museum.

The state of New York has not decided how, or if, they will use Camp Topridge. For five years it has sat empty—wooden Indians staring blankly into the great room, stuffed birds poised in midflight, ferocious bears gathering dust. Since its use as a Trujillo pleasure craft, *The Sea Cloud* has been owned by various American firms who have tried to operate it commercially. It turned up in Florida as a cruise ship. Students, in crude reference to the Trujillo ownership, had painted on the ship's side, "Zza Zza slept here." For a lark, Dina's daughter Nina Rumbough took a job on board for a brief time.

The biggest problem turned out to be Mar-A-Lago. The government, having accepted the estate as a retreat for visiting dignitaries, reversed itself when they learned the house sat beneath the flight lanes out of West Palm Beach airport, thus making it, they felt, too great a security risk for world leaders. The effort to return the property to the Post estate has been blocked by a congressman who says no legal machinery exists to return anything, once the United States government has accepted it. No one can prove him wrong.

More or less stuck with the property, the National Park Service has been considering plans for its future. The Carter Administration seems to favor the estate's preservation. When the Park Service took over the property, they hired Jim Griffin to run the house and grounds. A friend of Griffin's kidded him about becoming a governmental pencil-pusher after the excitement of working for Marjorie Merriweather Post.

Griffin came right back at him: "Once I'd worked for Mrs. Post, I couldn't work for anyone who wanted to cut corners. I figured the only person with more money than her was Uncle Sam."

Griffin figured wrong. He found the US government a far less openhanded employer than Marjorie. For the first time in his lifelong career at Mar-A-Lago, he had to maintain the place on a strict budget, and strict budgets are inimical to palaces.

If Mar-A-Lago sat on a lonely mountain top, like Hearst's San Simeon, there would be no problem. What makes it an unsolvable dilemma is its location, beginning with the air-traffic lanes and going on to its situation at a pivotal corner of Palm Beach's million-dollar beachfront. Wealthy neighbors would like it destroyed; they doubt it has a future as a private home, and any sort of museum arrangement would bring crowds the neighborhood is unable and unwilling to handle. Elements in the town and state governments would like the place demolished and the land developed; a museum or governmental facility would mean a sizable loss of tax revenues.

Some in the federal government would like to unload what they consider an unusable white elephant and a drain, perpetual and pointless, on the national treasury. Many would shrug at the demolition of what they consider an architectural abomination, or worse.

Those who would save Mar-A-Lago see it as the exuberant expression of one person's will, embodying a magnificence that transcends questions of beauty, taste, discretion, and financial good sense. Never again would one individual be able to indulge him-or herself to this extent, to convert castles in the air to castles of stone and mortar.

No one would have the money to spend on the scale of this residence or if they had the money, they would not be able to get the materials, the workmen, and the staff to maintain it. If through some miracle these conditions could be met, no sane person would choose to express his individuality in such an anachronistic, burdensome, and censurable way. Mar-A-Lago should be preserved because it exists, and it will never exist again.

As the country is paved over for efficient apartment complexes and standardized shopping centers, it is salubrious to experience anything so splendidly inefficient and idiosyncratic as Mar-A-Lago. A midwestern practicality had produced the wherewithal for this most impractical of all houses. In its zestful unorthodoxy, its unfettered extravagance, and its splendid vulgarity it is an apt symbol for both the woman who built it and the American economy's lusty adolescence. It also represents a capability for dream-building that will never be seen again.

INDEX

312